LINCOLN

on

RACE & SLAVERY

Abraham Lincoln *(1809–1865), taken at Mathew Brady's Studio, New York City, on February 28, 1860, a day after the Cooper Institute address.*

LINCOLN

on

RACE & SLAVERY

Edited and introduced by
Henry Louis Gates, Jr.

Coedited by Donald Yacovone

PRINCETON UNIVERSITY PRESS
PRINCETON AND OXFORD

Copyright 2009 by Henry Louis Gates, Jr.
Requests for permission to reproduce material from this work should be sent to Permissions, Princeton University Press

Published by Princeton University Press, 41 William Street, Princeton, New Jersey 08540
In the United Kingdom: Princeton University Press, 6 Oxford Street, Woodstock, Oxfordshire OX20 1TW

Library of Congress Cataloging-in-Publication Data

Lincoln, Abraham, 1809–1865.
  Lincoln on race and slavery / edited and introduced by Henry Louis Gates, Jr. ; coedited by Donald Yacovone.
    p. cm.
  Includes index.
  ISBN 978-0-691-14234-0 (hardcover : alk. paper) 1. Lincoln, Abraham, 1809–1865—Views on slavery. 2. Lincoln, Abraham, 1809–1865—Political and social views. 3. Lincoln, Abraham, 1809–1865—Relations with African Americans. 4. Slavery—United States—History—19th century—Sources. 5. Slaves—Emancipation—United States—Sources. 6. United States—Race relations—History—19th century—Sources. I. Gates, Henry Louis. II. Yacovone, Donald. III. Title.
  E457.2.L744 2009
  973.7092—dc22

                                                                    2008049960

British Library Cataloging-in-Publication Data is available

This book has been composed in PUP Monticello and Gloucester MT Extracondensed
Printed on acid-free paper.
press.princeton.edu

Designed by Isabella D. Palowitch, Artisa, LLC
Printed in the United States of America
1 2 3 4 5 6 7 8 9 10

For
Evelyn Brooks Higginbotham
and
in Memory of
George M. Fredrickson

CONTENTS

LIST OF ILLUSTRATIONS

ACKNOWLEDGMENTS

I would like to thank Donald Yacovone for bringing to bear his considerable expertise on the Civil War and Abraham Lincoln in the preparation of the headnotes that preface the selections of Lincoln's writings. In addition, I would like to thank John Sellers, Sheldon Cheek, Tom Wolejko, Julie Wolf, Aditya Basheer, and Joyce Clifford for their research assistance. Allen Guelzo, John Stauffer, Ira Berlin, Philip Kunhardt, Peter Kunhardt, Ted Widmer, Donald Yacovone, David Herbert Donald, James McPherson, and Tina Bennett read several drafts of my introduction, and provided quite helpful criticisms and suggestions.

This book grew out of my research for my PBS documentary, *Looking for Lincoln*, which marks the bicentennial of Abraham Lincoln's birth. I would like to thank Doris Kearns Goodwin, and my fellow executive producers, William Grant, Peter Kunhardt, and Dyllan McGee, and my producers, Barak Goodman, John Maggio, and Muriel Soenens, for helping me to understand my own relationship to Lincoln and Lincoln's relationship to our times.

I would also like to thank my agent, Tina Bennett, and my editor at Princeton University Press, Hanne Winarsky, for their support of the publication of this book to coincide with the airing of our documentary series. Lauren Lepow expertly edited my introduction, helping me to understand what it was I was trying to say.

The texts of Lincoln's writings and speeches are taken from *The Collected Works of Abraham Lincoln* [*CW*], edited by Roy P. Basler, published under the auspices of the Abraham Lincoln Association (New Brunswick: Rutgers University Press, 1953–1990), available online at http://quod.lib.umich.edu/l/lincoln.

Abraham Lincoln on Race and Slavery

What I would most desire would be the separation of the white and black races. . . .

   —SPEECH AT SPRINGFIELD, JULY 17, 1858

Certainly the negro is not our equal in color—perhaps not in many other respects; still, in the right to put into his mouth the bread that his own hands have earned, he is the equal of every other man, white or black.

   —SPEECH AT SPRINGFIELD, JULY 17, 1858

. . . I have expressly disclaimed all intention to bring about social and political equality between the white and black races, and, in all the rest, I have done the same thing by clear implication.

  I have made it equally plain that I think the negro is included in the word "men" used in the Declaration of Independence. . . .

  But it does not follow that social and political equality between whites and blacks, *must* be incorporated, because slavery must *not*. The declaration [of Independence] does not so require.

   —LETTER TO JAMES N. BROWN, OCTOBER 18, 1858

They say that between the nigger and the crocodile they go for the nigger. The proportion, therefore, is, that as the crocodile to the nigger so is the nigger to the white man.

   —SPEECH AT HARTFORD, MARCH 5, 1860

I am naturally anti-slavery. If slavery is not wrong, nothing is wrong. I can not remember when I did not so think, and feel.

   —LETTER TO ALBERT G. HODGES, APRIL 4, 1864

But what was A. Lincoln to the colored people or they to him? As compared with the long line of his predecessors, many of whom were merely the facile and servile instruments of the slave power, Abraham Lincoln, while unsurpassed in his devotion to the welfare of the white race, was also in a sense hitherto without example, emphatically, the black man's President: the first to show any respect for their rights as men.

—FREDERICK DOUGLASS, 1865

. . . Abraham Lincoln was not, in the fullest sense of the word, either our man or our model. In his interests, in his associations, in his habits of thought, and in his prejudices, he was a white man. He was pre-eminently the white man's President, entirely devoted to the welfare of white men. . . . You are the children of Abraham Lincoln. We are at best only his step-children, children by adoption, children by force of circumstances and necessity.

I have said that President Lincoln was a white man, and shared the prejudices common to his countrymen towards the colored race. . . . Though Mr. Lincoln shared the prejudices of his white fellow-countrymen against the negro, it is hardly necessary to say that in his heart of hearts he loathed and hated slavery.

—FREDERICK DOUGLASS, 1876

All throughout his debates with Stephen Douglas, Abraham Lincoln never allowed himself to be without a thin black leather notebook that he had converted into a scrapbook, preparation for the war of words in which he and his ardent foe were so passionately and desperately engaged. It served Lincoln almost as a cheat sheet, a ready-reference tool to which he could conveniently revert for facts and figures, opinions from editorials and letters to the editor, and clips from newspaper stories about all those pressing issues of the day over which he and Douglas so thoughtfully, if feverishly, were debating. The notebook, now housed in the Lincoln Papers at the Library of Congress—six inches high, three and three-quarters inches wide, an inch thick, its covers made of hardboard—was small enough to slip into his coat pocket, discreet enough for Lincoln to consult on the podium while preparing his rebuttals as Douglas redoubled his ferocious attacks. The notebook's metal clasp is broken; it is boxed closely for protection. What a wealth of information about slavery and the most important issues of his day does that slim volume contain! Lincoln knew what he needed to know, or didn't know, to hold his own with Douglas. And he consulted his commonplace book frequently, judging from the wear of the clasp and its well-thumbed, glue-stiff pages.

Among its many gems, two newspaper clippings—anonymous and undated—are especially arresting, because they offer diametrically opposed positions on three related but distinct issues: first, the institution of slavery as practiced in America, the right of whites to hold persons of African descent in bondage; second, race and the nature of the Negro (a complex subject often conflated with slavery in American historical discourse, but a very distinct thing, in fact, especially in Lincoln's mind); and, third, the colonization of former slaves in Africa, the Caribbean, or South America, an idea that Lincoln contemplated until late in his presidency.

One of the editorials that Lincoln clipped for his notebook is proslavery, vulgarly anti-Negro, yet anticolonization: slavery "is a thing that we cannot do without, that is righteously profitable and permanent and that belongs to southern society as inherently,

[handwritten margin note: anti slavery by proslavery newspapers in book - prove that he's a politician.]

intricately and durably as the white race itself. Yea, the white race will itself emigrate from the southern states to Africa, California or Polynesia, sooner than the African. Let us make up our minds, therefore to put up with and make the most of the institution. Let us not bother our brains about what Providence intends to do with our negroes in the distant future but glory in and profit to the utmost by what He has done for him in transplanting him here, and setting him to work on our plantations. . . . keep . . . slaves at hard work, under strict discipline, out of idleness and mischief, while they live . . . instead of sending them off to Africa, or manumitting them to a life of freedom, licentiousness and nuisance."

The other editorial, curiously enough, argues the opposite case: it is antislavery and pro-Negro: "We were brought up in a State where blacks were voters, and we do not know of any inconvenience resulting from it. . . . We have seen many a 'nigger' that we thought much more of than some white man." Yet the editorial writer is also procolonization: "Our opinion is that it would be best for all concerned to have the colored population in a State by themselves," either their own country or even a state within the United States. One can imagine Lincoln mulling over these two opinions while Stephen Douglas droned on, trying to decide where the voluntary colonization of the Negro figured into his firm opposition to the institution of slavery.

In preparation for writing, hosting, and narrating *Looking for Lincoln,* a television documentary about Abraham Lincoln to be aired in celebration of the bicentennial of his birth, since I am not a Lincoln scholar, I began to read for the first time in a systematic way Lincoln's collected speeches and writings, as well as the major biographies and studies of Lincoln's private and public life both before and during his presidency. One of the most striking conclusions that a close reading of Lincoln's speeches and writings yielded to me was that "slavery," "race," and "colonization," were quite often three separate issues for him. Sometimes these issues were intertwined in Lincoln's thinking, but far more often they seem to have remained quite distinct, even if we have difficulty understanding or explaining how this could have been so. And this difficulty has led far too many scholars, I believe, when writing about Lincoln's views on slavery, for example, to blur distinctions that were important to him and to his contemporaries as they reflected upon the institution of slavery, the status of African Americans both as human beings and as potential citizens in the United States, and whether or not voluntary colonization was an inseparable aspect of abolition.

In Lincoln's case, we can trace these three strands of thought clearly within three distinct discourses that braid their way through his speeches and writings: in his early and consistent abhorrence of slavery as a violation of natural rights, as an economic institution that created an uneven playing field for white men, and that dehumanized and brutalized black human beings; in the fascinating manner in which he wrestled with the deep-seated, conventional ambivalence about the status of Negroes vis-à-vis white people on the scale of civilization, his penchant for blackface minstrelsy and darky jokes, his initially strong skepticism about the native intellectual potential of people of color and the capacity of black men to serve with valor in a war against white men; and, finally, his long flirtation with the voluntary colonization of the freed slaves either in the West Indies, in Latin America, or back in Africa.

Interspersed, as it were, among these three separate but sometimes overlapping discourses is the manner in which he seems to have wrestled with his own use of the "n-word," which he used publicly at least until 1862, and which most Lincoln scholars today find so surprising and embarrassing that they consistently avoid discussing it, since for a politician to do so today would be quite scandalous, and since this is not in accord with the image most of us share of Lincoln as the Great Emancipator, the champion of black slaves. And for that reason alone, it deserves to be discussed, if only briefly, to help us to begin to understand how complex the issue of "race" actually was in Lincoln's era, and how very different it was from our discussions of race today.

It is worth noting that although Lincoln used the "n-word" far less than did Stephen Douglas (next to Douglas, who used it as much as possible, Lincoln, in his relatively rare usages, more closely resembles John Brown than a recovering racist), he did indeed use that word in prominent public contexts. Most of us would be surprised to learn that Lincoln used it twice in his first debate with Douglas, once in the Freeport debate, once in the debate at Jonesboro, seven times in a speech in 1860 in Hartford, and once in a letter to Newton Deming and George P. Strong in 1857. Even as late as April 1862, James Redpath recorded Lincoln's saying of President Geffard of Haiti (who had offered to send a white man as his ambassador to the United States), "You can tell the President of Haiti that I shan't tear my shirt if he does send a nigger here."[1]

Today, we often tend to think of the nineteenth-century rhetoric of antiblack and proslavery racist discourse as hyperbolic or melodramatic, and that when the Founders argued that "all men were created equal," they, of course, recognized that the sons and daughters of Africa were, indeed, human beings, even if they were systematically deprived of their rights. At its most extreme, however, the discourse of antiblack racism sought to exclude black women and men from the human community. To take just two of hundreds of examples, when the *Richmond Examiner,* as Frederick Douglass reported in a speech in 1854, declared in all capital letters that "[The Negro] is not a man," and when Alexander H. Stephens, vice president of the Confederacy, maintained in 1861 that the South represented "the highest type of civilization ever exhibited by man," because "its cornerstone rests upon the great truth that the Negro is not equal to the white man, that slavery—subordination to the superior race—is his natural and normal condition," neither was referring to a socially constructed difference between blacks and whites, a gap in condition that reflected the results of environmental variables.[2]

No, they were attempting to define black people as an "other species of men," as David Hume had put it in 1754, an opinion shared even as late as 1850 by the Harvard scholar Louis Agassiz, one of the most influential ethnologists of his day. "It was in Philadelphia," Agassiz wrote, "that I first found myself in prolonged contact with negroes; all the domestics in my hotel were men of color. I can scarcely express to you the painful impression that I received, especially since the feeling that they inspired in me is contrary to all our ideas about the confraternity of the human type [genre] and the unique origin of our species. But truth before all. . . . It is impossible for me to [ignore] the feeling that they are not of the same blood as us. In seeing their black faces with their thick lips and grimacing teeth, the wool on their head, their bent knees, their elongated hands, their large curved nails, and especially the livid color of the palm of their hands, I could not take my eyes off their face in order to tell them to stay far away. And when they advanced that hideous hand towards my plate in order to serve me, I wished I were able to depart in order to eat a piece of bread elsewhere, rather than dine with such service."[3]

Thomas Jefferson may or may not have understood, through his personal relations with Sally Hemings, for example, that black people were human beings, just like white people; but he never stated this in his writings, and he most certainly did not include black people within his definition of "men" when he wrote the Declaration of Independence. In fact, as Jefferson put it in *Notes on the State of Virginia,* "It is not their condition then, but nature, which has produced this distinction"[4]—a distinction between those of African descent, meant forever to be subordinate, and those of European descent, meant forever to be dominant. And distinctions in kind or type created by Nature itself could never be altered. All men may have been created equal; the real question was who was a man, and what being "a man," in fact, meant. Thomas Jefferson most certainly was not thinking of black men and women when he wrote the Declaration of Independence, and no amount of romantic historical wishful thinking can alter that fact. However, Abraham Lincoln most certainly and most impressively did, as he stated privately in 1858 and publicly throughout his career, a belief that boldly challenged the Dred Scott decision of 1857; but even this rather radical belief did not translate, in Lincoln's mind, into an embrace or advocacy of "social and political equality" between blacks and whites, as he put it in the same letter to James N. Brown, which I quote above in a epigraph. It is important for us to understand that Lincoln did not find these positions contradictory or inconsistent, even if we might today. How did his thinking about these issues evolve during his presidency, during the course of the deadly Civil War?

The Abraham Lincoln of the popular American imagination—Father Abraham, the Great Emancipator—is often represented almost as an island of pure reason in a sea of mid-nineteenth-century racist madness, a beacon of tolerance blessed with a certain cosmopolitan sensibility above or beyond race, a man whose attitudes about race and slavery transcended his time and place. It is this Abraham Lincoln that many writers have conjured, somewhat romantically—for example, as Ralph Ellison often did—to claim for him and those who fought to abolish slavery a privileged, noble status in the history of American race relations from which subsequent, lesser mortals disgracefully fell away. This is one reason that blacks such as Marian Anderson in 1939 and Martin Luther King, Jr., in 1963 used the Lincoln Memorial as the most ideal symbolic site through which to make a larger, implicit statement about race prejudice in their times, and why Barack Obama launched his campaign for president in Springfield, Illinois, Lincoln's home. Black people, to an extent that would no doubt have surprised Frederick Douglass, have done more perhaps than even white Americans have to confect an image of Lincoln as the American philosopher-king and patron saint of race relations, an image strenuously embraced and enthusiastically reproduced in lithographs by Booker T. Washington at the turn of the century to sanctify the authority of his leadership in a direct line of descent from both Frederick Douglass and Father Abraham himself.

However, contemporary views of Lincoln, and of the abolitionists, as the sources of the modern civil rights movement have sometimes been naive and have almost always been ahistorical. Black abolitionists, keenly aware of the vast difference between finding the economic institution of slavery a harmful and repugnant force of inequity in the marketplace, on the one hand, and embracing black people as equal human beings, on the other, were fond of saying that the only thing some of the white abolitionists hated more than slavery was the slave. While this was meant to criticize their white associates for unconscious forms of racism, it is certainly true that many white abolitionists treated black people paternalistically. But at least they advocated emancipation, both immediate and gradual, and in theory called for racial equality, even if they often had a difficult time realizing it in their personal relations with actual former slaves. What's more, many of the abolitionists came to define themselves against colonizationists, those who would free the slaves only to remove them outside of the country.

It should not surprise us that Lincoln was no exception to his times; what is exceptional about Abraham Lincoln is that, perhaps because of temperament or because of the shape-shifting contingencies of command during an agonizingly costly war, he wrestled with his often contradictory feelings and ambivalences and vacillations about slavery, race, and colonization, and did so quite publicly and often quite eloquently. It is the progress of his fraught journey through the thickets of slavery and race that this book seeks to chart, in Lincoln's own words, arranged chronologically between 1837 and his final speech, delivered just before his assassination in April 1865, a speech in which he said that he intended to secure the right to vote for "very intelligent negroes" and the 200,000 black Civil War veterans. It was this speech, overheard by John Wilkes Booth, by Booth's own admission, that led to his decision to assassinate the president.

It is fascinating to trace how these three strands of Lincoln's thought about the status of black people in America manifested themselves in his attitudes about voluntary colonization, for example. Lincoln favored colonization initially because of a genuine concern that blacks and whites could not live in social harmony. He continued to contemplate colonization for much of his term as president because of an equally genuine concern that the huge number of slaves who would ultimately be freed by the Thirteenth Amendment would never be accepted by the former Confederates and white people in the North, whither at least some of the former slaves would sooner or later migrate. There were 3.9 million slaves in 1860, and it is quite surprising to most people that, according to the historians David Blight and Allen Guelzo, only about 500,000 of these slaves were actually freed between 1863 and the end of the war by the Emancipation Proclamation;[5] the remainder would not be freed until passage of the Thirteenth Amendment.[6] It was certainly not unreasonable for Lincoln, and anyone else who took a moment to think about it, that it would be extraordinarily difficult to assimilate this mass of former slaves into an integrated American society without extended social, political, and economic conflict. But he was willing to accommodate those "very intelligent negroes," whom he never defined, but whom, at the maximum, we can define as the 488,000 Negroes who were free in 1860, and more realistically as those free Negroes who were literate, plus those 200,000 soldiers to whom he proudly referred as his "black warriors," whose right to vote he was determined to effect, and to whom he remained doggedly loyal.

Given the vexed history of race relations in America between the end of the Civil War and the election of President Barack Obama, 143 years after the final abolition of slavery, Lincoln would have been politically naive not to have these concerns, and he was not, by and large, a naive leader. In the end, however, both because the scheme of voluntary repatriation would have been too costly (not to mention too unpopular among blacks) ever to have succeeded, and because of the evolution in his own thinking about who blacks were as human beings in relation to whites and the capacity of at least some of them eventually to become fully vested American citizens, Lincoln seems to have lost confidence in his commitment to colonization as a possible solution to postwar race conflict. This collection of Lincoln's words enables us to chart the evolution of his thinking about this tangled mass of issues concerning slavery and race, so that we can, as it were, overhear the conversation that he was having with himself and with other Americans about these vexed issues. Some Lincoln scholars seem to examine his thoughts and feelings about slavery and race through the mediation of a certain rose-colored filter, apparently embarrassed by Lincoln's inconsistencies and his complexity, and determined to reinvent Lincoln as a race-relations patron saint, outside of his time and place, a man less complicated, flawed, contradictory, and interesting than he, in fact, actually was.

Make way for liberty! *by Henry Louis Stephens. Color Lithograph card, ca. 1863, Prints and Photographs Division, Library of Congress, LC-USZ62-53190.*

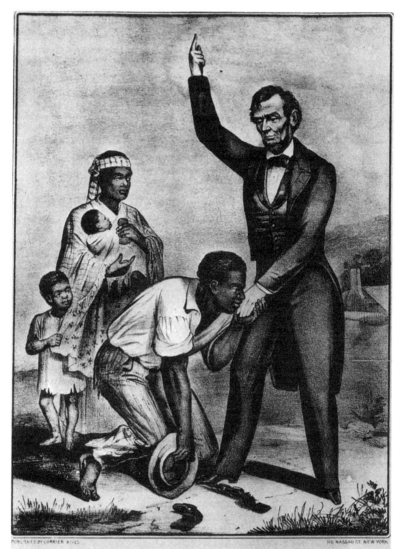

Freedom to the Slaves/Proclaimed January 1st 1863, by Abraham Lincoln, President of the United States. "Proclaim liberty throughout All the land unto All the inhabitants thereof."—Lev. XXV, 10. *ca. 1865, Currier & Ives, lithograph, New York.*

When we consider Lincoln today, we tend to forget that we are reading him—indeed, conceiving of him—through an interpretive frame forged in part, ironically enough, by the uses to which his image was put by blacks long after he was dead, at least since Booker T. Washington created his "Onward" series of lithographs at the turn of the century, with a noble Lincoln, on one side, and a fierce Frederick Douglass, on the other, both blessing their stepchild and logical heir, Booker T. Washington. Moreover, we hear Lincoln's words through the echo of the rhetoric of the civil rights movement, especially the "I have a dream" speech of Martin Luther King, Jr. It is easy to forget that when Lincoln made a public address, he was speaking primarily— certainly until his second inaugural address—to all-white or predominantly white audiences, who most certainly were ambivalent about blacks and black rights, if not ambivalent about slavery. When Lincoln talked about wrestling with the better angels of our nature, he knew whereof he spoke: about his audience and, just as important, about himself. And we do both Lincoln and ourselves a grave disservice by attempting to elide his contradictory feelings and thoughts and actions about the future of slavery in the Republic, and the future of the Republic's slaves and former slaves.

2

Lincoln made one of his earliest comments about slavery in a letter to Mary Speed, dated September 27, 1841, when he was thirty-two years old. Even here, we can begin to see the tension between his repugnance toward slavery and a certain tendency to "other" the slaves, to register their responses to hardships, "as we would think them," as quite different from our own. Lincoln remarks that while the slaves were facing the harshest fate—"being separated forever from the scenes of their childhood, their friends, their fathers and mothers, and brothers and sisters, and many of them, from their wives and children, and going into perpetual slavery where the lash of the master is proverbially more ruthless and unrelenting than any other where"—nevertheless, "amid all these distressing circumstances, as we would think them, they were the most cheerful and apparantly [*sic*] happy creatures on board." God "renders the worst of human conditions tolerable, while He permits the best, to be nothing better than tolerable." To Lincoln, God *endowed* blacks with the capacity to be happy and cheerful even in the worst human conditions. Whether Lincoln admires them for these seemingly transcendent reactions or sees them as the reactions of creatures a breed apart is not clear.

But what is clear is that Lincoln hated slavery, not only because of its brutality and inhumanity, but first and foremost because it constituted the theft of another person's labor—both the labor of the slave and that of the white men who had, in effect, to compete disadvantageously in the marketplace with slave labor—and he was exceptionally clear and forceful about saying so, as early as 1854. Indeed, Lincoln's central opposition to slavery seems to have been deeply rooted in this economic premise, rather than only or primarily stemming from humanitarian grounds. In a fragment on slavery, perhaps written in July 1854, he writes that "all *feel* and *understand*" the most fundamental aspect of the relation of a slave to his or her master: "The ant, who has toiled and dragged a crumb to his nest, will furiously defend the fruit of his labor, against whatever robber assails him." And this is "so plain, that the most dumb and stupid slave that ever toiled for a master, does constantly *know* that he is wronged." In other words, as Allen Guelzo puts it, this parable should be interpreted in terms of natural law: "a creature which functions solely according to natural law behaves in an anti-slavery fashion."[7]

And such a theft of the fruits of a person's labor was, as we would put it today, just about as un-American as a practice could be. "In our greedy chase to make profit of the negro," he said in a speech delivered at Peoria in October of that year, "let us beware, lest we 'cancel and tear to pieces' even the white man's charter of freedom." Slavery hurts the Negro most certainly, he is saying, but it hurts the white man, too, by trampling all over the implicit premise of the Declaration and the Constitution, that of equal economic opportunity. For Lincoln, economic mobility for white people is coterminous with America's peculiar contribution to the doctrine of natural rights. He makes this point explicitly in a speech he gave in Kalamazoo, Michigan, in August of 1856: "the free Territories of the United States," he declared, "should be kept open for the homes of free white people. . . . In this we have an interest—a deep and abiding interest." White men struggling to rise in society could not compete against white men who gained an unfair advantage in the marketplace using free black labor.

Perhaps to clarify this point about the motivation of his opposition to slavery, Lincoln sent a letter, in August 1855, to his friend Joshua Speed. Lincoln reminds Speed of a trip they took on a steamboat between Louisville and St. Louis in 1841, during which they saw "ten or a dozen slaves, shackled together with irons," a sight that was "a continual torment to me." He was by no means immune to the suffering of the slaves, he writes; nothing could be further from the truth: "It is hardly fair for you to assume, that I have no interest in a thing which has, and continually exercises, the power of making me miserable." One must wonder to what query about his motivations Lincoln is responding in this letter.

Even so, Lincoln made it clear in a speech delivered at Springfield on June 26, 1857, that his firm opposition to slavery must not be confused with a naive or romantic embrace of the slave. Stephen Douglas, whom Lincoln will famously debate starting in August of 1858, he says, is "especially horrified at the thought of the mixing blood by the white and black races," a sentiment with which, Lincoln says, he is "agreed for once—a thousand times agreed." And separation was the best way to prevent what was then called "amalgamation," Lincoln says, cleverly attempting to tie the abhorrence of interracial sexual relations, widespread among the members of his audience, to his opposition to the spread of slavery: "A separation of the races is the only perfect preventive of amalgamation but as an immediate separation is impossible the next best thing is to *keep* them apart *where* they are not already together. If white and black people never get together in Kansas," for example, he reasons, "they will never mix blood in Kansas." He will return to this theme in July 1858, in a reference to a comment made by Stephen Douglas, noting, "I protest, now and forever, against that counterfeit logic which presumes that because I do not want a negro woman for a slave, I do necessarily want her for a wife."

But the most effective way to prevent amalgamation, he continues, is by removing the black people in this country completely, through colonization: "Such separation, if ever effected at all, must be effected by colonization; and no political party, as such, is now doing anything directly for colonization." Lincoln aims to remedy that; both "moral sense" and "self-interest" demand it: "Let us be brought to believe that it is morally right, and, at the same time, favorable to, or, at least, not against, our interest, to transfer the African to his native clime, and we shall find a way to do it, however great the task may be." After all, he concludes, even "the children of Israel"—no fewer than 400,000 "fighting men"—left Egypt "in a body." We can find a way to ship the blacks out of the country as well.

Lincoln broaches the most vexed subject of all—whether Jefferson and the Founders included blacks in their claim that "all men are created equal"—in a speech he gave in Springfield in July 1858, about a month before his first debate with Stephen Douglas. And here, in one short paragraph, he makes plain the distinction we are charting among the nature of the Negro, what we might think of as the economic relation—a certain equality in the marketplace—and, finally, his passion for colonization. "I do not understand the Declaration to mean that all men were created equal in all respects," he begins. How are Negroes equal, how are they not? Well, "certainly, the negro is not our equal in color—perhaps not in many other respects," by which he means innate intellectual potential. Nevertheless, he continues, he is an equal agent in the economy, "in the right to put into his mouth the bread that his own hands have earned"; in this, Lincoln boldly declares, "he is the equal of every other man, white or black." Furthermore, "if you do not like him, let him alone." And precisely because of the tension between these contradictions—between, on the one hand, the economic rights of black men and white men, and, on the other, their fundamental natural differences, these two pivotal variants on the rights maintained by the

Declaration of Independence, there is only one way to resolve this quandary: "What I would most desire would be the separation of the white and black races." (Privately, Lincoln elaborated on this distinction three months later in his letter to James N. Brown of October 18, cited above.)

In his first debate with Douglas, in Ottawa, Illinois, on August 21, 1858, Lincoln says that there are only three options for dealing with the slaves. His "first impulse" would be to free them all "and send them to Liberia,—to their own native land." But they would all die "in the next ten days," if "they were all landed there in a day." Besides, he continues, we have neither the "surplus shipping" nor the "surplus money" to "carry them there in many times ten days." So that's out. "What next?" he asks his audience. Well, could we "free them, and make them politically and socially, our equals?" he asks again. Not really: "My own feelings will not admit of this," he says adamantly. And even if his did, "those of the great mass of white people will not. . . . We can not, then, make them equals." The alternative: "gradual emancipation," which Lincoln at one point estimates would take not less than one hundred years. As Lincoln put it, "I do not suppose that in the most peaceful way ultimate extinction would occur in less than a hundred years at the least; but that it will occur in the best way for both races in God's own good, time, I have no doubt."[8] At that rate, some black people born in my birth year, 1950, would have been born slaves.

As early as 1861, in his very first annual message to Congress, Lincoln requested funds to relocate the slaves who would be freed through the First Confiscation Act and slaves from the border states who might be freed; Lincoln also advocated "extending diplomatic recognition to Haiti and Liberia, partly to improve prospects for black emigration," as Eric Foner puts it.[9] Without a doubt, however, Lincoln's most bizarre and theatrical statements about slavery, race, and colonization were made on August 14, 1862, and at the White House, at that, just a month or so before he would sign the Preliminary Emancipation Proclamation. Through the Reverend James Mitchell, the commissioner of emigration in the Interior Department, Lincoln invited a group of blacks to assemble at his request at Henry McNeal Turner's Union Bethel AME Church at 2:00 p.m. When they arrived, they had expected that Lincoln would be present, but they discovered that he was inviting them to send a delegation of five men to meet with him personally at the White House two hours later to discuss his plan for the colonization of the freed slaves in South America, and their leadership of that plan. The group was headed by Edward M. Thomas, who embraced the idea in a letter he later sent to Lincoln, but he and his four colleagues were bitterly attacked in the black press for supporting Lincoln's proposal, especially by Frederick Douglass.[10]

Because he requested the presence of a reporter at the meeting— by the way, only once before had a black man been formally invited to the White House to discuss a matter of state (Paul Cuffe had an audience with James Madison there in 1812)—it is obvious that Lincoln held the meeting in an attempt to placate any opposition in the North to the abolition of slavery in the Confederacy (which he was about to effect) and its expected onslaught of freed black migrants into the North's marketplace, and to extend an olive branch to the rebellious citizens of the South, reassuring them that freeing their slaves would not lead to an inundation of the free labor force there, or the social chaos that could ensue from freed slaves' demanding equal social or political rights in the postwar society. Lincoln was declaring through this meeting that he was not liberating the slaves so that all of them could become Americans, necessarily; he was liberating them and hoping most ardently that many of them would become citizens of their own nation, a new nation that they would conceive and construct, and that these five men would take the lead in founding.

Lincoln asked Thomas and his colleagues that day to head a voluntary colonization movement, which would take the soon-to-be-freed Southern slaves to what is now the Isthmus of Panama. And this mass exit of blacks was necessary, he said, because "you and we are different races," and "this physical difference is a great disadvantage to us both," whites and blacks suffering "on each side," blacks no doubt suffering more, indeed "the greatest wrong inflicted on any people." But even when blacks are freed, "you are yet far removed from being placed on an equality with the white race." Accordingly, there is only one plausible alternative: blacks must leave the country, and he has invited these gentlemen to the White House, he informs them, to be the founding fathers of this mass, voluntary exodus. That Lincoln held this meeting knowing full well that he was about to proclaim the emancipation of the slaves in the Confederacy helps us to understand how inextricably entangled his revulsion at slavery was with his skepticism about the nature of the Negro, and how dubious he was about the prospects for a harmonious interracial, postslavery America, in the North or in the South.

The most astonishing aspect of Lincoln's remarks that day is his frank and blunt admission that slavery—again, as an economic institution inherently unfair to white men—and the presence of black people in America because of slavery are the conjoined causes of the Civil War, as inseparably connected as Siamese twins: "See our present condition—the country engaged in war!—our white men cutting one another's throats, none knowing how far it will extend; and then consider what we know to be the truth. But for your race among us there could not be war, although many men engaged on either side do not care for you one way or the other. Nevertheless, I repeat, without the institution of Slavery and the colored race as a basis, the war could not have an existence."

Impatient with the course of the war and the administration's apparent reluctance to end slavery, Horace Greeley publicly challenged Lincoln to make a stand. On August 20, 1862, under the title "The Prayer of Twenty Millions," Greeley published a long list of grievances in an editorial in his New York Tribune accusing Lincoln of failing to enforce the laws that Congress had already passed. Greeley drew special attention to the Second Confiscation Act, which authorized the president to institute an aggressive policy of emancipation and recruit freed slaves into the army— which the administration adamantly refused to consider. Lincoln, Greeley contended, was forming and enacting policy with an eye too much directed toward the border states, in which slavery remained legal. He denounced Lincoln for failing to instruct his generals to accept runaway slaves into their lines; instead, Union troops sometimes returned them and sometimes even murdered them. The time had long since passed, Greeley argued, for the president to follow the lead of Congress and attack the South where it would hurt most: in its heart, which was the institution of slavery itself.

In his response to Greeley, dated August 22, 1862, exactly a month before he signed the Preliminary Emancipation, Lincoln addressed the *Tribune*'s editor—speaking to the North and the border states—making it patently clear that his mandate as president, his first and ultimate priority as a citizen, was to save and restore the nation-state, not to dismantle slavery or to save black people: "I would save the Union," he writes, almost forlornly, keenly aware that this was going to be a very long and costly and deadly war, a war that the North was losing. "If I could save the Union without freeing *any* slave I would do it, and if I could save it by freeing *all* the slaves I would do it; and if I could save it by freeing some and leaving others alone I would also do that. What I do about slavery, and the colored race, I do because I believe it helps to save the Union." Slavery, an indirect cause of the war, was not his prime concern; protecting the integrity of the Constitution was: "My paramount object in this struggle is to save the Union, and is *not* either to save or to destroy slavery." Lincoln could live with slavery if he had to, if this was the only way to preserve the integrity of the country he thought he had been elected to serve, a point that he had emphasized during his run for the presidency, even if, temperamentally, he was opposed to the institution itself, and thought that its containment to the slave states would, ultimately, force it to collapse, through gradual, compensated emancipation and voluntary colonization.

The summer of 1862 saw the great sea change in Lincoln's attitudes about the cause of the war (at least how to represent that cause in public), about the conduct of the war, and about the fate of the slaves. The war was not going especially well; casualties were increasing, popular support in the North was waning, and the price of war, with no end in sight, was steadily rising. As Horace Greeley had noted, the Second Confiscation Act had given the president the authorization "to employ as many persons of African descent as he may deem necessary and proper for the suppression of this rebellion, and for this purpose he may organize and use them in such manner as he may judge best for the public welfare," as the act's section 11 plainly stated. And this included employing them as troops. (It also, in the very next section, authorized the president to ship "such persons of the African race, made free by the provisions of this act," to "some tropical country beyond the limits of the United States," still another indication of the separation even in the mind of the Republican Congress between the abolition of slavery and the integration of these newly freed slaves seamlessly into American society. I shall return to this point later in this essay.) But Lincoln was deeply skeptical; even as late as September 22, the date on which he signed the Preliminary Emancipation Proclamation following the Union victory at Antietam, he had included in it no provision for the freed slaves' serving as soldiers in the war.

Until about the middle of the fall of 1862, Lincoln seemed profoundly reluctant to allow black people to serve in the military and bear arms, for two predominant reasons. First of all, he felt worried, quite reasonably, that such a decision would so fundamentally alter the public definition of what a "negro" was and what the freed slaves could possibly become in all arenas of American society that the reaction, even in the North, would be quite negative. When the subject of black recruitment had come up for debate in the House of Representatives, for instance, one congressman howled that "This is a government of white men, made by white men for white men, to be administered, protected, defended, and maintained by white men."[11]

Second, Lincoln had the deepest doubts about the native abilities of blacks to fight white men effectively, in spite of the advocacy of people such as his first secretary of war, Simon Cameron, and a slew of abolitionists, including Charles Sumner and Frederick Douglass. In a meeting on September 13, 1862, Lincoln told a delegation of antislavery ministers from Chicago: "I admit that slavery is the root of the rebellion, or at least its *sine qua non*. The ambition of politicians may have instigated them to act, but they would have been impotent without slavery as their instrument."

Emancipation, he continued, would have a certain, dramatic, and practical impact on the uneven progress of the war, because "unquestionably it would weaken the rebels by drawing off their laborers, which is of great importance," since, as we have seen, the Confederates—as anyone thinking about the matter with a clear head should have anticipated—brought their slaves with them to war, where they performed the same functions in the military that they had performed back on the plantation or before the war. And though he recognized the cost to the North of slave labor among the Southern troops, he still remained profoundly skeptical of the capacities of blacks to serve as useful soldiers: "But I am not so sure we could do much with the blacks," Lincoln continued. "If we were to arm them, I fear that in a few weeks the arms would be in the hands of the rebels; and indeed thus far we have not had arms enough to equip our white troops." All that began to change, gradually if inevitably, in August of 1862. And it began to change, first and foremost, because Lincoln knew that the North was losing the war, and desperate—even heretofore unthinkable—measures now were called for.

As Allen Guelzo points out, Lincoln had every reason to be worried about the course of the war: "In the east, McClellan's grand army had bogged down on the Peninsula, was repelled from the gates of Richmond, and retreated to a fortified camp on the James River; Stonewall Jackson had scoured the Shenandoah, and Lee and Jackson together had administered a punishing defeat to John Pope at Second Bull Run. In the west, Grant had nearly fobbed away the entire game through inattention at Shiloh and Braxton Bragg was running free through Tennessee and up to Kentucky. The British cabinet was discussing an offer of mediation (i.e., sit down at the table, you fools, or we'll make you). And the Democratic opposition, which had been leaderless for a year after Stephen Douglas's death, was feeling its oats again and bidding to stage a return to power in Congress after the Fall elections."[12] Lincoln despaired of defeating the Confederacy, and felt that freeing the slaves in the seceded South was an urgent, practical, military necessity. (The pioneering research of Earl Ijames reveals that some slaves bore arms, and some free Negroes in the South actually enlisted and fought in the Confederate Army, as Frederick Douglass as early as 1861 warned Lincoln they would do, in an attempt to persuade Lincoln to authorize the use of black men as soldiers.)[13] But would he actually allow the freedmen to fight? How urgent was the need to reverse the course of the war?

The conduct of a very small number of black soldiers demonstrated their potential for courage and efficacy in battle, especially the First Kansas Colored Volunteer Infantry, which distinguished itself at Island Mound, Missouri, on October 29, 1862. But this action had little impact on the Union's commander-in-chief, and the unauthorized troops raised in South Carolina by General David Hunter only created protests in Congress. Lincoln continued to resist the possibilities offered by the idea of including black men in the Union army. His opposition to black recruitment changed, however, with an important, and little noted, subtle coup engineered by the Massachusetts abolitionist Senator Charles Sumner. Sumner quite cleverly gave the president a copy of a book that would both address Lincoln's doubts and fears about the courage and capacities of black soldiers and remind him that the Founders themselves had used black troops in combat during the Revolution. Lincoln was ever mindful of what the Founders had done; after all, his careful research into their attitudes about the future of slavery was crucial to his argument against slavery's spread to the territories in his pivotal Cooper Union speech. The book, *An Historical Research Respecting the Opinions of the Founders of the Republic on Negroes as Slaves, Citizens, and as Soldiers,* was written by George Livermore, a Boston merchant and bibliophile, and published after Lincoln issued his Preliminary Emancipation Proclamation. Livermore himself became intrigued by the history of black soldiers after reading the black abolitionist William C. Nell's *Colored Patriots of the American Revolution,* published in 1855. How important would this book be to Lincoln's thinking about the wisdom of employing black troops in his effort to save the Union? Lincoln supposedly even gave Livermore the pen that he used to sign the Emancipation Proclamation, though the list of claimants to that singular honor is no doubt a long one.

When Lincoln issued the final Emancipation Proclamation a few months later on January 1, 1863, he included a call to enlist black men into the army—ironically, blacks had served honorably in the navy since the beginning of the war, which inexplicably never entered into the calculation to include them in the army. "And I further declare and make known," Lincoln wrote, "that such persons ["the people so declared to be free"] of suitable condition, will be received into the armed service of the United States to garrison forts, positions, stations, and other places, and to man vessels of all sorts in said service." It was done. But the call was a cautious one and Lincoln and the War Department treated the idea as an experiment, one they thought was more than likely to fail. Early reports, however, especially from Union field commanders, proved encouraging. In a letter to Andrew Johnson, dated March 26, 1863, not even three full months after the Emancipation Proclamation became effective, Lincoln reinforced the case for the enormous potential benefits to the Union of the black troops: "The colored population is the great *available* and yet *unavailed* of, force for restoring the Union. The bare sight of fifty thousand armed, and drilled black soldiers on the banks of the Mississippi, would end the rebellion at once. And who doubts that we can present that sight, if we but take hold in earnest?" And take hold of this option Lincoln soon would, to great effect. On the one hand, freeing the slaves potentially eliminated an unremunerated source of labor for the army of the South; on the other hand, employing black troops would add significantly to the size of the North's fighting force. In other words, allowing black men to serve as troops would represent a negative factor for the South, and a positive factor for the North, a double benefit for the latter.

Andrew Johnson, by the way, never responded to Lincoln, at least not in writing, perhaps because the specter of fifty thousand armed and drilled black soldiers was a bit too much for him to imagine. And it was quite a sight to imagine for most Americans, black and white, but a desperate Lincoln had made the call, Livermore's treatise very much in mind. Precedent, after all, was of crucial importance to the lawyerly Lincoln, and no precedents were more important than those established by the Founders. Lincoln also listened carefully to his generals in the field, which increased his confidence in the change of policy. As Grant put it to Lincoln in a letter dated August 9, 1863, "I have given the subject of arming the negro my hearty support. This, with the emancipation . . . is the heavyest blow yet given the Confederacy." Grant was no abolitionist; he was writing to his president strictly as a military man. Not only did Lincoln, like Grant, become an enthusiastic convert; his stated loyalty to and praise of his black troops—he would frequently and with genuine emotion call them his "black warriors"—remained consistent until his death; indeed, his devotion to them and his determination to give them the right to vote following the war, as we have seen, led directly to Booth's decision to kill him. (Despite his declarations of support for the colored troops, it must be noted, Lincoln nevertheless refused to intervene to ensure their equal pay with white troops, an issue that nearly caused a mutiny of all the black troops; indeed, several were executed for opposing unequal pay. Only after an eighteen-month campaign by the Fifty-fourth Massachusetts Regiment and its supporters in Massachusetts did the government relent.)[14]

By the summer of 1863, the conduct of black soldiers had completely vindicated the president's decision. Black troops in the Louisiana Native Guard fought heroically at Port Hudson in May 27, 1863, and at Milliken's Bend on June 7, followed by the magnificent battle of the Fifty-fourth Regiment, of *Glory* fame, at Fort Wagner on July 18, which effectively ended Northern debate over black recruitment. A model of the fort and the battle actually circulated in New York, to much public acclaim. For all of his hesitancy and doubts, Lincoln, to his credit, changed his mind, recognizing the great practical impact the service of newly freed black troops would have upon the South's war effort by depriving it of its massive source of uncompensated labor, and understanding that the North needed more able bodies in combat. He was oddly silent, however, about the role of the free Negroes in the North, who numbered about 220,000 by 1860—another 260,000 lived in states in which slavery was legal—though many of them did fight, including J. R. Clifford, a great-uncle of mine.

3

So Lincoln freed the slaves in the rebellious, seceded South—and not in the border states, fearing their defection to the South—justifying his actions (about the constitutionality of which he had grave doubts) as a prerogative of the president during wartime. (As he wrote on August 26, 1863, in a letter for James C. Conkling to read aloud to a statewide Union rally in Springfield in September 1863—addressed to those who argued that the Emancipation was unconstitutional—"I think the constitution invests its commander-in-chief, with the law of war, in time of war. The most that can be said, if so much, is, that slaves are property. Is there—has there ever been—any question that by the law of war, property, both of enemies and friends, may be taken when needed?") Historians cannot agree about how many slaves Lincoln actually freed through the Emancipation Proclamation, but the numbers generally proposed are surprisingly low—about half a million, or 12 percent of the slaves, at most—considering that 3.9 million slaves are recorded in the 1860 federal census.[15] Between 180,000 and 200,000 newly liberated slaves and Negroes freed well before 1863 served the Union cause with distinction during the Civil War.

But if Lincoln successfully and quite fruitfully resolved the issue of black service in the military, what was his thinking about the matter of (voluntary) colonization of the mass of the slaves, who he knew by now would eventually, almost inevitably, have to be freed, unless the Confederacy won the war, or unless one of its preconditions for returning to the Union were to be abandonment of the Emancipation itself? With colonization, the story of Lincoln and slavery and race becomes even more complicated, and sometimes quite vexed, inextricably intertwined with the story of African American freedom through much of Lincoln's administration.

Just a month before the Emancipation Proclamation, in his annual message to Congress, on December 1, 1862, Lincoln formally announced that he intended to free the slaves in the Confederacy. At the same time, he was at pains to stress his continued support for voluntary colonization. "Many free Americans of African descent," he stresses, have made application to him "to favor their emigration" to other countries. However, since "several of the Spanish-American republics have protested against the sending of such colonies to their respective territories," Lincoln had hesitated to support migration there, until he could ensure "conditions which shall be equal, just, and humane." The freedmen, however, could go to Liberia and Haiti "with certainty of being received and adopted as citizens." Nevertheless, he continues, "I regret to say such persons, contemplating colonization, do not seem so willing to migrate to those countries, as to some others, nor so willing as I think their interest demands."

Lincoln, regardless of this stated reluctance, held out hope that the blacks would realize, sooner or later, that colonization was in their own best long-term interest: "I believe, however, opinion among them, in this respect, is improving; and that, ere long, there will be an augmented, and considerable migration to both these countries, from the United States." He urged Congress to "appropriate money, and otherwise provide, for colonizing free colored persons with their own consent, at any place or places without the United States." Lincoln went on to say that he wanted this to be part of a constitutional amendment. And that, of course, never happened, because most African Americans historically have found colonization a racist and repugnant idea, a thinly veiled form of negrophobia. Black leaders such as Martin R. Delany, Henry Highland Garnet, and James T. Holly supported colonization as early as the 1850s, just as Paul Cuffe had in 1815. Some blacks, of course, a very small number, did indeed migrate between 1815 and 1865 to Sierra Leone and Liberia—the African Colonization Society claimed to have transported about twelve thousand during this period[16]—while some black leaders called for migration with the collapse of Reconstruction, and the ensuing bitter backlash against black rights after 1876, including, among others, Henry McNeal Turner, by now a bishop in the African Methodist Episcopal Church, and Richard T. Greener, the first black graduate of Harvard College, who became dean of Howard University's Law Department in 1879. In 1876, Turner was elected honorary vice president of the American Colonization Society, and he played a pivotal role in the creation of the International Migration Society, which as late as 1895 and 1896 sponsored the return of two shiploads of African Americans to Liberia.[17] But for all this effort the numbers always remained small. Considering that 75 percent of the Africans who came to this country directly from the continent in the slave trade had arrived by 1775, one would think that this would be no surprise. After all, where else could "home" be, all of those decades later?

One reason for Lincoln's early embrace of colonization and long flirtation with it stemmed from his worry about the social and economic effects of immediate emancipation, which he did not favor except in the distant South, and only to further the North's campaign in the war. If colonization was not going to work, then prudent forethought about the pace of emancipation was demanded; indeed, he told General John M. Schofield, in a letter dated June 22, 1863, that "*gradual* [emancipation] can be made better than *immediate* [emancipation] for both black and white, except when military necessity changes the case." And where emancipation was upon us, Lincoln urged caution, asking General Nathaniel P. Banks, in a letter dated August 5, 1863, to consider for Louisiana "some practical system by which the two races could gradually live themselves out of their old relation to each other, and both come out better prepared for the new." The key to such gradual and mutual accommodation and social acceptance, he continued, would be "education for young blacks. After all," he mused, "the power, or element, of 'contract' may be sufficient for this probationary period; and, by it's simplicity, and flexibility, may be the better."

The sea change in Lincoln's attitudes toward what we might think of as the concept of the Negro, of his or her "nature," occurred, without a doubt, because of his perception of the valor of the black soldiers during the conflict, and perhaps through his meetings with the most extraordinary black man of all, the great writer and orator Frederick Douglass. In the August 26 letter that he had Conkling read at the Union rally on his behalf, Lincoln made the case for his decision not only to free the slaves, as we have seen, but also to use freed slaves as soldiers. "You say you will not fight to free negroes. Some of them seem willing to fight for you; but no matter. Fight you, then, exclusively to save the Union." And in the "struggle for the Union," he continues with great force and barely disguised anger wrapped in biting irony, there was no choice but to make the black former slaves soldiers: "to whatever extent the negroes should cease helping the enemy, to that extent it weakened the enemy in his resistance to you. Do you think differently? I thought that whatever negroes can be got to do as soldiers, leaves just so much less for white soldiers to do, in saving the Union. Does it appear otherwise to you?" We cannot win the war without the Negroes, Lincoln is saying; can't you see that? Are your prejudices so deep that you can't see what is in the best interests of the North?

But the most telling part of Lincoln's letter for Conkling is his unconscious testament about the view he has come to hold of Negroes, as human beings, just like white people. "But negroes," he maintains, "like other people, act upon motives. Why should they do any thing for us, if we will do nothing for them? If they stake their lives for us, they must be prompted by the strongest motives—even the promise of freedom." Negroes, in fighting to save the Union, have fought themselves out of slavery. Like it or not, they are people, just as we are; and just like us, they are motivated by what is best for them. We have entered into a contract with them. And, having done so, Lincoln concludes with a rhetorical hammer, there is no turning back: "And the promise being made, must be kept."

Lincoln's loyalty to the colored troops—whom he usually represented as consisting exclusively of former slaves, though Negroes long free served as well, of course—is the most impressive aspect of the transformation in his attitudes toward blacks. Reading his words today, and attempting to understand how Lincoln actually felt about "Americans of African descent," as he once put it, we can, I think, make the case that for him the colored troops were the Noble Negroes, a precursor to W.E.B. Du Bois's "talented tenth," though Lincoln would come to include that unspecified small number of "very intelligent negroes" in this group as well.

(Indeed, Lincoln's secretary William O. Stoddard described them in similar terms, calling them "a new race of freemen.")[18] In other words, Lincoln abstracted from the large mass of black people, slave and free, a much smaller subgroup, an elite within a nation-within-a-nation, one comprising two distinct parts: those who had demonstrated their capacity to be valiant in war—those who were physically superior, we might say—and those, like Frederick Douglass, who were intellectually superior. These were the natural aristocrats of the race, that signal core group upon whom Lincoln eventually became willing to confer the perquisites of American citizenship, as he said in his final speech.

I believe that Lincoln honestly felt, for both humanitarian and economic reasons, that, as he wrote in the letter for Conkling, "all men could be free." But perhaps because of nature, or because of the confining limits of the cruel environment of slavery, all men weren't yet equal, and perhaps would never be; hence the appeal to him at least of the idea of removing the mass of black people elsewhere, out of the country, and retaining what we might think of as an elite remnant. Nevertheless, we are a long way from "niggers and crocodiles" when the president of the United States, in an interview with Alexander W. Randall and Joseph T. Mills on August 16, 1864, asserts his determination to ensure the ideals of democracy and keep faith with his own promise of freedom to the black soldiers: "There have been men who have proposed to me to return to slavery the black warriors of Port Hudson & Olustee to their masters to conciliate the South." And to those who urge this action, Lincoln's answer is unequivocal: "I should be damned in time & in eternity for so doing." Moreover, "the world shall know that I will keep my faith to friends & enemies, come what will." He has pursued a course of abolition, he says bluntly, "for the sole purpose of restoring the Union." And why has he done so? Why has he been forced to do so? He must pursue a course of abolition in the slave states because "no human power can subdue this rebellion without using the Emancipation lever as I have done. Freedom has given us the control of 200,000 able bodied men, born & raised on southern soil. It will give us more yet." Abolition is essential to victory: "My enemies condemn my emancipation policy. Let them prove by the history of this war, that we can restore the Union without it." Lincoln had come full circle since his debates with Stephen Douglas, and it was the need for and actions of the colored troops that had transformed his attitudes so fundamentally. If he remained skeptical about the capacity of the larger society to absorb the mass of slaves that a Union victory would, through the Thirteenth Amendment, liberate, his commitment to his elite group of warriors was impressively total and absolute.

4

On March 4, 1865, just about a month before he died, Lincoln delivered what for Frederick Douglass, and many other African Americans, was his most resonant speech, a speech more about them and for them than any of Lincoln's other speeches or writings, not excluding the Emancipation Proclamation. As Ted Widmer notes, "His oration consisted of 703 words, 505 of which were words of one syllable, neatly distributed across 25 sentences tucked into four paragraphs. . . . In all of American expression, it would be difficult to imagine a higher ratio of thought-per-word."[19] It lasted all of six minutes. But in three distinct sections of his third paragraph, Lincoln pronounced, more powerfully than he ever had, the institution of slavery to be the inextricable cause of the war that would soon grind to an end, a war that had left 623,000 Americans dead.

"These slaves," he wrote ("one eighth of the whole population"), "constituted a peculiar and powerful interest. All knew that this interest was, somehow, the cause of the war." This would seem to be the most direct statement that Lincoln made about slavery as the origin of the war, since his meeting with the black delegation at the White House in August 1862. While he had referred to slavery in relation to the war on several occasions by now, he had never before stated the matter so clearly. For instance, in his first inaugural address, Lincoln said that "the only substantial dispute" between the North and the South was, in fact, over the extension of slavery, even though "one section of our country believes slavery is *right* . . . while the other believes it is *wrong*." During the first year of the war, he declared flatly, "We didn't go into the war to put down slavery, but to put the flag back, and to act differently at this moment, would, I have no doubt, not only weaken our cause but smack of bad faith; for I never should have had votes enough to send me here if the people had supposed I should try to use my power to upset slavery." If for no other reason, he continued, "the first thing you'd see, would be a mutiny in the army." No, for this reason among others, "we must wait until every other means has been exhausted. This thunderbolt will keep."

Even more important, in his first annual message to Congress, Lincoln declared that "the insurrection is largely, if not exclusively, a war upon the first principle of popular government—the rights of our people." And Lincoln made the direct connection between slavery and the origins of the war again just a week before issuing the Proclamation—during his conversation with the delegation of antislavery ministers, when he said "I admit that slavery is the root of the rebellion," then qualifying it somewhat by adding "or at least its *sine qua non*." But by the time he wrote the second inaugural, all qualifications had disappeared. There, before the most integrated audience that a president had ever addressed, Lincoln, curiously, seemed to have accepted the mantle of "Father Abraham" to the newly freed slaves.

According to the *Times of London,* "at least half the multitude were colored," newly freed slaves and free Negroes, among them Frederick Douglass, and this speech seemed tailor-made for them.[20] Following his often cited comment that "Both [the North and the South] read the same Bible and pray to the same God; and each invokes His aid against the other," Lincoln slyly implies that it is slavery that makes all the difference: "It may seem strange that any men should dare to ask a just God's assistance in wringing their bread from the sweat of other men's faces; but let us judge not that we be not judged." Then, most astonishingly and boldly, Lincoln dares to suggest that perhaps— just perhaps—the reason why 623,000 Americans would lie dead, Americans North and South who "both read the same Bible, and pray to the same God," is that this is the price God is extracting for the history of slavery: "Fondly do we hope—fervently do we pray—that this mighty scourge of war may speedily pass away. Yet, if God wills that it continue, until all the wealth piled by the bond-man's two hundred fifty years of unrequited toil shall be sunk, and until every drop of blood drawn with the lash, shall be paid by another drawn with the sword, . . . so still it must be said 'the judgments of the Lord, are true and righteous altogether.'" It is safe to say that never before in the history of the American presidency had the political economy of suffering, the rhetoric of a white eye for a black eye, been applied to the condition of the black enslaved. No wonder the reporter of the *Times of London* was struck by the call-and-response of Lincoln's black audience, the shouts and murmurs of "bless the Lord" and similar phrases still familiar in the black church, which must have reached a crescendo as he hit his stride in that remarkable third paragraph of his speech.

Frederick Douglass would later note "a leaden stillness" about the white half of the crowd. For black folks in attendance that day, Abraham Lincoln had come home, and blacks had every reason to believe that, at long last, they had found a permanent home in America as freedmen at last. On that day, within that third paragraph, Abraham Lincoln became the president of black men and women, far more so than he had before, even through the Emancipation. No wonder Douglass, who had to fight his way past two racist guards to gain entrance to the White House immediately following the speech, told the president in response to his questioning, "Mr. Lincoln, that was a sacred effort." Never before had anyone but the most rabid abolitionist—the sentiment calls to mind any number of pronouncements by John Brown— ever dared to argue that the God of the white man was punishing him for his treatment of blacks.

Forty-one days later, Lincoln would be killed by John Wilkes Booth, who was in the audience that day, as he was on the day of Lincoln's final speech, an informal address from the second floor of the White House in which he favored giving the vote to "very intelligent" blacks, and to those black men who had fought to save the Union. That speech, as Booth himself confessed in a letter, led to his decision to assassinate Lincoln. A year before the second inaugural, Lincoln had floated this idea to Michael Hahn, the governor of Louisiana, in almost the identical words he would use in his final speech, suggesting that the state of Louisiana might consider enfranchising "very intelligent . . . colored people" and those black warriors who had served "gallantly in our ranks," who "would probably help, in some trying time to come, to keep the jewel of liberty within the family of freedom." This idea, however, he was quick to add, "is only a suggestion, not to the public, but to you alone." Bear in mind that all Lincoln had the authority to do was to suggest a course of action to the governor of a state; enfranchisement, we often forget, remained a state prerogative until passage of the Fifteenth Amendment. In his last public address, on April 11, 1865, it was these few words about black enfranchisement that so infuriated Booth, and, one must imagine, his fellow Confederate sympathizers: "It is also unsatisfactory to some that the elective franchise is not given to the colored man. I would myself prefer that it were now conferred on the very intelligent, and on those who serve our cause as soldiers." If we do not take this course, Lincoln maintains, it would be as if "to the blacks we say 'This cup of liberty which these, your old masters, hold to your lips, we will dash from you, and leave you to the chances of gathering the spilled and scattered contents in some vague and undefined when, where, and how.'" Nowhere had Lincoln been stronger on the case for the enfranchisement of these two segments of the soon-to-be-born black citizenry; universal black male suffrage was not, of course, even secured by the Thirteenth Amendment. That right was still two constitutional amendments away.

If the second inaugural was Lincoln's black speech, then why would Frederick Douglass, just eleven years later, after Lincoln had been transformed into the American Christ, remember him at the dedication of the Freedmen's Monument, in the presence of President U. S. Grant, his cabinet, the Chief Justice and all of the associate justices of the Supreme Court, and just about anyone who was anyone in Washington on April 14, 1876, as "preeminently the white man's President, entirely devoted to the welfare of white men"? Douglass said that "truth compels me to admit even here in the presence of the monument we have erected to his memory, Abraham Lincoln was not, in the fullest sense of the word, either our man or our model. . . . The race to which we belong were not the special objects of his consideration. . . . First, midst and last you and yours were the object of his deepest affection and his most earnest solicitude. You are the children of Abraham Lincoln. We are at best only his step-children, children by adoption, children by force of circumstances and necessity."

Douglass—himself once a fugitive slave—was keenly aware that Lincoln had supported the Fugitive Slave Act of 1850, an act that was anathema to Douglass and his fellow abolitionists, and most certainly to any fugitive slave. As John Stauffer puts it, "unlike many of his antislavery colleagues," Lincoln "never questioned the validity of the Fugitive Slave Act of 1850, either politically or constitutionally. . . . Lincoln believed that the Constitution called for 'an efficient fugitive slave law.'" Douglass, once a slave in Maryland, also recalled that the very day on which Lincoln "revoked General Hunter's emancipation proclamation," in 1862; as Stauffer puts it, "he publicly told Maryland's slaveholders that he would rigorously defend the Fugitive Slave Act."[21] For Douglass, these were twin offenses, of the gravest consequences. In addition, a large measure of Douglass's frustration with Lincoln stemmed from his decision at the end of the war to endorse a lenient view of Reconstruction that would allow the seceded states back into the Union based on pledges of loyalty from 10 percent of the prewar population, but without enfranchising the most loyal part of the South: the former slaves and free blacks. But most of all, Douglass reminded his audience of the meeting with the black delegation in 1862, when Lincoln "strangely told us that we were the cause of the war . . . [and] were to leave the land in which we were born."[22] It was Lincoln's determined advocacy of colonization that most deeply disturbed Douglass, even eleven years after he had been assassinated.

In spite of these surprisingly critical remarks, Douglass's assessment of Lincoln was quite nuanced. In fact, he defended Lincoln's priority of union over abolition: "Had he put the abolition of slavery before the salvation of the Union," he would have alienated large numbers of people and "rendered resistance to rebellion impossible. Viewed from the genuine abolition ground, Mr. Lincoln seemed tardy, cold, dull, and indifferent; but measuring him by the sentiment of his country, a sentiment he was bound as a statesman to consult, he was swift, zealous, radical, and determined." Curiously, here Douglass is reversing himself; Douglass consistently argued during the war that abolishing slavery immediately (just after war broke out) would bring a swift end to the conflict.

Douglass confessed a second reason for his unease with Lincoln: to what must have been a shocked audience, he said that Lincoln "came into the Presidential chair upon one principle alone, namely, opposition to the extension of slavery. His arguments in furtherance of this policy had their motive and mainspring in his patriotic devotion to the interest of his own race." Like most African Americans of my generation, I was raised to believe that Lincoln hated slavery because he loved the slaves. Anyone who has given Lincoln's writings even a cursory glance comes quickly to understand that Lincoln did indeed hate slavery, but he hated it because he thought that human bondage was evil and because he thought that it created unfair competition in the marketplace, first and foremost for other white men. Some historians believe that it is not clear that Lincoln had completely abandoned at least a theoretical interest in voluntary colonization for the bulk of the freed slaves. Even if he had abandoned it, he had done so only a year or two before his death. It is noteworthy that Douglass referred to Lincoln's views on colonization, as well as his curious twists and turns about slavery, abolition, and Negro rights. No doubt, all these things informed Douglass's surprisingly critical assessment of Lincoln's legacy rendered at such a solemn and august occasion, but none more than his enthusiasm for voluntary colonization, which Douglass abhorred.

Lincoln put into action two colonization schemes during his presidency, the first in August 1862, when he invited those five black men to the White House and urged them to lead a settlement of other freed blacks to the Isthmus of Chiriqui, in

Colombia (now part of Panama). But the black abolitionists and the neighboring countries of Honduras, Nicaragua, and Costa Rica objected, and Lincoln abandoned the plan. Lincoln launched the second plan in early 1863, after he had signed the Emancipation, this time to L'Ile a Vache, Cow Island, off the southern peninsula of Haiti. In fact, on the very day before the Emancipation Proclamation became official, Lincoln signed a contract with Bernard Kock, who was the genius behind the Ile a Vache plan. In mid-April, 1863, 453 former slaves set sail on the *Ocean Ranger* for Cow Island. Most of the émigrés died from smallpox and malarial fevers; even the Haitian government was opposed. The few remaining survivors returned to the United States.

Moreover, as late as November 30, 1864, as Michael Lind reports, Lincoln asked Edward Bates, his attorney general, whether James Mitchell could continue to serve as Bates's "assistant or aid [*sic*] in the matter of executing the several acts of Congress relating to the emigration or colonizing of the freed Blacks," even though Lincoln's secretary, John Hay, had famously written in his diary of July 1, 1864, "I am happy that the President has sloughed off that idea of colonization."[23]

And then there are the deeply problematic and troubling recollections about the matter by General Benjamin F. Butler, which for complex reasons have driven historians to distraction. Butler claimed, in an article he wrote for the *North American Review* in 1886, ten years after Douglass's speech (and which he included in his autobiography, *Butler's Book,* published in 1892), that on February 3, 1865, just two months before his death, Lincoln had commissioned him to investigate the practicability of colonization. "I wish you would carefully examine the question and give me your views upon it and go into the figures, as you did before in some degree, so as to show whether the negroes can be exported." Butler says he told him, two days later, that "it will be impossible for you to transport them to the nearest place that can be found fit for them,—and that is the island of San Domingo,—half as fast as Negro children will be born here." Butler devoted three pages to this conversation in his memoirs.[24] In part to contextualize Butler's claim, Lind reminds us that colonization most certainly did not die in 1864: President Ulysses S. Grant favored "the annexation of the Dominican Republic," according to Lind, "as a new home for the entire colored population of the United States, should it choose to emigrate."[25]

Most scholars have dismissed Butler's recollections out of hand primarily because Butler was "a thoroughly untrustworthy witness," as David Herbert Donald said to me.[26] If Butler's statements about Lincoln's continuing support of colonization as late as 1865 turned out to be true, our image of the Lincoln who had wrestled with and by the end of his life had transcended antiblack racism, and who had decided that the future of the former slaves was inextricably intertwined with the future of the Republic, would be deeply troubled. The most convincing refutation of Butler's claims is that of Mark E. Neely, Jr., who in a careful and thoughtful analysis argues quite persuasively that Butler's is, at best, a most "spurious testimony," both because he gets many key facts about the date and circumstances surrounding their supposed meeting wrong, but especially because Butler claimed that Lincoln wanted to remove the former colored troops following the war, seeing in them a certain danger: "I fear a race war," Butler recalled Lincoln telling him, in direct quotation; "and it will be at least a guerilla war because we have taught these men how to fight."[27]

Now were these sentiments proven to be true, given the great faith in and fondness for the black troops that Lincoln had so publicly professed, this would be not only deeply disturbing, but profoundly chilling. Here, Neely is most convincing; at the least, we must doubt Butler's memory of Lincoln's angst about the potential for bad behavior among his black troops, since Butler claimed that this conversation with Lincoln occurred so close to the second inaugural and Lincoln's final speech. Actually, because of brilliant historical detective work by Phillip W. Magness, we now know that Butler *did* meet with Lincoln, but on April 11, 1865, the very day he delivered his final speech about black suffrage.[28] It seems scarcely possible for Lincoln to have said this privately to Butler about the black troops, and then to have delivered his speech just a few hours later making his intentions about their right to suffrage public for the first time. For Butler's claims about Lincoln to be true, Abraham Lincoln—mouthing all those lofty words about the inherent nobility of, and his loyalty to, the colored troops—would have to have been the most convincing actor in the history of the presidency before Ronald Reagan, and one of the most duplicitous. I have to confess that I find it a most chilling thought just contemplating the possibility that Butler's claims might be true, and am convinced that, for whatever reasons, Butler was either genuinely misremembering, or else engaging in his own attempt to press Lincoln into service for Butler's own personal and political cause.

Although they have not received the attention of Butler's claims about Lincoln and colonization, far more troubling are the recollections of Gideon Welles, Lincoln's secretary of the navy, with whom he shared "a relationship of mutual respect and admiration though not one of intimacy like that between Lincoln and Seward or Lincoln and Stanton," as Doris Kearns Goodwin puts it.[29] Lerone Bennett, Jr., has thoroughly examined Welles's diary entries made following cabinet meetings at which Lincoln discussed colonization, and two essays published seven years after Lincoln's death.[30] But I find even more intriguing Welles's final assessment of Lincoln, made in a third essay published in the *Galaxy* magazine (the first two were published in the same magazine in 1872—the first on "Lincoln and Johnson" and the second entitled "The History of Emancipation"—while the third one was published in 1877).

What gives Welles's recollections so much of their troubling power and authority is the fact that he is at pains to say that he disagreed with Lincoln about colonization but not about the supposed equality of the races: "I for one did not fully concur, from a conviction of the impracticability of general deportation, or sending from the country millions of its inhabitants; not," he is quick to add, "that I adopted the scheme of social and political equality of the races."[31] In the third essay, entitled "Administration of Abraham Lincoln," and published just a year after Douglass's Freedmen's Memorial Monument speech and a year before he died, Welles is at pains to tie Lincoln's support of emancipation to his unwavering support of colonization. Welles says that Lincoln "doubted if the Africans as a race were themselves capable of organizing as a community and successfully maintaining a government without supervision, or individually susceptible of high intellectual cultivation. There might be and were exceptional cases, but they were by nature dull, inert, dependent, and of little foresight—an ignorant and inferior race, who needed to be governed." As a consequence of their limited innate abilities, Welles continues, Lincoln was concerned that "if they remained with us, a war more terrible than that in which we were now engaged might be expected. It was, accordingly, "the duty of all who were entrusted with public affairs to take the subject into consideration, and foresee and guard against these threatened but he thought certainly impending evils. Colonization," therefore, "he believed to be the only remedy. His own speeches and writings disclose his sentiments, which are much misrepresented and misunderstood. He was not a political Abolitionist."

After repeating this directly and quite forcefully several times throughout the essay, Welles concludes adamantly that "Mr. Lincoln was always an anti-slavery man; but, as I have said, was never a political Abolitionist. Events and war necessity compelled him to adopt a policy of emancipation, for which he has received and deserved merited honors; but those who applaud his course in that respect omit to mention that colonization and deportation of the slaves when set free was deemed by him an essential part of his emancipation policy. Whether right or wrong on that subject it is not necessary to discuss, but the truth need not be suppressed. He believed it would be best for both the whites and blacks that the latter should leave the country, or, as he expressed it in his interview with the colored representatives [the August 1862 meeting], 'it is better for us both to be separated.' Knowing his convictions and earnest solicitude on this branch of his policy, I have sometimes doubted whether he would not have hesitated longer in issuing the decree of emancipation had he been aware that colonization would not be accepted as an accompaniment."

Why did Lincoln favor colonization? For two reasons, Welles argues: to ensure postwar social harmony and because he felt that black people were inherently inferior to white people: "Long before he yielded to emancipation, and in the belief that it was necessary to rid the country of the African race, he had schemes for their migration more advanced than those of the colonizationists. From a conviction that the white and black races could not abide together on terms of social and political equality, he thought they could not peaceably occupy the same territory—that one must dominate the other. Opposed to the whole system of enslavement, but believing the Africans were mentally an inferior race, he believed that any attempt to make them and the whites one people would tend to the degradation of the whites without materially elevating the blacks, but that separation would promote the happiness and welfare of each."

It is noteworthy that Welles wonders aloud why his contemporaries seem to wish to suppress Lincoln's views about colonization, which perhaps helps us to understand why he repeats his point again and again throughout the essay; it is equally noteworthy that Welles's views have largely escaped the rancorous debates that Butler's have elicited, perhaps because his are certainly more measured and persuasive than Butler's, and perhaps because he doesn't say explicitly whether or not he thought that Lincoln ever changed his mind, though he suggests that Lincoln did not: "President Lincoln, though disappointed in these experiments [the various colonization schemes tried during his administration], by no means abandoned his policy of deportation and emancipation, for the two were in his mind indispensably and indissolubly connected." A little later in the essay, Welles says again, grimly, that "at the time the preliminary emancipation proclamation was issued, he wished it distinctly understood that deportation was in his mind inseparably connected with that measure; that he considered the two to be parts of one system, and that they must be carried forward together." The clear implication of his argument, however, is that Lincoln held on to the idea of the inseparability of emancipation and colonization long after he issued the Emancipation Proclamation, though how long he never says explicitly. But for Welles, the unpopularity of the idea among blacks and the sheer logistical unfeasibility of the plan to relocate so many millions of former slaves out of the country caught Lincoln off guard; by the time he had committed to emancipating the Confederacy's slaves, there was no turning back, as Lincoln said himself. But that, of course, is not what Benjamin Butler argued. And it is not what Welles strongly implies either, though he feels no need to claim that Lincoln discussed the matter with him outside of cabinet meetings. While the discovery that Butler actually did have a final meeting with the president will no doubt open this debate once again, within this context and without claiming too much for them, Welles's contentions also warrant close and careful consideration of the matter of Lincoln's views on the voluntary colonization of at least some of the newly freed slaves after 1863.

Welles's reflections seem to have received less attention than Butler's, because Butler's have far more radical implications. If they were true, it would mean that our theories about Lincoln's complete transformation from the white man's president, as Douglass put it, to the black man's president that he would become in death and legend were problematic, to say the least. Magness's discovery of the actual date of Butler's meeting with the president makes his contentions all the more difficult to accept. But given what we know now about the history of race relations in this country since the Civil War, and given what we know of Lincoln's determination to reunite the North with the South, I find it perfectly reasonable that a war-weary Abraham Lincoln, who we know was still dreaming about the merits of colonization only two years before his death, might have allowed himself to wonder about—metaphorically "doing the figures" one more time—the feasibility of shipping the bulk of the former slaves out of this domain. I think many political leaders at the time wondered about this option as well, given the enormous hurdles presented by the integration of almost four million slaves into postwar American society. The dream of repatriating the mass of freed slaves back to Africa, after all, did not die with the death of Abraham Lincoln, and continued to be embraced by black and white leaders through the remainder of the century.

After all, common sense suggests that it would have been far easier to assimilate the relatively small numbers of black veterans and the elite Negroes into postwar America, in urgent need of healing between Southern and Northern white men, than it would have been to assimilate the remaining 3.4 million slaves who would be freed by the Thirteenth Amendment, the black underclass, as it were. (A century and a half after Lincoln's death, despite the election of a black president, we are still struggling to assimilate the large black underclass into the mainstream American working- and middle-class economy.) A prescient, sober, and practical Lincoln would most certainly have been aware of the social turmoil that surely faced a reunited America because of the liberation of all of these slaves. It seems perfectly reasonable to me that a man as brilliant as Abraham Lincoln, a man who loved the concept of country so much more than any single component of it, would have continued to wonder about the merits and efficacy of the colonization of the mass of these former black slaves. We underestimate Lincoln's commitment to reuniting the Union, at all costs, and diminish his complexity as a man still rooted deeply in his age and time when we romanticize him as the first American president completely to transcend racism and race. Lincoln was, if anything, "big enough to be inconsistent," as George M. Fredrickson, quoting W.E.B. Du Bois, so memorably said of the arc of his career, in his Du Bois Lectures at Harvard.[32] And I believe that his keen understanding of Lincoln's anguished twists and turns in his thinking about the Negro question over the course of the Civil War explains why Frederick Douglass felt justified when he said of Abraham Lincoln to that astonished audience that "The race to which we belong were not the special objects of his consideration. . . . To you it especially belongs to sound his praises, to preserve and perpetuate his memory, to multiply his statues, to hang his pictures on your walls, and commend his example, for to you he was a great and glorious friend and benefactor." How ironic it would be to Frederick Douglass that by the turn of the century, African Americans—most notably Booker T. Washington, Douglass's heir as the leader of the race—had assumed the leading role in sculpting Lincoln's image as the black man's president.

5

Despite the fact that Douglass would come to think of Lincoln as a friend, and consult with him at the White House on three occasions, nevertheless Douglass had been slow to trust Lincoln, and his sober, balanced remarks in 1876 must be read in the context of this history. Douglass's frustration with Lincoln first manifested itself in most dramatic form in late March 1861. As John Stauffer shows in great detail, Douglass announced in his newspaper that he planned to leave the United States for Haiti on April 25, with the intention of relocating there permanently, if indeed, as he hoped, it would prove to be a new, black "city set on a hill," the fulfillment at long last of the black person's dream of a republic in the New World in which the rights and privileges of citizenship would be extended to persons of color.

Just a month before, Douglass had responded to a correspondent that he would never emigrate to Haiti "under any circumstances now existing or apprehended." In Stauffer's words, "what induced him to suddenly abandon his faith in America"[33] was Abraham Lincoln's first inaugural address and the "first" Thirteenth Amendment, the unratified amendment passed by Congress in 1861, which would have guaranteed the existence of slavery forever: "Congress had just passed a proposed Thirteenth Amendment in the hope of wooing the traitors back into the Union. Although it was never ratified, this 'first' Thirteenth Amendment was the exact opposite of the 'actual' one that abolished slavery (in 1865). It was an *unamendable* amendment guaranteeing slavery in the slave states *forever*. Lincoln refers to it in his inaugural: 'I understand a proposed amendment to the Constitution . . . has passed Congress, to the effect that the Federal Government shall never interfere with slavery in the slave states. I have no objection to its being made express and irrevocable.'" He also vowed to uphold the Fugitive Slave Act, leading Douglass to label him "an excellent slave hound."

In addition, while most scholars would concur with David Herbert Donald in his praise of Lincoln's speech of April 11, 1865, in which he advocated suffrage for a limited number of black people—"never before had any American President publicly announced that he was in favor of Negro suffrage," as Donald puts it—black abolitionists to a man wanted the suffrage extended immediately to all free black people, and they wanted all black people to be free and to be citizens.[34] The pace of Lincoln's reform—and just as important the extent to which this reform would apply to members of the black community—was deeply troubling to Frederick Douglass and his black abolitionist peers.

Then, too, there were certain disturbing forms of address about black people in which Lincoln persisted at least until 1864. Don Fehrenbacher, in *Recollected Words of Abraham Lincoln,* records a conversation between the president and Henry Samuel, secretary of a committee concerned with the recruitment of black troops, about equal wages for blacks employed by the army. Samuel says that Lincoln said in a humorous tone, "Well, gentlemen, you wish the pay of Cuffie raised," Cuffee being a racist name for blacks widely in use in the nineteenth century. Samuel protested Lincoln's use of that term, to which the president responded, "I stand corrected, young man, but you know I am by birth a southerner and in our section that term is applied without any idea of an offensive nature. I will, however, at the earliest possible moment, do all in my power to accede to your request."[35] While John G. Nicolay, Lincoln's former secretary, later labeled this account "utterly untrustworthy," we have absolutely no reason to doubt it. Lincoln's prepresidential discourse about blacks was certainly peppered with words such as "Sambo," "boy," "auntie," "nigger," as well as Cuffee, and occasionally these slippages occurred even after he was president, such as the day he referred to Sojourner Truth as "Aunty" during her visit to the White House.[36] And this unfortunate practice, as trite perhaps as it might strike us today, most certainly would not have endeared him to members of the black community.

Historians have sought to sweep Douglass's 1876 assessment of Lincoln under the carpet of revision by portraying Douglass as a fervent admirer of the president, citing brief but deeply respectful remarks about Lincoln that Douglass made both before and after 1876. And, indeed, at several ceremonial occasions, Douglass praised Lincoln for being the Great Emancipator, as he most certainly was, especially through his advocacy of the (second) Thirteenth Amendment, which in fact freed all of the slaves. In December 1865, for instance, Douglass eulogized Lincoln by contrasting him to other presidents: "As compared with the long line of his predecessors, many of whom were merely the facile and servile instruments of the slave power, Abraham Lincoln, while unsurpassed in his devotion to the white race, was also in a sense hitherto without example, emphatically the black man's president."[37] After meeting Lincoln, he wrote that "I have never seen a more transparent countenance. There was not the slightest shadow of embarrassment after the first moment. . . . I was never in any way reminded of my humble origin, or of my unpopular color."[38] After Lincoln's death, Douglass frequently referred to him as "the king of self-made men," "the greatest statesman that ever presided over the destinies of this Republic" and the man most responsible for "American liberty."[39] We can see in Frederick Douglass's attitudes toward Lincoln's legacy the roots of the very duality in assessment that continues to manifest itself among black politicians and scholars, ranging from the untroubled adoration expressed by Booker T. Washington (who clearly sought to position Lincoln as his long-lost white metaphorical father figure) through the bitter denunciations of Malcolm X and the searching critiques of Lerone Bennett,[40] to the more nuanced yet strongly favorable assessment of Barack Obama.[41]

For his part, however, Douglass never intended his polite, sometimes quite sentimental, and genuinely heartfelt remarks about Lincoln's considerable strengths to deconstruct his considered assessment of Lincoln overall. In fact, he endeavored to avoid any confusion about his feelings, seeking to ensure that the force and impact of his 1876 speech would not be lost by appending the entire Freedom Monument speech to the last two editions of his third and final book, his autobiography, *The Life and Times of Frederick Douglass,* published in 1881, and revised in a final edition published just three years before his death, in 1892. Douglass knew Lincoln, and he came to like and admire him as a man and as his president, but he refused to whitewash what he considered Lincoln's flaws when it came to slavery and race, perhaps most important among them the president's refusal to embrace full emancipation as early as July 1861, which Douglass believed would have led to a swift Union victory, saving hundreds of thousands of lives, despite the fact that Lincoln believed that he did not have the power to do this, and that such an attempt would have been unconstitutional. Douglass also consistently abhorred Lincoln's attempts to encourage voluntary colonization, and continued to stand firm about emigration after Lincoln's death, even when it experienced an upsurge of support among both black and white leaders in the mid-1870s, as Reconstruction was being systematically and often violently dismantled.

W.E.B. Du Bois, Frederick Douglass's most legitimate heir within the black political tradition, shared Douglass's measured assessment of Lincoln on slavery and race. In 1922, Du Bois wrote that "As sinners, we like to imagine righteousness in our heroes. As a result, when a great man dies, we begin to whitewash him. We seek to forget all that was small and mean and unpleasant, and remember only the fine and brave and good. We slur over and explain away his inconsistencies until there appears before us, not the real *man* but the myth—immense, perfect, cold, and dead." Du Bois loved Lincoln but refused to deify him. "I love him not because he was perfect but because he was not and yet triumphed," he said. Lincoln was among those white folks "whose taste was educated in the gutter. The world is full of people born hating and despising their fellows. To these I love to say: See this man. He was one of you and yet he became Abraham Lincoln." For Du Bois, Lincoln was "big enough to be inconsistent," the phrase that proved so resonant for George M. Fredrickson in his last reflections on Lincoln's views on race, by which both Du Bois and Fredrickson meant that Lincoln grew and evolved, he faced and confronted his own prejudices, and, to a remarkable extent, overcame them.[42] Lincoln remade himself as a proponent of black freedom, fully aware of how far he had come in doing so.

We can do Lincoln no greater service than to walk that path with him, and we can do him no greater disservice than to whitewash it, seeking to give ourselves an odd form of comfort by pretending that he was even one whit less complicated than he actually was. And this is especially crucial in this, the very year in which a black man, Barack Obama—145 years after the Emancipation Proclamation—became the man who is destined be thought of as Lincoln's most direct heir, the forty-fourth president of the United States.

If I can risk a speculation, however, it seems to me that even if we did in fact learn that Lincoln held on to the very end to the idea that colonization was a way "to erase the original sin by returning blacks to their homeland," as Adam Gopnik so brilliantly put it to me,[43] this would not sully his reputation in any meaningful way, if we judge him by nineteenth-century standards, and when we recall how very far Lincoln had come in his thinking about race and the abolition of slavery, from the debates with Stephen Douglas through the signing of the Emancipation Proclamation and finally to the passage of the Thirteenth Amendment, which he insisted upon signing and which he clearly supported, understood, and championed as it made its way through congressional debate, and which, ultimately, was responsible for abolishing slavery. Moreover, I believe that the most radical thing that Abraham Lincoln did, as Adam Gopnik argues, given what we know about Thomas Jefferson's views of the "nature" of blacks and his limited definition of "men" in the Declaration, was his invocation of its opening line unequivocally on behalf of African Americans in a public debate well before the Civil War, and his insistence upon the inclusion of blacks in that definition consistently through his presidency.[44] Against his flirtation with colonization—and, indeed, trumping this—is the fact that he worked his way to declaring his support for limited black suffrage in the final speech of his life, which, as David Donald tells us, made him the very first president to do so, and which turned out to be the final speech of his life, in fact, precisely because of this declaration of support.[45] Perhaps this, in the end, was Abraham Lincoln's most "sacred effort" of all.

Henry Louis Gates, Jr.

Notes

1. I would like to thank John Sellers at the Library of Congress for showing me Lincoln's notebook. The Lincoln comment about the Haitian ambassador is in John R. McKivigan, *Forgotten Firebrand: James Redpath and the Making of Nineteenth-Century America* (Ithaca: Cornell University Press, 2008), 78.
2. Frederick Douglass, "The Claims of the Negro Ethnologically Considered," in *Racial Thought in America: From the Puritans to Abraham Lincoln, A Documentary History*, ed. Louis Ruchames, vol. 1 (New York: Grosset & Dunlap, 1969), 479–492.
3. David Hume, "Of National Characters," 1754/1776, in Emmanuel Chukwudi Eze, *Race and the Enlightenment: A Reader* (Cambridge, Mass.: Blackwell, 1997). For the Agassiz quotation, see Stephen Jay Gould, *The Mismeasure of Man*, rev. and expanded (New York: W. W. Norton, 1996), 76–77.
4. Thomas Jefferson, *Notes on the State of Virginia*, ed. William Peden (New York: W. W. Norton, 1972), 142.
5. Blight, correspondence, August 10, 2008.
6. As Allen Guelzo states: "There is a certain muddling among historians about who, and how many, were freed by the Proclamation, and that hangs on the ambiguous use of the word 'freed.' If we mean de facto, then the number is indeed vanishingly small, out of the population of 3.9 million slaves; but if we mean de jure, then the Proclamation freed every one of the slaves in the areas it was applied to. Freedom, in the fullest sense, requires both. A fugitive slave may run away and become de facto free, but so can any escapee from prison, and such fugitives are liable to recapture and rendition at any time. But a slave declared de jure free cannot, once an escape is made to Union lines, ever be returned to slavery; and slaves who are overrun by the advance of the Union armies are thus rendered both de facto and de jure free. They would not be, however, without the Proclamation. Any slave who achieved de facto freedom—what Lincoln called 'actual freedom'—was always liable to reenslavement without the change in legal status conferred by the Proclamation. So, just as it is often said that Lincoln's Proclamation freed no one because it did not instantly work de facto freedom, it can just as easily be said that without the Proclamation, no slave who escaped (or was liberated by the Union army) from slavery ever stopped being a slave— except, of course, for the Emancipation Proclamation. I know this sounds tendentious, but it's tendentious, too, to hear people

blather on about how Lincoln never 'really' freed any slave. That's like saying the Voting Rights Act and the Civil Rights Act never gave any black person an 'actual' vote" (Guelzo, correspondence, November 13, 2008). See also n. 12, below.

7. Guelzo, correspondence, October 3, 2008.
8. Charleston debate, in *Created Equal? The Complete Lincoln-Douglas Debates of 1858*, ed. Paul Angle (Chicago: University of Chicago Press, 1958), 270.
9. Eric Foner, ed., *Our Lincoln: New Perspectives on Lincoln and His World* (New York: W. W. Norton, 2008), 151.
10. *Christian Recorder,* August 30, 1862; Eric Foner, "Lincoln and Colonization," in Foner, *Our Lincoln*, 155–156; see also Manisha Sinha, "Allies for Emancipation? Lincoln and Black Abolitionists," in Foner, 167–199. Henry McNeal Turner, by the way, was the first African American appointed chaplain (by Lincoln in 1863) to the U.S. Army. He was attached to the First Regiment of the U.S. Colored Troops. Ironically, Turner in the 1870s would become an ardent proponent of black colonization in Liberia. On Douglass's reaction, see David W, Blight, *Frederick Douglass' Civil War: Keeping Faith in Jubilee* (Baton Rouge: Louisiana State University Press, 1989), 139.
11. Quoted in Forrest G. Wood, *Black Scare: The Racist Response to Emancipation and Reconstruction* (Berkeley and Los Angeles: University of California Press, 1968), 43.
12. Guelzo, correspondence, October 3, 2008. See also n. 6, above.
13. Earl L. Ijames, correspondence, November 17, 2008; John Stauffer, *Giants: The Parallel Lives of Frederick Douglass and Abraham Lincoln* (New York: Twelve, 2008), 229; Philip S. Foner, ed., *The Life and Writings of Frederick Douglass* (New York: International Publishers, 1950–1975), 3:156–157. Ijames, the curator of the North Carolina Museum of History, says that, among others, the Fortieth Regiment of North Carolina Troops, Company D, included several free black men who enlisted voluntarily and fought with guns in combat against the North. His book *Colored Confederates* is forthcoming.
14. Donald Yacovone, "The Fifty-fourth Massachusetts Regiment, the Pay Crisis, and the 'Lincoln Despotism,'" in *Hope and Glory: Essays on the Legacy of the Fifty-fourth Massachusetts Regiment*, ed. Martin H. Blatt, Thomas J. Brown, and Donald Yacovone (Amherst: University of Massachusetts Press, 2001), 35–51.
15. Guelzo, correspondence, October 3, 2008; Blight, correspondence, August 10, 2008.
16. P. J. Staudenraus, *The African Colonization Movement, 1816–1865* (New York: Columbia University Press, 1961).

17. See the article, by Greener and others, "The Future of the Negro," *North American Review* 139, no. 332 (July 1884): 79–100: "The negro will not only migrate, he will also emigrate; but only when impelled by absolute poverty or despair, or when led by prospects of pecuniary gain, and not in sufficient numbers to affect appreciably his social or political status in the South. He will become, however, more and more interested in the capabilities of the fatherland. From the United States the stream of civilization will inevitably lead to Africa. The rich table-lands east of Liberia will be occupied first, and we may look for many radiating currents therefrom. It would be poetic justice to see a Negro-American civilization redeeming Africa. The antipathy formerly felt by the Negro-American to colonization has passed away. He now sees quite clearly that to civilize Africa is to exalt the negro race. Our own Government, through its Department of State, could aid in this, by appointing every diplomatic and consular officer on the African continent from among the large number of ambitious and able colored men. It would be a brilliant stroke of policy for the spread of our commerce, and for allaying the phantom of negro supremacy, while it would open up a career to many of the colored people of the country in the way of business, and give a renewed impetus to emigration" (89). See also the entry on Turner in *African American National Biography*, ed. Henry Louis Gates, Jr., and Evelyn Brooks Higginbotham (New York: Oxford University Press, 2008).
18. Foner, *Our Lincoln,* 163.
19. Edward Widmer, "Lincoln's Apotheosis," forthcoming in *A New Literary History of America*, ed. Greil Marcus and Werner Sollors (Cambridge: Harvard University Press, Belknap Press, 2009).
20. Ronald C. White, *Lincoln's Greatest Speech: The Second Inaugural* (New York: Simon and Schuster, 2002), 32.
21. Stauffer, *Giants,* 240–241. For a different perspective, see James Oakes, *The Radical and the Republican: Frederick Douglass, Abraham Lincoln, and the Triumph of Antislavery Politics* (New York: W. W. Norton, 2007).
22. Foner, *Our Lincoln,* 156.
23. Michael Lind, *What Lincoln Believed: The Values and Convictions of America's Greatest President* (New York: Doubleday, 2004), 224.
24. Benjamin F. Butler, *Autobiography and Personal Reminiscences of . . . : Butler's Book* (Boston: A. M. Thayer, 1892), 903–904.
25. Lind, *What Lincoln Believed,* 225.
26. Donald, correspondence, November 13, 2008.
27. Mark E. Neely, Jr., "Abraham Lincoln and Black Colonization: Benjamin Butler's Spurious Testimony," *Civil War History* 25 (1970): 77–83.

28. Phillip W. Magness, "Benjamin Butler's Colonization Testimony Re-evaluated," *Journal of the Abraham Lincoln Association* 29, no. 1 (Winter 2008).

29. Goodwin, correspondence, November 29, 2008.

30. Lerone Bennett, Jr., *Forced Into Glory: Abraham Lincoln's White Dream* (Chicago: Johnson Publishing Company, 2000), 509–511, and passim; Gideon Welles, "Lincoln and Johnson," *Galaxy* (April 1872): 521–532, and Welles, "The History of Emancipation," *Galaxy* (December 1872): 838–851.

31. Gideon Welles, "Administration of Abraham Lincoln," *Galaxy* 24, no. 4 (October 1877): 437ff.

32. Cited in George M. Fredrickson, *Big Enough to Be Inconsistent: Abraham Lincoln Confronts Slavery and Race* (Cambridge: Harvard University Press, 2008).

33. Stauffer, *Giants*, 216–219; quotation from p. 217.

34. David Herbert Donald, *Lincoln* (New York: Simon and Schuster, 1995), 585.

35. *Recollected Words of Abraham Lincoln*, ed. Don E. Fehrenbacher and Virginia Fehrenbacher (Stanford: Stanford University Press, 1996), 389–390.

36. On "Sambo," see *Collected Works*, 3:204–205; on "boy," *Collected Works*, 4: 277 and 5:33; on "Cuffie," see Fehrenbacher, *Recollected Words of Abraham Lincoln*, 389–390; on "auntie," see Philip and Peter Kunhardt, *Looking for Lincoln: The Making of an American Icon* (New York: Alfred A. Knopf, 2008), 252–253.

37. Douglass, "Abraham Lincoln," December 1865 [holograph], Frederick Douglass Papers, Library of Congress, reel 19; Guelzo, correspondence, October 3, 2008.

38. Stauffer, *Giants*, 66; Douglass to George Stearns, August 12, 1863, Historical Society of Pennsylvania.

39. Stauffer, *Giants*, 24, 311.

40. Bennett, *Forced into Glory*.

41. Barack Obama, "What I See in Lincoln's Eyes," *Time Magazine*, June 26, 2005, http://www.time.com/time/printout/0,8816, 1077287,00.html.

42. W.E.B. Du Bois, *Writings* (New York: Library of America, 1986), 1196–1198.

43. Gopnik, correspondence, December 1, 2008.

44. Adam Gopnik, *Angels and Ages: A Short Book about Darwin, Lincoln, and Modern Life* (New York: Alfred A. Knopf, 2009).

45. Donald, *Lincoln*, 585.

LINCOLN
on
RACE & SLAVERY

1

Protest in Illinois Legislature on Slavery
CW, 1:74–75

Although Illinois abolished slavery in its 1818 constitution, the state remained hostile to African Americans throughout the nineteenth century. Its 1848 constitution, for instance, barred black immigration and remained the law until 1865, although officials did not rigorously enforce it. The state's white citizens demanded exclusion of new black settlers and threatened to "take the matter into their own hands, and commence a war of extermination." In January 1837, the Illinois legislature passed a resolution stating that "we highly disapprove of the formation of abolition" societies, "and of the doctrines promulgated by them," while admitting that slavery was indeed an "unfortunate condition of our fellow men, whose lots are cast in thralldom in a land of liberty and peace." The legislature, however, asserted that "the General government has no power to strike their fetters from them." The phrasing indicated the complexity of the slavery question for whites who generally disdained slavery *and* the slave. Throughout his career, Lincoln freely confessed to opposing the institution of slavery but remained equally opposed to the agitation of antislavery societies. Since the explosive debates surrounding the 1820 Missouri Compromise, the future of slavery remained the single greatest threat to the Union. Lincoln followed the example of his political hero Henry Clay and dedicated his career to preserving the Union and diminishing the strength of slavery. Lincoln, with state legislator Daniel Stone, a Whig lawyer originally from Vermont, went on record with this protest of the legislature's resolution. Although Lincoln clearly agreed with its principles, he criticized the phrasing of the original legislation, perhaps reflecting his desire to distinguish himself among his peers and to appeal to residents from New England, rather than those from the South who dominated Illinois. Lincoln and Stone characterized slavery as an "injustice" and "bad policy," but underscored their belief in the constitutionality of slavery where it already existed. Lincoln backed legislation where he believed the Constitution permitted action, in this case in the District of Columbia and, later, in the territories. More important, in one of his first public documents, Lincoln established his stand on the institution of slavery. For racial conditions in Illinois, see: Leon F. Litwack, *North of Slavery: The Negro in the Free States, 1790–1860* (Chicago: University of Chicago Press, 1961), 69.

March 3, 1837

The following protest was presented to the House, which was read and ordered to be spread on the journals, to wit:

"Resolutions upon the subject of domestic slavery having passed both branches of the General Assembly at its present session, the undersigned hereby protest against the passage of the same.

They believe that the institution of slavery is founded on both injustice and bad policy; but that the promulgation of abolition doctrines tends rather to increase than to abate its evils.

They believe that the Congress of the United States has no power, under the constitution, to interfere with the institution of slavery in the different States.

They believe that the Congress of the United States has the power, under the constitution, to abolish slavery in the District of Columbia; but that that power ought not to be exercised unless at the request of the people of said District.

The difference between these opinions and those contained in the said resolutions, is their reason for entering this protest."

Dan Stone,
A. Lincoln,
Representatives from the county of Sangamon.

2

Address Before the Young Men's Lyceum of Springfield, Illinois
CW, 1:108, 109–112

Beginning in the 1820s, rioting became an all-too-common oc-currence in America's cities and towns. Sparked by the market economic revolution and cyclical depressions, immigration, rapid urbanization, and racism, the blight of increasing violence spared few of the nation's growing population centers. This turmoil was compounded by the escalating debate over the morality of slavery, and by Nat Turner's 1831 slave insurrection; a young man like Lincoln might well express apprehension for the future. As a state legislator, Lincoln helped orchestrate the relocation of the state capital to Springfield in 1837, where he moved in April. In January of the next year, in one of his first speeches in the new capital, Lincoln addressed the growing unrest he saw. He had only to allude to Elijah P. Lovejoy, murdered the previous year in Alton, Illinois, for publishing an antislavery newspaper, to illustrate his warning that a new level of chaos endangered the entire nation. He even condemned the lynching of a black murderer as a wanton violation of the legal order and pointed to the killing of a recently freed slave for the crime of "attending to his own business, and at peace with the world." Lincoln feared for the future, presciently admonishing his audience that the greatest threat to national security would come from within. The only effective protection he could imagine lay in devotion to the principles of liberty established by the Founding Fathers with the "blood of the revolution." In this remarkable speech, one can see the principles that would in the years ahead lead a rising lawyer and politician to challenge Stephen A. Douglas, whom Lincoln saw as the greatest threat to the liberty won in the American Revolution.

The Perpetuation of Our Political Institutions

. . . At what point then is the approach of danger to be expected? I answer, if it ever reach us, it must spring up amongst us. It cannot come from abroad. If destruction be our lot, we must ourselves be its author and finisher. As a nation of freemen, we must live through all time, or die by suicide.

I hope I am over wary; but if I am not, there is, even now, something of ill-omen amongst us. I mean the increasing disregard for law which pervades the country; the growing disposition to substitute the wild and furious passions, in lieu of the sober judgement [*sic*] of Courts; and the worse than savage mobs, for the executive ministers of justice. This disposition is awfully fearful in any community; and that it now exists in ours, though grating to our feelings to admit, it would be a violation of truth, and an insult to our intelligence, to deny. Accounts of outrages committed by mobs, form the every-day news of the times. They have pervaded the country, from New England to Louisiana;—they are neither peculiar to the eternal snows of the former, nor the burning suns of the latter;—they are not the creature of climate—neither are they confined to the slaveholding, or the non-slaveholding States. Alike, they spring up among the pleasure hunting masters of Southern slaves, and the order loving citizens of the land of steady habits. Whatever, then, their cause may be, it is common to the whole country.

It would be tedious, as well as useless, to recount the horrors of all of them. Those happening in the State of Mississippi, and at St. Louis, are, perhaps, the most dangerous in example, and revolting to humanity. In the Mississippi case, they first commenced by hanging the regular gamblers: a set of men, certainly not following for a livelihood, a very useful, or very honest occupation; but one which, so far from being forbidden by the laws, was actually licensed by an act of the Legislature, passed but a single year before. Next, negroes, suspected of conspiring to raise an insurrection, were caught up and hanged in all parts of the State: then, white men, supposed to be leagued with the negroes; and finally, strangers, from neighboring States, going thither on business, were, in many instances, subjected to the same fate. Thus went on this process of hanging, from gamblers to negroes, from negroes to white citizens, and from these to strangers; till, dead men were seen literally dangling from the boughs of trees upon every road side; and in numbers almost sufficient, to rival the native Spanish moss of the country, as a drapery of the forest.

Turn, then, to that horror-striking scene at St. Louis. A single victim was only sacrificed there. His story is very short; and is, perhaps, the most highly tragic, of any thing of its length, that has ever been witnessed in real life. A mulatto man, by the name of McIntosh, was seized in the street, dragged to the suburbs of the city, chained to a tree, and actually burned to death; and all within a single hour from the time he had been a freeman, attending to his own business, and at peace with the world.

Such are the effects of mob law; and such are the scenes, becoming more and more frequent in this land so lately famed for love of law and order; and the stories of which, have even now grown too familiar, to attract any thing more, than an idle remark.

But you are, perhaps, ready to ask, "What has this to do with the perpetuation of our political institutions?" I answer, it has much to do with it. Its direct consequences are, comparatively speaking, but a small evil; and much of its danger consists, in the proneness of our minds, to regard its direct, as its only consequences. Abstractly considered, the hanging of the gamblers at Vicksburg, was of but little consequence. They constitute a portion of population, that is worse than useless in a[ny community; and their death, if no perni]cious example be set by it, is never matter of reasonable regret with any one. If they were annually swept, from the stage of existence, by the plague or small pox, honest men would, perhaps, be much profited, by the operation. Similar too, is the correct reasoning, in regard to the burning of the negro at St. Louis. He had forfeited his life, by the perpetration of an outrageous murder, upon one of the most worthy and respectable citizens of the city; and had he not died as he did, he must have died by the sentence of the law, in a very short time afterwards. As to him alone, it was as well the way it was, as it could otherwise have been. But the example in either case, was fearful. When men take it in their heads to day, to hang gamblers, or burn murderers, they should recollect, that, in the confusion usually attending such transactions, they will be as likely to hang or burn some one, who is neither a gambler nor a murderer [as] one who is; and that, acting upon the [exam]ple they set, the mob of to-morrow, may, an[d] probably will, hang or burn some of them, [by th]e very same mistake. And not only so; the innocent, those who have ever set their faces against violations of law in every shape, alike with the guilty, fall victims to the ravages of mob law; and thus it goes on, step by step, till all the walls erected for the defence of the persons and property of individuals, are trodden down, and disregarded. But all this even, is not the full extent of the evil. By such examples, by instances of the perpetrators of such acts going unpunished, the lawless in spirit, are encouraged to become lawless in practice; and having been used to no restraint, but dread of punishment, they thus become, absolutely unrestrained. Having ever regarded Government as their deadliest bane, they make a jubilee of the suspension of its operations; and pray for nothing so much, as its total annihilation. While, on the other hand, good men, men who love tranquility, who desire to abide by the laws, and enjoy their benefits, who would gladly spill their blood in the defence of their country;

seeing their property destroyed; their families insulted, and their lives endangered; their persons injured; and seeing nothing in prospect that forebodes a change for the better; become tired of, and disgusted with, a Government that offers them no protection; and are not much averse to a change in which they imagine they have nothing to lose. Thus, then, by the operation of this mobocratic spirit, which all must admit, is now abroad in the land, the strongest bulwark of any Government, and particularly of those constituted like ours, may effectually be broken down and destroyed—I mean the *attachment* of the People. Whenever this effect shall be produced among us; whenever the vicious portion of population shall be permitted to gather in bands of hundreds and thousands, and burn churches, ravage and rob provision stores, throw printing presses into rivers, shoot editors, and hang and burn obnoxious persons at pleasure, and with impunity; depend on it, this Government cannot last. By such things, the feelings of the best citizens will become more or less alienated from it; and thus it will be left without friends, or with too few, and those few too weak, to make their friendship effectual. At such a time and under such circumstances, men of sufficient tal[ent and ambition will not be want]ing to seize [the opportunity, strike the blow, and over-turn that fair fabric], which for the last half century, has been the fondest hope, of the lovers of freedom, throughout the world.

I know the American People are *much* attached to their Government;—I know they would suffer *much* for its sake;—I know they would endure evils long and patiently, before they would ever think of exchanging it for another. Yet, notwithstanding all this, if the laws be continually despised and disregarded, if their rights to be secure in their persons and property, are held by no better tenure than the caprice of a mob, the alienation of their affections from the Government is the natural consequence; and to that, sooner or later, it must come.

Here then, is one point at which danger may be expected.

The question recurs "how shall we fortify against it?" The answer is simple. Let every American, every lover of liberty, every well wisher to his posterity, swear by the blood of the Revolution, never to violate in the least particular, the laws of the country; and never to tolerate their violation by others. As the patriots of seventy-six did to the support of the Declaration of Independence, so to the support of the Constitution and Laws, let every American pledge his life, his property, and his sacred honor;—let every man remember that to violate the law, is to trample on the blood of his father, and to tear the character [charter?] of his own, and his children's liberty. Let reverence for the laws, be breathed by every American mother, to the lisping babe, that prattles on her lap—let it be taught in schools, in seminaries, and in colleges;—let it be written in Primmers, spelling books, and in Almanacs;—let it be preached from the pulpit, proclaimed in legislative halls, and enforced in courts of justice. And, in short, let it become the *political religion* of the nation; and let the old and the young, the rich and the poor, the grave and the gay, of all sexes and tongues, and colors and conditions, sacrifice unceasingly upon its altars.

3

AL to Mary Speed
CW, 1:260

Lincoln said that he grew up hating slavery, and his few recorded reactions to seeing actual slaves reinforced his professed revulsion. In this letter to Mary Speed, the half sister of his best friend, Joshua, Lincoln depicted his experience of seeing a coffle of slaves in St. Louis. The slaves recently had been purchased in his home state of Kentucky and were destined for the owner's farm somewhere in the South. Lincoln imagined how it would feel to be "separated forever from the scenes of their childhood, their friends, their fathers and mothers, and brothers and sisters, and many of them, from their wives and children, and going into perpetual slavery where the lash of the master is proverbially more ruthless and unrelenting than any other where." Yet he believed that the poor slaves endured their misfortune with laughter and song, God's or nature's way of permitting a person to endure hardship. As a teenager, Lincoln had sailed to New Orleans on a flatboat with a local storeowner's son to transport supplies. Somewhere in Louisiana, "seven negroes" attacked the pair, intending, or so Lincoln believed, to rob and kill them both. The incidents strongly suggest how Lincoln could have developed such deep animosity for the institution of slavery side by side with such unbending belief in the necessity of racial segregation. For Lincoln's early experience with African Americans, see: David Herbert Donald, *Lincoln* (London: Jonathan Cape, 1995), 34.

Miss Mary Speed   Bloomington, Illinois,
Louisville, Ky.   *Sept. 27ᵗʰ. 1841*

. . . You remember there was some uneasiness about Joshua's health when we left. That little indisposition of his turned out to be nothing serious; and it was pretty nearly forgotten when we reached Springfield. We got on board the Steam Boat Lebanon, in the locks of the Canal about 12. o'clock. M. of the day we left, and reached St. Louis the next monday at 8 P.M. Nothing of interest happened during the passage, except the vexatious delays occasioned by the sand bars be thought interesting. By the way, a fine example was presented on board the boat for contemplating the effect of *condition* upon human happiness. A gentleman had purchased twelve negroes in different parts of Kentucky and was taking them to a farm in the South. They were chained six and six together. A small iron clevis was around the left wrist of each, and this fastened to the main chain by a shorter one at a convenient distance from, the others; so that the negroes were strung together precisely like so many fish upon a trot-line. In this condition they were being separated forever from the scenes of their childhood, their friends, their fathers and mothers, and brothers and sisters, and many of them, from their wives and children, and going into perpetual slavery where the lash of the master is proverbially more ruthless and unrelenting than any other where; and yet amid all these distressing circumstances, as we would think them, they were the most cheerful and apparantly [*sic*] happy creatures on board. One, whose offence for which he had been sold was an over-fondness for his wife, played the fiddle almost continually; and the others danced, sung, cracked jokes, and played various games with cards from day to day. How true it is that "God tempers the wind to the shorn lamb," or in other words, that He renders the worst of human conditions tolerable, while He permits the best, to be nothing better than tolerable.

4

Temperance Address
CW, 1:278–279

Although early in his career Lincoln sold alcohol in his New
Salem store, once he rose in the legal profession and entered the
middle class, he adopted temperance principles. Temperance advocates, much like the modern antidrug movement, identified addiction as the root cause of social disintegration and threats to
the family. While some proponents advanced total abstinence as
the only means to end the threat posed by alcohol, others sought
only an end to the manufacture and sale of distilled (but not fer-
mented) beverages. In either case, temperance reformers mar-
shaled impressive statistics on the terrible impact of alcohol or
crafted passionate essays, books, and novels to advance the cause.
Every state and most localities could boast of a temperance society,
and one's career as a public figure or as a businessman might
depend upon a reputation for probity and temperance. The loss
of liberty through addiction represented a natural corollary to the
loss of liberty in slavery, as Lincoln affirmed in this 1842 address
at an Illinois Presbyterian church on the birthday of George
Washington—a figure who loomed large in temperance circles.
Lincoln condemned the tyranny of drink and slavery, hoping for
the day when both scourges would be eliminated from the earth.
His lofty vision, a future in which "there shall be neither a slave
nor a drunkard on the earth," honored the memory of the nation's Founding Father, but rendered African Americans as little
more than an abstraction. Most important, the address provides
keen insight into Lincoln's view of social reformers. He preferred
the modest, voluntary approach of the Washingtonians—usually
former alcoholics who saw those addicted to drink as victims,
rather than sinners, and tried to lead them to good health and
stability—and repudiated strident temperance measures and the
radical reformers' penchant for denouncing the *sin* and the *sinner*.
Such an approach, he thought, was foolishly counterproductive
and calculated to alienate those whom advocates sought to reach.
"It is an old and a true maxim, that a 'drop of honey catches

more flies than a gallon of gall.'" From this early address, we can better understand why Lincoln perceived radical abolitionists of any stripe as self-defeating, disruptive, and a greater threat to the social order than defenders of slavery.

February 22, 1842

... For this new and splendid success, we heartily rejoice. That that success is so much greater *now* than *heretofore*, is doubtless owing to rational causes; and if we would have it to continue, we shall do well to enquire what those causes are. The warfare heretofore waged against the demon of Intemperance, has, some how or other, been erroneous. Either the champions engaged, or the tactics they adopted, have not been the most proper. These champions for the most part, have been Preachers, Lawyers, and hired agents. Between these and the mass of mankind, there is a want of *approachability*, if the term be admissible, partially at least, fatal to their success. They are supposed to have no sympathy of feeling or interest, with those very persons whom it is their object to convince and persuade.

And again, it is so easy and so common to ascribe motives to men of these classes, other than those they profess to act upon. The *preacher*, it is said, advocates temperance because he is a fanatic, and desires a union of Church and State; the *lawyer*, from his pride and vanity of hearing himself speak; and the *hired agent*, for his salary. But when one, who has long been known as a victim of intemperance, bursts the fetters that have bound him, and appears before his neighbors "clothed, and in his right mind," a redeemed specimen of long lost humanity, and stands up with tears of joy trembling in eyes, to tell of the miseries *once* endured, *now* to be endured no more forever; of his once naked and starving children, now clad and fed comfortably; of a wife long weighed down with woe, weeping, and a broken heart, now restored to health, happiness, and renewed affection; and how easily it all is done, once it is resolved to be done; however simple his language, there is a logic, and an eloquence in it, that few, with human feelings, can resist. They cannot say that *he* desires a union of church and state, for he is not a church member; they can not say *he* is vain of hearing himself speak, for his whole demeanor shows, he would gladly avoid speaking at all; they cannot say *he* speaks for pay for he receives none, and asks for none. Nor can his sincerity in any way be doubted; or his sympathy for those he would persuade to imitate his example, be denied.

In my judgment, it is to the battles of this new class of champions that our late success is greatly, perhaps chiefly, owing. But, had the old school champions themselves, been of the most wise selecting, was their *system* of tactics, the most judicious? It seems to me, it was not. Too much denunciation against dram sellers and dram-drinkers was indulged in. This, I think, was both impolitic and unjust. It was *impolitic*, because, it is not much in the nature of man to be driven to any thing; still less to be driven about that which is exclusively his own business; and least of all, where such driving is to be submitted to, at the expense of pecuniary interest, or burning appetite. When the dram-seller and drinker, were incessantly told not in the accents of entreaty and persuasion, diffidently addressed by erring man to an erring brother; but in the thundering tones of anathema and denunciation, with which the lordly Judge often groups together all the crimes of the felon's life, and thrusts them in his face just ere he passes sentence of death upon him, that *they* were the authors of all the vice and misery and crime in the land; that *they* were the manufacturers and material of all the thieves and robbers and murderers that infested the earth; that *their* houses were the workshops of the devil; and that *their persons* should be shunned by all the good and virtuous, as moral pestilences—I say, when they were told all this, and in this way, it is not wonderful that they were slow, *very slow*, to acknowledge the truth of such denunciations, and to join the ranks of their denouncers, in a hue and cry against themselves.

To have expected them to do otherwise than as they did—to have expected them not to meet denunciation with denunciation, crimination with crimination, and anathema with anathema, was to expect a reversal of human nature, which is God's decree, and never can be reversed. When the conduct of men is designed to be influenced, *persuasion*, kind, unassuming persuasion, should ever be adopted. It is an old and a true maxim, that a "drop of honey catches more flies than a gallon of gall." So with men. If you would win a man to your cause, *first* convince him that you are his sincere friend. Therein is a drop of honey that catches his heart, which, say what he will, is the great high road to his reason, and which, when once gained, you will find but little trouble in convincing his judgment of the justice of your cause, if indeed that cause really be a just one. On the contrary, assume to dictate to his judgment, or to command his action, or to mark him as one to be shunned and despised, and he will retreat within himself, close all the avenues to his head and his heart; and tho' your cause be naked truth itself, transformed to the heaviest lance, harder than steel, and sharper than steel can be made, and tho' you throw it with more than Herculean force and precision, you shall no more be able to pierce him, than to penetrate the hard shell of a tortoise with a rye straw.

Such is man, and so *must* he be understood by those who would lead him, even to his own best interest.

On this point, the Washingtonians greatly excel the temperance advocates of former times. Those whom *they* desire to convince and persuade, are their old friends and companions. They know they are not demons, nor even the worst of men. *They* know that generally, they are kind, generous and charitable, even beyond the example of their

more staid and sober neighbors. *They* are practical phi-
lanthropists; and *they* glow with a generous and brotherly
zeal, that mere theorizers are incapable of feeling. Benev-
olence and charity possess *their* hearts entirely; and out
of the abundance of their hearts, their tongues give ut-
terance. "Love through all their actions runs, and all their
words are mild." In this spirit they speak and act, and in
the same, they are heard and regarded. And when such is
the temper of the advocate, and such of the audience, no
good cause can be unsuccessful. . . .

. . . Turn now, to the temperance revolution. In *it*, we
shall find a stronger bondage broken; a viler slavery,
manumitted; a greater tyrant deposed. In *it*, more of want
supplied, more disease healed, more sorrow assuaged. By
it no orphans starving, no widows weeping. By *it*, none
wounded in feeling, none injured in interest. Even the
dram-maker, and dram seller, will have glided into other
occupations *so* gradually, as never to have felt the shock
of change; and will stand ready to join all others in the
universal song of gladness.

And what a noble ally this, to the cause of political
freedom. With such an aid, its march cannot fail to be on
and on, till every son of earth shall drink in rich fruition, the
sorrow quenching draughts of perfect liberty. Happy day,
when, all appetites controled, [*sic*] all passions subdued,
all matters subjected, *mind*, all conquering *mind*, shall live
and move the monarch of the world. Glorious consummation! Hail fall of Fury! Reign of Reason, all hail!

And when the victory shall be complete—when there
shall be neither a slave nor a drunkard on the earth—how
proud the title of that *Land*, which may truly claim to be
the birth-place and the cradle of both those revolutions,
that shall have ended in that victory. How nobly distinguished that People, who shall have planted, and nurtured
to maturity, both the political and moral freedom of their
species. . . .

5

AL to Williamson Durley
CW, 1:347–348

In this letter to a Putnam County, Illinois, supporter and his brother, Lincoln vented his frustration over the consequences of abolitionists entering the political process. He clearly saw antislavery politicians (even Whigs) as a separate political breed, one that brought mayhem to the political process, ruined the prospects for the national Whig Party, and strengthened, rather than weakened, the institution of slavery. Lincoln explained to Durley that the high moralism of political abolitionists, which led them to create the Liberty Party, had proven lethal to Whigs in the 1844 election, which sent the proslavery expansionist James K. Polk to the White House. If New York Whigs had not split their vote over James G. Birney of the Liberty Party, Henry Clay would be president, and the annexation of Texas—which abolitionists vehemently opposed—would have been halted. The moral stance of Liberty Party members repelled Lincoln since the results of their actions betrayed their intentions. "By the *fruit* the tree is to be known. An *evil* tree can not bring forth *good* fruit. If the fruit of electing Mr. Clay would have been to prevent the extension of slavery," Lincoln explained in frustration, "could the act of electing have been *evil*?" Lincoln also admitted that the great question of Texas annexation that had so riled abolitionists in the North did not mean much to him. Slavery already existed in the republic, he explained, and annexing that country to the United States would not have changed the status of slavery. He went on to advise Durley—who admitted to being an abolitionist—that Americans could safeguard their liberty only by letting "the slavery of the other states alone." As Lincoln stated here and would repeat throughout his career, he thought the only workable national policy was to allow the peculiar institution to die "a natural death." However, he also implied that if slaves took matters into their own hands to gain their freedom, he would support crushing them.

H. Clay

Henry Clay *(1777–1852). Engraving, unidentified artist, n.d. Kentucky senator Henry Clay was the leading politician of the Whig Party, gathering widespread popular support even from New Englanders, and was Abraham Lincoln's model statesmen. From Portraits of American Abolitionists collection, courtesy of the Massachusetts Historical Society.*

Friend Durley: Springfield, *Octr. 3. 1845*

When I saw you at home, it was agreed that I should write to you and your brother Madison [Durley]. Until I then saw you, I was not aware of your being what is generally called an abolitionist, or, as you call yourself, a Liberty-man; though I well knew there were many such in your county. I was glad to hear you say that you intend to attempt to bring about, at the next election in Putnam, a union of the whigs proper, and such of the liberty men, as are whigs in principle on all questions save only that of slavery. So far as I can perceive, by such union, neither party need yield any thing, on *the* point in difference between them. If the whig abolitionists of New York had voted with us last fall, Mr. Clay would now be president, whig principles in the ascendent, [*sic*] and Texas not annexed; whereas by the division, all that either had at stake in the contest, was lost. And, indeed, it was extremely probable, beforehand, that such would be the result. As I always understood, the Liberty-men deprecated the annexation of Texas extremely; and, this being so, why they should refuse to so cast their votes as to prevent it, even to me, seemed wonderful. What was their process of reasoning, I can only judge from what a single one of them told me. It was this: "We are not to do *evil* that *good* may come." This general, proposition is doubtless correct; but did it apply? If by your votes you could have prevented the *extention*, &c. of slavery, would it not have been *good* and not *evil* so to have used your votes, even though it involved the casting of them for a slaveholder? By the *fruit* the tree is to be known. An *evil* tree can not bring forth *good* fruit. If the fruit of electing Mr. Clay would have been to prevent the extension of slavery, could the act of electing have been *evil*?

But I will not argue farther. I perhaps ought to say that individually I never was much interested in the Texas question. I never could see much good to come of annexation; inasmuch, as they were already a free republican people on our own model; on the other hand, I never could very clearly see how the annexation would augment the evil of slavery. It always seemed to me that slaves would be taken there in about equal numbers, with or without annexation. And if more *were* taken because of annexation, still there would be just so many the fewer left, where they were taken from. It is possibly true, to some extent, that with annexation, some slaves may be sent to Texas and continued in slavery, that otherwise might have been liberated. To whatever extent this may be true, I think annexation an evil. I hold it to be a paramount duty of us in the free states, due to the Union of the states, and perhaps to liberty itself (paradox though it may seem) to let the slavery of the other states alone; while, on the other hand, I hold it to be equally clear, that we should never knowingly lend ourselves directly or indirectly, to prevent that slavery from dying a natural death—to find new places for it to live in, when it can no longer exist in the old. Of course I am not now considering what would be our duty, in cases of insurrection among the slaves.

To recur to the Texas question, I understand the Liberty men to have viewed annexation as a much greater evil than I ever did; and I, would like to convince you if I could, that they could have prevented it, without violation of principle, if they had chosen.

I intend this letter for you and Madison together; and if you and he or either shall think fit to drop me a line, I shall be pleased.

Yours with respect
A. Lincoln

6

AL to Josephus Hewett
CW, 1:450

Patrick W. Tompkins, a Kentucky-born Whig congressman from Mississippi who lived in the same boardinghouse as Lincoln during his one term in Congress, shared with his fellow Whig a letter he had received from Josephus Hewett, a mutual friend. Ten years earlier, Hewett had practiced law in Springfield, Illinois, and Lincoln used the correspondence to renew their acquaintance. What moved Hewett to consider rejecting the electoral college system of holding national elections is unknown. Lincoln admitted to having once agreed with his correspondent, but came back to the formulation conceived by the Founding Fathers to balance the three parts of government. He did so in part, as this letter makes clear, because direct elections would actually *decrease* the power of the slave states, since they could no longer count three-fifths of the black population as specified in the Constitution. A master strategist in the mold of Henry Clay, Lincoln rejected proposals that would upset the power relationship between free and slave states. According to Lincoln, Hewett, another transplanted Kentuckian, had not considered the unintended consequences of his idea. "Have you ever reflected on these things?" he inquired.

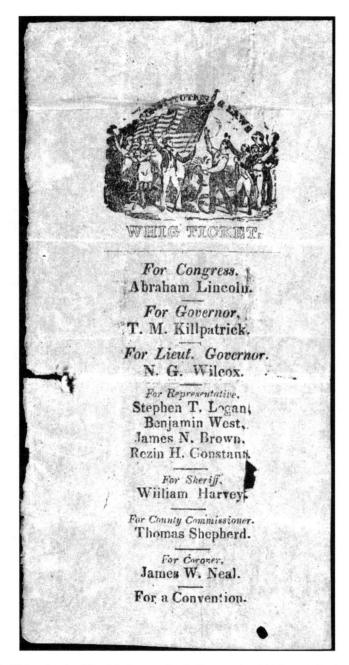

Whig Ticket *showing Lincoln's first run for the Congress in 1846; he served only one term as an Illinois U.S. representative. Courtesy, Chicago History Museum.*

Dear Hewett: Washington, *Feb. 13. 1848.*

Your whig representative from Mississippi, P. W. Tompkins, has just shown me a letter of yours to him. I am jealous because you did not write to me. Perhaps you have forgotten me. Dont you remember a long black fellow who rode on horseback with you from Tremont to Springfield nearly ten years ago, swiming [*sic*] your horses over the Mackinaw on the trip? Well, I am that same one fellow yet. I was once of your opinion, expressed in your letter, that presidential electors should be dispensed with; but a more thorough knowledge of the causes that first introduced them, has made me doubt. Those causes were briefly these. The convention that framed the constitution had this difficulty: the small states wished to so frame the new government as that they might be equal to the large ones regardless of the inequality of population; the large ones insisted on equality in proportion to population. They compromised it, by basing the House of Representatives on *population,* and the Senate on *states* regardless of population; and the executive on both principles, by electors in each state, equal in numbers to her senators *and* representatives. Now, throw away the machinery of electors, and the compromise is broken up, and the whole yielded to the principle of the large states. There is one thing more. In the slave states, you have representatives, and consequently, electors, partly upon the basis of your black population, which would be swept away by the change you seem to think desireable. [*sic*] Have you ever reflected on these things? . . .

7

Speech at Worcester, Massachusetts
CW, 2:2–4

Seeking to buttress the declining fortunes of the Whig Party in face of the rising Free Soil Party, Lincoln attended the Massachusetts Whig convention that met on September 13 in Worcester, a hotbed of antislavery sentiment. Many former Whigs with strong abolitionist sentiments abandoned the party of Henry Clay for an unlikely coalition of former Democrats, abolitionists, and even some African Americans, including, briefly, Frederick Douglass. The party nominated the former one-term Democratic president Martin Van Buren for president and Charles Francis Adams for vice president. A report of Lincoln's remarks, which appeared in a Boston newspaper, highlighted his drive to maintain the Whig Party as a bulwark against slavery and its expansion into the territories acquired as a result of the Mexican War. Lincoln exaggerated the level of antislavery sentiment in Illinois for his Massachusetts audience. He rightly warned that if the Free Soilers gained sufficient strength, it would be at the expense of Zachary Taylor and would put the much-hated Lewis Cass of Michigan into the White House, where he would do the bidding of the slave states. Back in Illinois at the beginning of November, he delivered a similar address at Lacon but offered a harsher assessment of abolitionists for their failure to recognize the political necessity of voting for Taylor as a way to avoid electing Cass.

September 12, 1848

... Mr. Lincoln proceeded to examine the absurdity of an attempt to make a platform or creed for a national party, to *all* parts of which *all* must consent and agree, when it was clearly the intention and the true philosophy of our government, that in Congress all opinions and principles should be represented, and that when the wisdom of all had been compared and united, the will of the majority should be carried out. On this ground he conceived (and the audience seemed to go with him) that General Taylor held correct, sound republican principles.

Mr. Lincoln then passed to the subject of slavery in the States, saying that the people of Illinois agreed entirely with the people of Massachusetts on this subject, except perhaps that they did not keep so constantly thinking about it. All agreed that slavery was an evil, but that we were not responsible for it and cannot affect it in States of this Union where we do not live. But, the question of the *extension* of slavery to new territories of this country, is a part of our responsibility and care, and is under our control. In opposition to this Mr. L. believed that the self named "Free Soil" party, was far behind the Whigs. Both parties opposed the extension. As he understood it the new party had no principle except this opposition. If their platform held any other, it was in such a general way that it was like the pair of pantaloons the Yankee peddler offered for sale, "large enough for any man, small enough for any boy." They therefore had taken a position calculated to break down their single important declared object. They were working for the election of either Gen. Cass or Gen. Taylor.

The Speaker then went on to show, clearly and eloquently, the danger of extension of slavery, likely to result from the election of General Cass. To unite with those who annexed the new territory to prevent the extension of slavery in that territory seemed to him to be in the highest degree absurd and ridiculous. Suppose these gentlemen succeed in electing Mr. Van Buren, they had no specific means to *prevent* the extension of slavery to New Mexico and California, and Gen. Taylor, he confidently believed, would not encourage it, and would not prohibit its restriction. But if Gen. Cass was elected, he felt certain that the plans of farther extension of territory would be encouraged, and those of the extension of slavery would meet no check.

The "Free Soil" men in claiming that name indirectly attempted a deception, by implying the Whigs were *not* Free Soil men. In declaring that they would "do their duty and leave the consequences to God," merely gave an excuse for taking a course that they were not able to maintain by a fair and full argument. To make this declaration did not show what their duty was. If it did we should have no use for judgment, we might as well be made without intellect, and when divine or human law does not clearly point out what *is* our duty, we have no means of finding out what it is by using our most intelligent judgment of the consequences. If there were divine law, or human law for voting for Martin Van Buren, or if a fair examination of the consequences and first reasoning would show that voting for him would bring about the ends they pretended to wish—then he would give up the argument. But since there was no fixed law on the subject, and since the whole probable result of their action would be an assistance in electing Gen. [Lewis] Cass, he must say that they were behind the Whigs in their advocacy of the freedom of the soil. . . .

8

Remarks and Resolution Introduced in United States House of Representatives Concerning Abolition of Slavery in the District of Columbia
CW, 2:20–22

At the close of 1848 when Abraham Lincoln returned to Congress after campaigning for the presidency of Zachary Taylor, some two thousand slaves lived in the District of Columbia. Congressmen like John Gorham Palfrey, a Free Soiler from Massachusetts, and Daniel Gott, a New York Whig, lamented that one could see the warehouse of the nation's largest slave trader standing in the shadow of the Capitol. To help repair the nation's image, the two men often presented bills to abolish slavery in the federal district. Lincoln, on the other hand, consistently voted against such resolutions, despite his personal distaste for the sight of chained humans, fearing that such a measure would agitate Southern Whigs and divide his party. In an effort to maintain party unity, Lincoln prepared a compromise proposal, which met with the approval of only a few antislavery congressmen. A critical element of the new measure, which had been part of his 1837 Illinois "protest," remained Lincoln's insistence that nothing regarding the institution of slavery could be done without the approval of whites living there, despite his belief that Congress possessed the power to legislate in all matters regarding the District. His proposal offended several antislavery congressmen who opposed legitimizing the institution of slavery by offering federal dollars to compensate slaveowners for the freedom of their "property." Southerners, on the other hand, rallied against Lincoln's bill, seeing it as a covert step toward abolishing slavery nationwide. On January 13, Lincoln stated that he intended to introduce the bill himself, but found himself "abandoned by [his] former backers" and, "having little personal influence," dropped the measure.

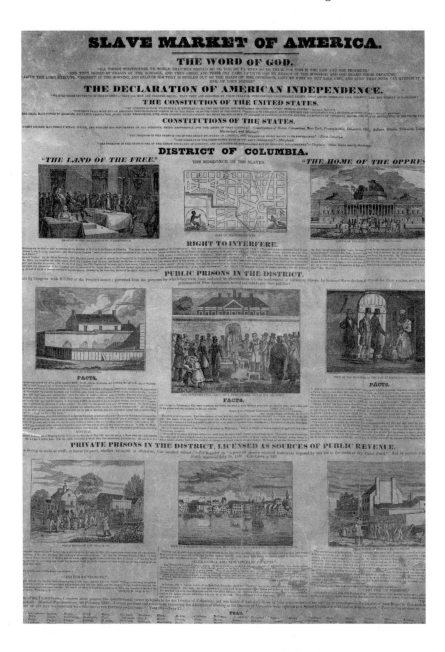

Slave Market of America. *Broadside, American Anti-Slavery Society, New York, 1836. Early antislavery effort to promote the abolition of slavery in the District of Columbia. Courtesy of the Massachusetts Historical Society.*

Congress would not abolish slavery in the District until April 16, 1862, with Lincoln still urging colonization for the former slaves and compensation to their owners.

January 10, 1849

. . . That the Committee on the District of Columbia be instructed to report a bill in substance as follows, to wit:

Section 1. Be it enacted by the Senate and House of Representatives of the United States of America, in Congress assembled: That no person not now within the District of Columbia, nor now owned by any person or persons now resident within it, nor hereafter born within it, shall ever be held in slavery within said District.

Section 2. That no person now within said District, or now owned by any person, or persons now resident within the same, or hereafter born within it, shall ever be held in slavery without the limits of said District: *Provided,* that officers of the government of the United States, being citizens of the slave-holding states, coming into said District on public business, and remaining only so long as may be reasonably necessary for that object, may be attended into, and out of, said District, and while there, by the necessary servants of themselves and their families, without their right to hold such servants in service, being thereby impaired.

Section 3. That all children born of slave mothers within said District on, or after the first day of January in the year of our Lord one thousand, eight hundred and fifty shall be free; but shall be reasonably supported and educated, by the respective owners of their mothers or by their heirs or representatives, and shall owe reasonable service, as apprentices, to such owners, heirs and representatives until they respectively arrive at the age of —— years when they shall be entirely free; and the municipal authorities of Washington and Georgetown, within their respective jurisdictional limits, are hereby empowered and required to make all suitable and necessary provisions for enforcing obedience to this section, on the part of both masters and apprentices.

Section 4. That all persons now within said District lawfully held as slaves, or now owned by any person or persons now resident within said District, shall remain such, at the will of their respective owners, their heirs and legal representatives: *Provided* that any such owner, or his legal representative, may at any time receive from the treasury of the United States the full value of his or her slave, of the class in this section mentioned, upon which such slave shall be forthwith and forever free: and *provided further* that the President of the United States, the Secretary of State, and the Secretary of the Treasury shall be a board for determining the value of such slaves as their owners may desire to emancipate under this section; and whose duty it shall be to hold a session for the purpose, on the first monday of each calendar month; to receive all applications; and, on satisfactory evidence in each case, that the person presented for valuation, is a slave, and of the class in this section mentioned, and is owned by the applicant, shall value such slave at his or her full cash value, and give to the applicant an order on the treasury for the amount; and also to such slave a certificate of freedom.

Section 5[.] That the municipal authorities of Washington and Georgetown, within their respective jurisdictional limits, are hereby empowered and required to provide active and efficient means to arrest, and deliver up to their owners, all fugitive slaves escaping into said District.

Section 6[.] That the election officers within said District of Columbia, are hereby empowered and required to open polls at all the usual places of holding elections, on the first monday of April next, and receive the vote of every free white male citizen above the age of twentyone years, having resided within said District for the period of one year or more next preceding the time of such voting, for, or against this act; to proceed, in taking said votes, in all respects not herein specified, as at elections under the municipal laws; and, with as little delay as possible, to transmit correct statements of the votes so cast to the President of the United States. And it shall be the duty of the President to canvass said votes immediately, and, if a majority of them be found to be for this act, to forthwith issue his proclamation giving notice of the fact; and this act shall only be in full force and effect on, and after the day of such proclamation.

Section 7. That involuntary servitude for the punishment of crime, whereof the party shall have been duly convicted shall in no wise be prohibited by this act.

Section 8. That for all the purposes of this act the jurisdictional limits of Washington are extended to all parts of the District of Columbia not now included within the present limits of Georgetown.

Mr. Lincoln then said, that he was authorized to say, that of about fifteen of the leading citizens of the District of Columbia to whom this proposition had been submitted, there was not one but who approved of the adoption of such a proposition. He did not wish to be misunderstood. He did not know whether or not they would vote for this bill on the first Monday of April; but he repeated, that out of fifteen persons to whom it had been submitted, he had authority to say that every one of them desired that some proposition like this should pass.

9

Eulogy on Henry Clay
& Outline for Speech to the Colonization Society
CW, 2:127–129, 130–132 & 298–299

Next to temperance, colonization proved one of the most popular reform movements in America prior to the Civil War. The American Colonization Society, founded in the halls of Congress in December 1816, included men like the political powerhouse Henry Clay, Supreme Court Justice Bushrod Washington, and Francis Scott Key. The organization quickly recruited President James Monroe and most of the nation's political elite into its fold. To Speaker of the House Clay, colonization held out the hope of purging the nation of its free blacks, "a useless and pernicious, if not a dangerous portion of its population." According to Clay, by resettling in Africa, blacks would Christianize the "dark continent" and help bring it into the modern world. How so "useless" a population in America could work such wonders in Africa remains unclear, but Clay and his associates saw themselves as benevolent reformers who had the best interests of all blacks and all Americans at heart. Clay, a major slaveholder, refused to consider abolition when helping to found the society, but by 1831 came to see slavery as a violation of human rights and in Kentucky and elsewhere sought ways to end the practice. He understood intimately the obstacles to emancipation and sought compromises that would gradually and painlessly move the nation away from reliance on slave labor. While many Northerners sympathized with Clay and supported gradual emancipation, Southerners increasingly saw colonization as a means to buttress the "peculiar institution" by eliminating those most likely to challenge white domination: free blacks. In his eulogy to his political hero Clay and in his notes for an 1855 speech on colonization, Lincoln expressed his lifelong commitment to the colonization of black Americans as a vital part of the plan to end slavery and keep the nation true to the vision of the Founding Fathers. In the writings of men like Jefferson and in the nation's political history, Lincoln contended, one could see a clear path into the future. To Lincoln, Henry Clay embodied the highest ideals of the Fathers, and his commitment to colonization proved his fidelity to the past and offered indispensable guidance for the future. As his 1855 speech notes make clear, Lincoln viewed colonization as the fruit of two hundred years of slavery history and the course Americans must pursue to avoid the dire outcome of which Jefferson had warned. Together, the two speeches also reveal Lincoln's failure to include African Americans in what he called "the white-man's charter of freedom—the declaration that 'all men are created free and equal,'" despite what he would later assert during the famed debates with Stephen A. Douglas. For general information about Henry Clay and the American Colonization Society, see: Claude A. Clegg III, *The Price of Liberty: African Americans and the Making of Liberia* (Chapel Hill: University of North Carolina Press, 2004), 30.

July 6, 1852

Honors to Henry Clay

. . . Mr. Clay's predominant sentiment, from first to last, was a deep devotion to the cause of human liberty—a strong sympathy with the oppressed every where, and an ardent wish for their elevation. With him, this was a primary and all controlling passion. Subsidiary to this was the conduct of his whole life. He loved his country partly because it was his own country, but mostly because it was a free country; and he burned with a zeal for its advancement, prosperity and glory, because he saw in such, the advancement, prosperity and glory, of human liberty, human right and human nature. He desired the prosperity of his countrymen partly because they were his

Henry Clay. *Engraving by John Sartain after the original presidential campaign portrait by John Neagle, 1843. The image expresses Clay's patriotism and depicts him as the nation's defender of liberty and commerce. Prints and Photographs Division, Library of Congress,* LC-USZ62-71603.

Life Membership Certificate for American Colonization Society, ca. 1840. Henry Clay succeeded former president James Madison as president of the American Colonization Society
and served from 1836 to 1849. The ACS remained popular throughout the North and formed
state auxiliaries even during the Civil War. American Colonization Society Papers, Manu-
script Division, Library of Congress.

countrymen, but chiefly to show to the world that freemen
could be prosperous. . . .

Important and exciting as was the War question, of
1812, it never so alarmed the sagacious statesmen of the
country for the safety of the republic, as afterwards did
the Missouri question. This sprang from that unfortunate
source of discord—negro slavery. When our Federal Constitution was adopted, we owned no territory beyond
the limits or ownership of the states, except the territory
North-West of the River Ohio, and East of the Mississippi. What has since been formed into the States of
Maine, Kentucky, and Tennessee, was, I believe, within the
limits of or owned by Massachusetts, Virginia, and North
Carolina. As to the North Western Territory, provision had

been made, even before the adoption of the Constitution, that slavery should never go there. On the admission of the States into the Union carved from the territory we owned before the constitution, no question—or at most, no considerable question—arose about slavery—those which were within the limits of or owned by the old states, following, respectively, the condition of the parent state, and those within the North West territory, following the previously made provision. But in 1803 we purchased Louisiana of the French; and it included with much more, what has since been formed into the State of Missouri. With regard to it, nothing had been done to forestall the question of slavery. When, therefore, in 1819, Missouri, having formed a State constitution, without excluding slavery, and with slavery already actually existing within its limits, knocked at the door of the Union for admission, almost the entire representation of the non-slave-holding states, objected. A fearful and angry struggle instantly followed. This alarmed thinking men, more than any previous question, because, unlike all the former, it divided the country by geographical lines. Other questions had their opposing partizans in all localities of the country and in almost every family; so that no division of the Union could follow such, without a separation of friends, to quite as great an extent, as that of opponents. Not so with the Missouri question. On this a geographical line could be traced which, in the main, would separate opponents only. This was the danger. Mr. Jefferson, then in retirement wrote:

"I had for a long time ceased to read newspapers, or to pay any attention to public affairs, confident they were in good hands, and content to be a passenger in our bark to the shore from which I am not distant. But this momentous question, like a fire bell in the night, awakened, and filled me with terror. I considered it at once as the knell of the Union. It is hushed, indeed, for the moment. But this is a reprieve only, not a final sentence. A geographical line, co-inciding with a marked principle, moral and political, once conceived, and held up to the angry passions of men, will never be obliterated; and every irritation will mark it deeper and deeper. I can say, with conscious truth, that there is not a man on earth who would sacrifice more than I would to relieve us from this heavy reproach, in any *practicable* way. The cession of that kind of property, for so it is misnamed, is a bagatelle which would not cost me a second thought, if, in that way, a general emancipation, and *expatriation* could be effected; and, gradually, and with due sacrifices I think it might be. But as it is, we have the wolf by the ears and we can neither hold him, nor safely let him go. Justice is in one scale, and self-preservation in the other."

Mr. Clay was in congress, and, perceiving the danger, at once engaged his whole energies to avert it. It began, as I have said, in 1819; and it did not terminate till 1821. Missouri would not yield the point; and congress—that is, a majority in congress—by repeated votes, showed a determination to not admit the state unless it should yield. After several failures, and great labor on the part of Mr. Clay to so present the question that a majority could consent to the admission, it was, by a vote, rejected, and as all seemed to think, finally. A sullen gloom hung over the nation. All felt that the rejection of Missouri, was equivalent to a dissolution of the Union: because those states which already had, what Missouri was rejected for refusing to relinquish, would go with Missouri. All deprecated and deplored this, but none saw how to avert it. For the judgment of Members to be convinced of the necessity of yielding, was not the whole difficulty; each had a constituency to meet, and to answer to. Mr. Clay, though worn down, and exhausted, was appealed to by members, to renew his efforts at compromise. He did so, and by some judicious modifications of his plan, coupled with laborious efforts with individual members, and his own over-mastering eloquence upon the floor, he finally secured the admission of the State. Brightly, and captivating as it had previously shown, it was now perceived that his great eloquence, was a mere embellishment, or, at most, but a helping hand to his inventive genius, and his devotion to his country in the day of her extreme peril. . . .

Having been led to allude to domestic slavery so frequently already, I am unwilling to close without referring more particularly to Mr. Clay's views and conduct in regard to it. He ever was, on principle and in feeling, opposed to slavery. The very earliest, and one of the latest public efforts of his life, separated by a period of more than fifty years, were both made in favor of gradual emancipation of the slaves in Kentucky. He did not perceive, that on a question of human right, the negroes were to be excepted from the human race. And yet Mr. Clay was the owner of slaves. Cast into life where slavery was already widely spread and deeply seated, he did not perceive, as I think no wise man has perceived, how it could be at *once* eradicated, without producing a greater evil, even to the cause of human liberty itself. His feeling and his judgment, therefore, ever led him to oppose both extremes of opinion on the subject. Those who would shiver into fragments the Union of these States; tear to tatters its now venerated constitution; and even burn the last copy of the Bible, rather than slavery should continue a single hour, together with all their more halting sympathisers, have received, and are receiving their just execration; and the name, and opinions, and influence of Mr. Clay, are fully, and, as I trust, effectually and enduringly, arrayed against them. But I would also, if I could, array his name, opinions, and influence against the opposite extreme— against a few, but an increasing number of men, who, for the sake of perpetuating slavery, are beginning to assail and to ridicule the white-man's charter of freedom—the declaration that "all men are created free and equal." So far as I have learned, the first American, of any note, to do or attempt this, was the late John C. Calhoun; and if I mistake not, it soon after found its way into some of the messages of the Governors of South Carolina. We, however, look for, and are not much shocked by, political eccentricities and heresies in South Carolina. But, only last year, I saw with astonishment, what purported to be a letter of a very distinguished and influential clergyman of Virginia, copied, with apparent approbation, into a St. Louis newspaper, containing the following, to me, very extraordinary language—

"I am fully aware that there is a text in some Bibles that is not in mine. Professional abolitionists have made more use of it, than of any passage in the Bible. It came, however, as I trace it, from Saint Voltaire, and was baptized by Thomas Jefferson, and since almost universally regarded as canonical authority '*All men are born free and equal.*'

"This is a genuine coin in the political currency of our generation. I am sorry to say that I have never seen two men of whom it is true. But I must admit I never saw the Siamese twins, and therefore will not dogmatically say that no man ever saw a proof of this sage aphorism."

This sounds strangely in republican America. The like was not heard in the fresher days of the Republic. Let us contrast with it the language of that truly national man, whose life and death we now commemorate and lament. I quote from a speech of Mr. Clay delivered before the American Colonization Society in 1827.

"We are reproached with doing mischief by the agitation of this question. The society goes into no household to disturb its domestic tranquility; it addresses itself to no slaves to weaken their obligations of obedience. It seeks to affect no man's property. It neither has the power nor the will to affect the property of any one contrary to his consent. The execution of its scheme would augment instead of diminishing the value of the property left behind. The society, composed of free men, concerns itself only with the free. Collateral consequences we are not responsible for. It is not this society which has produced the great moral revolution which the age exhibits. What would they, who thus reproach us, have done? If they would repress all tendencies towards liberty, and ultimate emancipation, they must do more than put down the benevolent efforts of this society. They must go back to the era of our liberty and independence, and muzzle the cannon which thunders its annual joyous return. They must renew the slave trade with all its train of atrocities. They must suppress the workings of British philanthropy, seeking to meliorate the condition of the unfortunate West Indian slave. They must arrest the career of South American deliverance from thraldom. They must blow out the moral lights around us, and extinguish that greatest torch of all which America presents to a benighted world—pointing the way to their rights, their liberties, and their happiness. And when they have achieved all those purposes their work will be yet incomplete. They must penetrate the human soul, and eradicate the light of reason, and the love of liberty. Then, and not till then, when universal darkness and despair prevail, can you perpetuate slavery, and repress all sympathy, and all humane, and benevolent efforts among free men, in behalf of the unhappy portion of our race doomed to bondage."

The American Colonization Society was organized in 1816. Mr. Clay, though not its projector, was one of its earliest members; and he died, as for the many preceding years he had been, its President. It was one of the most cherished objects of his direct care and consideration; and the association of his name with it has probably been its very greatest collateral support. He considered it no demerit in the society, that it tended to relieve slave-holders from the troublesome presence of the free negroes; but this was far from being its whole merit in his estimation. In the same speech from which I have quoted he says: "There is a moral fitness in the idea of returning to Africa her children, whose ancestors have been torn from her by the ruthless hand of fraud and violence. Transplanted in a foreign land, they will carry back to their native soil the rich fruits of religion, civilization, law and liberty. May it not be one of the great designs of the Ruler of the universe, (whose ways are often inscrutable by short-sighted mortals,) thus to transform an original crime, into a signal blessing to that most unfortunate portion of the globe?" This suggestion of the possible ultimate redemption of the African race and African continent, was made twenty-five years ago. Every succeeding year has added strength to the hope of its realization. May it indeed be realized! Pharaoh's country was cursed with plagues, and his hosts were drowned in the Red Sea for striving to retain a captive people who had already served them more than four hundred years. May like disasters never befall us! If as the friends of colonization hope, the present and coming generations of our countrymen shall by any means, succeed in freeing our land from the dangerous presence of slavery; and, at the same time, in restoring a captive people to their long-lost father-land, with bright prospects for the future; and this too, so gradually, that neither races nor individuals shall have suffered by the change, it will indeed be a glorious consummation. And if, to such a consummation, the efforts of Mr. Clay shall have contributed, it will be what he most ardently wished, and none of his labors will have been more valuable to his country and his kind. . . .

Outline for Speech to the Colonization Society

January 4, 1855?

1434–	A portaguse [*sic*] captain, on the coast of Guinea, seizes a few Affrican [*sic*] lads, and sells them in the South of Spain.
1501–2–3.	Slaves are carried from Africa to the Spanish colonies in America.

1516–17	Charles 5th. of Spain gives encouragement to the African Slave trade.
1562–	John Hawkins carries slaves to the British West Indies.
1620	A dut[c]h ship carries a cargo of African slaves to Virginia.
1626–	Slaves introduced into New-York.
1630 to 41.	Slaves introduced into Massachusetts.
1776.	The period of our revolution, there were about 600-000 slaves in the colonies; and there are now in the U.S. about 3¼ millions.
	Soto, the catholic confessor of Charles 5. opposed Slavery and the Slave trade from the beginning; and, in 1543, procured from the King some amelioration of its rigors.
	The American colonies, from the beginning, appealed to the British crown, against the Slave trade; but without success.
1727–	Quakers begin to agitate for the abolition of Slavery within their own denomination
1751–	Quakers succeed in abolishing Slavery within their own denomination.
1787–	Congress, under the confederation, passes an Ordinance forbidding Slavery to go to the North Western Teritory. [*sic*]
1808–	Congress, under the constitution, abolishes the Slave trade, and declares it piracy.
1776. to 1800–	Slavery abolished in all the States North of Maryland and Virginia.

All the while — Individual conscience at work.

1816   Colonization Society is organized—it's direct object—history—and present prospects of success. Its colateral [*sic*] objects—Suppression of Slave trade—commerce—civilization and religion.

Objects of this meeting.

10

Speech to the Springfield Scott Club
CW, 2:156–157

The Fugitive Slave Law of 1850, part of the compromise package
constructed by Henry Clay and rammed through Congress by
Stephen A. Douglas, aimed to quiet secessionist threats from
the South. Other components of the compromise, especially the
admission of California as a free state, were intended to mollify
Northerners offended by the more extreme defenders of slavery.
Contrary to expectations, the compromise pleased no one and
within a short period of time appeared to offend everyone. The
Northern antislavery movement, which had failed to gain anything
other than a minority of adherents, suddenly appeared prescient.
By violating elementary principles of justice, the extralegal system
established to implement the 1850 law attracted new people to
the antislavery movement who saw slavery as an inherent threat
to their own rights and privileges. In his first speech in the U.S.
Senate chambers, William Henry Seward of New York explained
that the Fugitive Slave Law might be legal and constitutional, but
Americans must answer to the "higher law" of equality embodied
in the Declaration of Independence. Lincoln claimed to be unfa-
miliar with Seward's memorable address; if this is true, he may
have been the only politician of his day not to have read it. The
political fallout from the speech and its possible impact on voter
perception of the Whig Party's presidential candidate for 1852,
General Winfield Scott, hero of the Mexican War, deeply concerned Lincoln. Senator Stephen A. Douglas, to whom Lincoln
would always refer as "Judge Douglas," used Seward's remarks
to attack the Whigs in a July speech in support of the Democratic
candidate, the suave New Hampshirite Franklin Pierce. Lincoln
sought to distance himself and the Whig Party from Seward, a
man well known for his support of black rights and abolitionist
rhetoric. Lincoln offered a calculating assessment, as he had done
in 1848, of the necessity of carrying New York if the Whigs were

to stand a chance of electing Scott. He ended his remarks with a wry and racially tinged warning that Pierce, if elected, would be a mixed-breed political leader, part Northern, but mostly Southern—a "dough face": in the end, he concluded, "a good deal darker" than a mulatto.

August 14 & 26, 1852

Hon A. Lincoln's Address, Before the Springfield Scott Club, In Reply to Judge Douglas' Richmond Speech

... I come now to the key-notes of the Richmond speech—Seward—Abolition—free soil, &c. &c. It is amusing to observe what a "Raw Head and Bloody Bones" Seward is to universal Locofocoism [radical Democrats]. That they do really hate him there is no mistake; but that they do not choose to tell the true reason of their hatred, is manifest from the vagueness of their attacks upon him. His supposed proclamation of a "higher law" is the only specific charge I have seen for a long time. I never read the speech in which that proclamation is said to have been made; so that I cannot by its connection, judge of its import and purpose; and I therefore have only to say of it now, that in so far as it may attempt to foment a disobedience to the constitution, or to the constitutional laws of the country, it has my unqualified condemnation. But this is not the true ground of democratic hatred to Seward; else they would not so fondly cherish so many "higher law" men in their own ranks. The real secret is this: whoever does not get the State of New York will not be elected president. In 1848, in New York, Taylor had 218 538 votes—Cass 114 319, and free soilism, under Van Buren 120 497, Taylor only lacking 16 234 of beating them both. Now in 1852, the free soil organization is broken up, Van Buren has gone back to Locofocoism, and his 120 thousand votes

Stephen A. Douglas *(1813–1861). Photomechanical, n.d. The Illinois senator was Abraham Lincoln's primary rival. By introducing the Kansas-Nebraska Act in 1854, Douglas incited deadly sectional antagonism that led to the formation of the Republican Party and ultimately to Civil War. His nomination for president in 1860 split the Democratic Party and helped propel Lincoln into the White House. From Portraits of American Abolitionists collection, courtesy of the Massachusetts Historical Society.*

are the stakes for which the game in New York is being played. If Scott can get nine thousand of them he carries the State, and is elected; while Pierce is beaten unless he can get about one hundred and eleven thousand of them. Pierce has all the leaders, and can carry a majority; but that won't do—he cannot live unless he gets nearly all. Standing in the way of this Seward is thought to be the greatest obstacle. In this division of free soil effects, they greatly fear he may be able to get as many as nine out of each hundred, which is more than they can bear; and hence their insane malice against him. The indispensable necessity with the democrats of getting these New York free soil votes, to my mind, explains why they nominated a man who "loathes the Fugitive Slave Law." In December or January last Gen. [Franklin] Pierce made a speech, in which, according to two different news paper reports, published at the time in his vicinity and never questioned by him or any one else till after the nomination, he publicly declared his loathing of the Slave law. Now we shall allow ourselves to be very green, if we conclude the democratic convention did not know of this when they nominated him. On the contrary, its supposed efficacy to win free soil votes, was the very thing that secured his nomination. His Southern allies will continue to bluster and pretend to disbelieve the report, but they would not, for any consideration, have him to contradict it. And he will not contradict it—mark me, *he will not contradict it.* I see by the despatches [*sic*] he has already written a letter on the subject; but I have not seen the letter, or any quotation from it. When we shall see it, we shall also see it does not contradict the report—that is, it will not specifically deny the charge that he declared his loathing for the Fugitive Slave Law. I know it will not, because I know the *necessity* of the party will not permit it to be done. The letter will deal in generalities, and will be framed with a view of having it to pass at the South for a denial; but the specific point will not be made and met.

And this being the necessity of the party, and its action and attitude in relation to it, is it not particularly bright— in Judge Douglas to stand up before a slave-holding audience, and make flings at the Whigs about free soil and abolition! Why Pierce's only chance for presidency, is to be born into it, as a cross between New York old hunkerism, [conservative Democrats] and free soilism, the latter predominating in the offspring. [Frederick] Marryat, in some one of his books, describes the sailors, weighing anchor, and singing:

"Sally is a bright Mullatter,
Oh Sally Brown—
Pretty gal, but can't get at her,
Oh, Sally Brown."

Now, should Pierce ever be President, he will, politically speaking, not only be a mulatto; but he will be a good deal darker one than Sally Brown.

11

Fragments on Slavery

CW, 2:222–223

In the following fragments deleted from different unidentified speeches—which may have been given as late as 1859—Lincoln attacked apologists for slavery, especially those who characterized the peculiar institution as a "positive good." He drew on free labor ideology to appeal to those, perhaps of the working class, who would be sympathetic to the idea that even the lowest ant is justified in defending the fruit of his own labor. In the tradition of the Founding Fathers, Lincoln distinguished between aristocracies and democracies: the one based on the inequality of man and the other on the "equal rights of men." He implied that fidelity to what the nation stood for demanded that one oppose the institution of slavery. By equating "brutes and creeping insects" with "the most dumb and stupid slave," however, he reflexively damaged his case for black freedom. In the briefer but more significant fragment, Lincoln flirted with a true egalitarian vision of emancipation—which may explain its absence from all of his published addresses. Whether on the basis of color or on that of intelligence, Lincoln wrote, justifications of slavery could not stand logical tests without unintentionally exposing the advocate and others to enslavement. If the pieces were written after 1857, Lincoln may have had George Fitzhugh's *Cannibals All* in mind. Fitzhugh, the South's most ardent defender of slave society, believed that the corrupt "free" North proved that only enslavement could provide the care necessary for those unable to support themselves, regardless of race. The "peculiar institution," Fitzhugh predicted, would prove beneficial for Northern wage workers and all others who might be perceived as posing a threat to the social order. The second document is a direct adaptation of *Elements of Moral Science* (New York: Cooke and Co., 1835), 191, by the minister, moral philosopher, and president of Brown University Francis Wayland: ". . . if A, on the ground of intellectual superiority, have a right to improve his own means of happiness, by diminishing those which the Creator has given to B, B would have the same right over A, on the ground of superior muscular strength; while C would have a correspondent right over them both, on the ground of superiority of wealth; and so on indefinitely."

[July 1, 1854?]

... Made so plain by our good Father in Heaven, that all *feel* and *understand* it, even down to brutes and creeping insects. The ant, who has toiled and dragged a crumb to his nest, will furiously defend the fruit of his labor, against whatever robber assails him. So plain, that the most dumb and stupid slave that ever toiled for a master, does constantly *know* that he is wronged. So plain, that no one, high or low, ever does mistake it, except in a plainly *selfish* way; for although volume upon volume is written to prove slavery a very good thing, we never hear of the man who wishes to take the good of it, *by being a slave himself.*

Most governments have been based, practically, on the denial of equal rights of men, as I have, in part, stated them; *ours* began, by *affirming* those rights. *They* said, some men are too *ignorant*, and *vicious*, to share in government. Possibly so, said we; and, by your system, you would always keep them ignorant, and vicious. We proposed to give *all* a chance; and we expected the weak to grow stronger, the ignorant, wiser; and all better, and happier together.

We made the experiment; and the fruit is before us. Look at it—think of it. Look at it, in it's aggregate grandeur, of extent of country, and numbers of population—of ship, and steamboat, and rail-

If A. can prove, however conclusively, that he may, of right, enslave B.—why may not B. snatch the same argument, and prove equally, that he may enslave A?—

You say A. is white, and B. is black. It is *color*, then; the lighter, having the right to enslave the darker? Take care. By this rule, you are to be slave to the first man you meet, with a fairer skin than your own.

You do not mean *color* exactly?—You mean the whites are *intellectually* the superiors of the blacks, and, therefore have the right to enslave them? Take care again. By this rule, you are to be slave to the first man you meet, with an intellect superior to your own.

But, say you, it is a question of *interest*; and, if you can make it your *interest*, you have the right to enslave another. Very well. And if he can make it his interest, he has the right to enslave you.

12

Speech at Bloomington, Illinois
CW, 2:230–233

The young Whig Richard Yates sought reelection in 1854 to the congressional seat once occupied by Lincoln. Campaigning vigorously for his friend Yates and against Stephen A. Douglas's Kansas-Nebraska Act, Lincoln also hoped that his efforts would convince the state legislature to select him as the state's new U.S. senator in the fall. Both campaigns failed. Douglas and Lincoln spoke in Bloomington, where Lincoln returned about two weeks later to give similar remarks, reflecting the contentious debate over the expansion of slavery. In this address, Lincoln avoided demonizing Southerners, asserting that anyone in their position would have become an advocate of slavery, "and we never ought to lose sight of this fact in discussing the subject." Accepting the slaveholders' constitutional rights was one thing, Lincoln asserted, but spreading slavery over areas traditionally free of it was an entirely different matter. He then launched into a concise chronological history of the spread of slavery in the United States since the ratification of the Constitution to show that Douglas's party represented a radical break from the past. In this selection, Lincoln defended the compromises Congress had made to satisfy the competing interests of the North and South, but never, according to Lincoln, abandoning the Founding Fathers' goal of keeping the "peculiar institution" on the road to extinction. In comments not reported, Lincoln vigorously defended enforcement of the hated Fugitive Slave Law for the sake of national comity. The people of Illinois, he exclaimed, should demand restoration of the Missouri Compromise and not "oppose the Fugitive Slave Law, which would be repelling wrong with wrong. It was a compromise, and as citizens we were bound to stand up to it, and enforce it."

He first declared that the Southern slaveholders were neither better, nor worse than we of the North, and that we of the North were no better than they. If we were situated as they are, we should act and feel as they do; and if they were situated as we are, they should act and feel as we do; and we never ought to lose sight of this fact in discussing the subject. With slavery as existing in the slave States at the time of the formation of the Union, he had nothing to do. There was a vast difference between tolerating it there, and protecting the slaveholder in the rights granted him by the Constitution, and extending slavery over a territory already free, and uncontaminated with the institution. When our federal compact was made, almost all of the valley of the Mississippi belonged to the French, not us; and what little territory we had belonged to different States; Virginia owning almost all of what now constitutes the State of Ohio, Indiana, Illinois, Michigan, and Wisconsin. Thomas Jefferson, being a Virginian, proposed the cession of this territory to the general government, and in carrying out the measure, had the clause especially inserted, that slavery should never be introduced into it. Kentucky belonged also to Virginia, but was settled as a part of the State of Virginia, so that slavery was carried there by the first settlers from Virginia, and was admitted into the Union with the institution as existing there. Tennessee belonged to North Carolina, and was settled by emigrants from that State, and was afterwards admitted into the Union as Kentucky was. Alabama was settled from South Carolina and admitted in a similar manner. Thus three slave States were made from territories that belonged to individual slaveholding States.

Jefferson saw the necessity of our government possessing the whole valley of the Mississippi; and though he acknowledged that our Constitution made no provision for the purchasing of territory, yet he thought that the exigency of the case would justify the measure, and the purchase was made. When the lower part of this territory comprising the State of Louisiana, wished to be admitted, the institution of slavery having existed there long before the territory was bought, she was admitted with the institution without any opposition, as a right that belonged to her citizens.

There was an old French settlement in St. Louis and vicinity, with slaves; and that territory comprising what is now the State of Missouri, was settled in part by Slaveholders. And when that territory, according to the law, gave notice that they should apply for admission into the Union, the North voted that she should not be admitted unless she framed a State Constitution excluding involuntary servitude, and they were the majority. Neither the North nor the South would yield, and the discussion became angry and endangered the peace of the Union. A compromise was made by agreeing that all territory bought of the French, north of 36 deg. 30', should be free, which secured the whole of Nebraska, Iowa and Minnesota to freedom, and left the balance of the French purchase south of the line to come in as free or not, as they might choose to frame their state Constitution.

Missouri chose to come in a slave-state, and was so admitted, as was afterwards Arkansas, according to the compromise. And afterwards, when first the Democrats and afterwards the Whigs held their Conventions at Baltimore, in forming their platforms they both declared that compromise to be a "finality," as to the subject of slavery, and the question of slave territory was by agreement settled forever.

There was no more agitation of the subject till near the close of our war with Mexico, when three millions were appropriated with the design that the President might purchase territory of Mexico, which resulted in our obtaining possession of California, New Mexico, and Utah. This was new territory, with which Jefferson's provision and the Missouri Compromise had nothing to do. The gold in California led to such a rush of immigration that that territory soon became filled with the requisite number of inhabitants, and they formed a constitution, and requested an admission into the Union. But the South objected because her constitution excluded slavery. This gave rise to the "Wilmot proviso," no more slave territory; next the "Omnibus bill," and finally what are called the "compromise measures of 1850," which comprised among other things the following:

> 1st. The "fugitive slave law," which was a concession on the part of the North to the South.

> 2d. California was admitted as a free State, called a concession of the South to the North.

> 3d. It was left with New Mexico, and Utah to decide when they became States, whether they would be free or not. This was supposed by the North to settle the question of slavery in this new territory, as the question with regard to the former territories had been settled forever.

The matter with regard to slavery was now settled, and no disturbance could be raised except by tearing up some of the Compromises with regard to the territory where it was already settled. The South had got all they claimed, and all the territory south of the compromise line had been appropriated to slavery; they had gotten and eaten their half of the loaf of bread; but all the other half had not been eaten yet; there was the extensive territory of Nebraska secured to freedom, that had not been settled yet. And the slaveholding power attempted to snatch that away. So on Jan. 4, 1854, Douglas introduced the famous Nebraska

Bill, which was so constructed before its passage as to repeal the Missouri Compromise, and open all of the territory to the introduction of slavery. It was done without the consent of the people, and against their wishes, for if the matter had been put to vote before the people directly, whether that should be made a slave territory, they would have indignantly voted it down. But it was got up unexpectedly by the people, hurried through, and now they were called upon to sanction it. . . .

13

Speech at Peoria, Illinois
CW, 2:255–256, 262–269, 270–272, 274–276

In the congressional election of 1854 Democrats suffered a staggering blow, losing seventy-three seats. Party leaders attributed their loss to hatred of the Kansas-Nebraska Act, signed into law on May 22, 1854. Senator Stephen A. Douglas, chairman of the Senate Committee on Territories, intended the act to quell the increasingly violent national debate over slavery and establish a government for an area rapidly filling with settlers. Asserting that the 1850 Compromise had ended the 1820 Compromise's prohibition against slavery in the Louisiana Territory, he maintained that the settlers themselves should determine whether or not slavery should exist in the West. The legislation, however, annihilated the political party system, sparked creation of the Republican Party, incited more opposition to slavery in the North than ever had existed in the nation's history, and moved slaveowners to insist on their "right" to take their "property" anywhere in the country. Particularly disheartened by congressional losses in Iowa and Maine, formerly Democratic strongholds, Douglas launched a campaign to explain his Kansas-Nebraska Act to the voters of Illinois. On October 3, after Douglas gave a speech at the Illinois State Fair in Springfield, Lincoln announced that either he or Lyman Trumbull (who eventually edged out Lincoln to become U.S. senator the following year) would answer Douglas the next day. On October 4, Lincoln delivered a three-hour rebuttal, reviewing the legislative history of slavery, the necessity for compromise between the sections, Douglas's views on African Americans, and the immorality of slavery in all its forms. Lincoln then followed Douglas to Peoria, where on October 16 he elaborated on his Springfield address. His speech offered the fullest accounting to date of his views on the political and social equality of African Americans, which he opposed, and the moral equality of all humanity, which he asserted underpinned

American democracy and republicanism. Lincoln's description of the Declaration of Independence as the "white man's charter of freedom," however, revealed the striking limits to his conception of black rights. Following Peoria, Lincoln repeated his speech in Urbana on October 24 and then in Chicago on October 27. The warm receptions Lincoln received led him to embark on his first bid for a seat in the U.S. Senate.

October 16, 1854

. . . When southern people tell us they are no more responsible for the origin of slavery, than we; I acknowledge the fact. When it is said that the institution exists; and that it is very difficult to get rid of it, in any satisfactory way, I can understand and appreciate the saying. I surely will not blame them for not doing what I should not know how to do myself. If all earthly power were given me, I should not know what to do, as to the existing institution. My first impulse would be to free all the slaves, and send them to Liberia,—to their own native land. But a moment's reflection would convince me, that whatever of high hope, (as I think there is) there may be in this, in the long run, its sudden execution is impossible. If they were all landed there in a day, they would all perish in the next ten days; and there are not surplus shipping and surplus money enough in the world to carry them there in many times ten days. What then? Free them all, and keep them among us as underlings? Is it quite certain that this betters their condition? I think I would not hold one in slavery, at any rate; yet the point is not clear enough for me to denounce people upon. What next? Free them, and make them politically and socially, our equals? My own feelings will not admit of this; and if mine would, we well know that those of the great mass of white people will not. Whether this feeling accords with justice and sound judgment, is not the sole question, if indeed, it is any part of it. A universal feeling, whether well or ill-founded, can not be safely disregarded. We can not, then, make them equals. It does seem to me that systems of gradual emancipation might be adopted; but for their tardiness in this, I will not undertake to judge our brethren of the south.

When they remind us of their constitutional rights, I acknowledge them, not grudgingly, but fully, and fairly; and I would give them any legislation for the reclaiming of their fugitives, which should not, in its stringency, be more likely to carry a free man into slavery, than our ordinary criminal laws are to hang an innocent one.

But all this; to my judgment, furnishes no more excuse for permitting slavery to go into our own free territory, than it would for reviving the African slave trade by law. The law which forbids the bringing of slaves *from* Africa; and that which has so long forbid the taking them *to* Nebraska, can hardly be distinguished on any moral principle; and the repeal of the former could find quite as plausible excuses as that of the latter. . . .

Let me here drop the main argument, to notice what I consider rather an inferior matter. It is argued that slavery will not go to Kansas and Nebraska, *in any event*. This is a *palliation*—a *lullaby*. I have some hope that it will not; but let us not be too confident. As to climate, a glance at the map shows that there are five slave States—Delaware, Maryland, Virginia, Kentucky, and Missouri—and also the District of Columbia, all north of the Missouri compromise line. The census returns of 1850 show that, within these, there are 867,276 slaves—being more than one-fourth of all the slaves in the nation.

It is not climate, then, that will keep slavery out of these territories. Is there any thing in the peculiar nature of the country? Missouri adjoins these territories, by her entire western boundary, and slavery is already within every one of her western counties. I have even heard it said that there are more slaves, in proportion to whites, in the north western county of Missouri, than within any county of the State. Slavery pressed entirely up to the old western boundary of the State, and when, rather recently, a part of that boundary, at the north-west was moved out a little farther west, slavery followed on quite up to the new line. Now, when the restriction is removed, what is to prevent it from going still further? Climate will not. No peculiarity of the country will—nothing in nature will. Will the disposition of the people prevent it? Those nearest the scene, are all in favor of the extension. The yankees, who are opposed to it may be more numerous; but in military phrase, the battle-field is too far from *their* base of operations.

But it is said, there now is *no* law in Nebraska on the subject of slavery; and that, in such case, taking a slave there, operates his freedom. That is good book-law; but is not the rule of actual practice. Wherever slavery is, it has been first introduced without law. The oldest laws we find concerning it, are not laws introducing it; but *regulating* it, as an already existing thing. A white man takes his slave to Nebraska now; who will inform the negro that he is free? Who will take him before court to test the question of his freedom? In ignorance of his legal emancipation, he is kept chopping, splitting and plowing. Others are brought, and move on in the same track. At last, if ever the time for voting comes, on the question of slavery, the institution already in fact exists in the country, and cannot well be removed. The facts of its presence, and the difficulty of its removal will carry the vote in its favor. . . .

The African slave trade is not yet effectually suppressed; and if we make a reasonable deduction for the white people amongst us, who are foreigners, and the descendants of foreigners, arriving here since 1808, we shall find the increase of the black population out-running that of the white, to an extent unaccountable, except by supposing that some of them too, have been coming from Africa. If this be so, the opening of new countries to the institution, increases the demand for, and augments the price of slaves, and so does, in fact, make slaves of freemen by causing them to be brought from Africa, and sold into bondage.

But, however this may be, we know the opening of new countries to slavery, tends to the perpetuation of the institution, and so does KEEP men in slavery who otherwise would be free. This result we do not FEEL like favoring, and we are under no legal obligation to suppress our feelings in this respect.

Equal justice to the south, it is said, requires us to consent to the extending of slavery to new countries. That is to say, inasmuch as you do not object to my taking my hog to Nebraska, therefore I must not object to you taking your slave. Now, I admit this is perfectly logical, if there is no difference between hogs and negroes. But while you thus require me to deny the humanity of the negro, I wish to ask whether you of the south yourselves, have ever been willing to do as much? It is kindly provided that of all those who come into the world, only a small percentage are natural tyrants. That percentage is no larger in the slave States than in the free. The great majority, south as well as north, have human sympathies, of which they can no more divest themselves than they can of their sensibility to physical pain. These sympathies in the bosoms of the southern people, manifest in many ways, their sense of the wrong of slavery, and their consciousness that, after all, there is humanity in the negro. If they deny this, let me address them a few plain questions. In 1820 you joined the north, almost unanimously, in declaring the African slave trade piracy, and in annexing to it the punishment of death. Why did you do this? If you did not feel that it was wrong, why did you join in providing that men should be hung for it? The practice was no more than bringing wild negroes from Africa, to sell to such as would buy them. But you never thought of hanging men for catching and selling wild horses, wild buffaloes or wild bears.

Again, you have amongst you, a sneaking individual, of the class of native tyrants, known as the "SLAVE-DEALER." He watches your necessities, and crawls up to buy your slave, at a speculating price. If you cannot help it, you sell to him; but if you can help it, you drive him from your door. You despise him utterly. You do not recognize him as a friend, or even as an honest man. Your children must not play with his; they may rollick freely with the little negroes, but not with the "slave-dealers" children. If you are obliged to deal with him, you try to get through the job without so much as touching him. It is common with you to join hands with the men you meet; but with the slave dealer you avoid the ceremony—instinctively shrinking from the snaky contact. If he grows rich and retires from business, you still remember him, and still keep up the ban of non-intercourse upon him and his family. Now why is this? You do not so treat the man who deals in corn, cattle or tobacco.

And yet again; there are in the United States and territories, including the District of Columbia, 433,643 free blacks. At $500 per head they are worth over two hundred millions of dollars. How comes this vast amount of property to be running about without owners? We do not see free horses or free cattle running at large. How is this? All these free blacks are the descendants of slaves, or have been slaves themselves, and they would be slaves now, but for SOMETHING which has operated on their white owners, inducing them, at vast pecuniary sacrifices, to liberate them. What is that SOMETHING? Is there any mistaking it? In all these cases it is your sense of justice, and human sympathy, continually telling you, that the poor negro has some natural right to himself—that those who deny it, and make mere merchandise of him, deserve kickings, contempt and death.

And now, why will you ask us to deny the humanity of the slave? and estimate him only as the equal of the hog? Why ask us to do what you will not do yourselves? Why ask us to do for nothing, what two hundred million of dollars could not induce you to do?

But one great argument in the support of the repeal of the Missouri Compromise, is still to come. That argument is "the sacred right of self government." It seems our distinguished Senator has found great difficulty in getting his antagonists, even in the Senate to meet him fairly on this argument—some poet has said

"Fools rush in where angels fear to tread."

At the hazzard [*sic*] of being thought one of the fools of this quotation, I meet that argument—I rush in, I take that bull by the horns. . . .

The doctrine of self government is right—absolutely and eternally right—but it has no just application, as here attempted. Or perhaps I should rather say that whether it has such just application depends upon whether a negro is *not* or *is* a man. If he is *not* a man, why in that case, he who *is* a man may, as a matter of self-government, do just as he pleases with him. But if the negro *is* a man, is it not to that extent, a total destruction of self-government, to say that he too shall not govern *himself*? When the white man governs himself that is self-government; but when he governs himself, and also governs *another* man, that is *more* than self-government—that is despotism. If the negro is a *man*, why then my ancient faith teaches me that "all men are created equal;" and that there can be no moral right in connection with one man's making a slave of another. . . .

What I do say is, that no man is good enough to govern another man, *without that other's consent*. I say this is the leading principle—the sheet anchor of American republicanism. Our Declaration of Independence says:

"We hold these truths to be self evident: that all men are created equal; that they are endowed by their Creator with certain inalienable rights; that among these are life, liberty and the pursuit of happiness. That to secure these rights, governments are instituted among men, DERIVING THEIR JUST POWERS FROM THE CONSENT OF THE GOVERNED. . . ."

Let it not be said I am contending for the establishment of political and social equality between the whites and blacks. I have already said the contrary. I am not now combating the argument of NECESSITY, arising from the fact that the blacks are already amongst us; but I am combating what is set up as MORAL argument for allowing them to be taken where they have never yet been—arguing against the EXTENSION of a bad thing, which where it already exists, we must of necessity, manage as we best can. . . .

But you say this question should be left to the people of Nebraska, because they are more particularly interested. If this be the rule, you must leave it to each individual to say for himself whether he will have slaves. What better moral right have thirty-one citizens of Nebraska to say, that the thirty-second shall not hold slaves, than the people of the thirty-one States have to say that slavery shall not go into the thirty-second State at all?

But if it is a sacred right for the people of Nebraska to take and hold slaves there, it is equally their sacred right to buy them where they can buy them cheapest; and that undoubtedly will be on the coast of Africa; provided you will consent to not hang them for going there to buy them. You must remove this restriction too, from the sacred right of self-government. I am aware you say that taking slaves from the States of Nebraska, does not make slaves of freemen; but the African slave-trader can say just as much. He does not catch free negroes and bring them here. He finds them already slaves in the hands of their black captors, and he honestly buys them at the rate of about a red cotton handkerchief a head. This is very cheap, and it is a great abridgement of the sacred right of self-government to hang men for engaging in this profitable trade! . . .

Whether slavery shall go into Nebraska, or other new territories, is not a matter of exclusive concern to the people who may go there. The whole nation is interested that the best use shall be made of these territories. We want them for the homes of free white people. This they cannot be, to any considerable extent, if slavery shall be planted within them. Slave States are places for poor white people to remove FROM; not to remove TO. New free States are the places for poor people to go to and better their condition. For this use, the nation needs these territories. . . .

Finally, I insist, that if there is ANY THING which it is the duty of the WHOLE PEOPLE to never entrust to any hands but their own, that thing is the preservation and perpetuity, of their own liberties, and institutions. And if they shall think, as I do, that the extension of slavery endangers them, more than any, or all other causes, how recreant to themselves, if they submit the question, and with it, the fate of their country, to a mere hand-full of men, bent only on temporary self-interest. If this question of slavery extension were an insignificant one—one having no power to do harm—it might be shuffled aside in this way. But being, as it is, the great Behemoth of danger, shall the strong gripe of the nation be loosened upon him, to entrust him to the hands of such feeble keepers? . . .

Slavery is founded in the selfishness of man's nature— opposition to it, is [in?] his love of justice. These principles are an eternal antagonism; and when brought into collision so fiercely, as slavery extension brings them, shocks, and throes, and convulsions must ceaselessly follow. Repeal the Missouri compromise—repeal all compromises— repeal the declaration of independence—repeal all past history, you still can not repeal human nature. It still will be the abundance of man's heart, that slavery extension is wrong; and out of the abundance of his heart, his mouth will continue to speak. . . .

Some yankees, in the east, are sending emigrants to Nebraska, to exclude slavery from it; and, so far as I can judge, they expect the question to be decided by voting, in some way or other. But the Missourians are awake too. They are within a stone's throw of the contested ground. They hold meetings, and pass resolutions, in which not the slightest allusion to voting is made. They resolve that slavery already exists in the territory; that more shall go there; that they, remaining in Missouri will protect it; and that abolitionists shall be hung, or driven away. Through all this, bowie-knives and six-shooters are seen plainly enough; but never a glimpse of the ballot-box. And, really, what is to be the result of this? Each party WITHIN, having numerous and determined backers WITHOUT, is it not probable that the contest will come to blows, and bloodshed? Could there be a more apt invention to bring about collision and violence, on the slavery question, than this Nebraska project is? I do not charge, or believe, that such was intended by Congress; but if they had literally formed a ring, and placed champions within it to fight out the controversy, the fight could be no more likely to come off, than it is. And if this fight should begin, is it likely to take a very peaceful, Union-saving turn? Will not the first drop of blood so shed, be the real knell of the Union? . . .

I particularly object to the NEW position which the avowed principle of this Nebraska law gives to slavery in the body politic. I object to it because it assumes that there CAN be MORAL RIGHT in the enslaving of one man by another. I object to it as a dangerous dalliance for a few [free?] people—a sad evidence that, feeling prosperity we forget right—that liberty, as a principle, we have ceased to revere. I object to it because the fathers of the republic eschewed, and rejected it. The argument of "Necessity" was the only argument they ever admitted in favor of slavery; and so far, and so far only as it carried them, did they ever go. They found the institution existing among us, which they could not help; and they cast blame upon the British King for having permitted its introduction. BEFORE the constitution, they prohibited its introduction into the north-western Territory—the only country we owned, then free from it. AT the framing and adoption of the constitution, they forbore to so much as mention the word "slave" or "slavery" in the whole instrument. In the provision for the recovery of fugitives, the slave is spoken of as a "PERSON HELD TO SERVICE OR LABOR." In that prohibiting the abolition of the African slave trade for twenty years, that trade is spoken of as "The migration or importation of such persons as any of the States NOW EXISTING, shall think proper to admit," &c. These are the only provisions alluding to slavery. Thus, the thing is hid away, in the constitution, just as an afflicted man hides away a wen or a cancer, which he dares not cut out at once, lest he bleed to death; with the promise, nevertheless, that the cutting may begin at the end of a given time. Less than this our fathers COULD not do; and NOW [MORE?] they WOULD not do. Necessity drove them so far, and farther, they would not go. But this is not all. The earliest Congress, under the constitution, took the same view of slavery. They hedged and hemmed it in to the narrowest limits of necessity.

In 1794, they prohibited an out-going slave-trade—that is, the taking of slaves FROM the United States to sell.

In 1798, they prohibited the bringing of slaves from Africa, INTO the Mississippi Territory—this territory then comprising what are now the States of Mississippi and Alabama. This was TEN YEARS before they had the authority to do the same thing as to the States existing at the adoption of the constitution.

In 1800 they prohibited AMERICAN CITIZENS from trading in slaves between foreign countries—as, for instance, from Africa to Brazil.

In 1803 they passed a law in aid of one or two State laws, in restraint of the internal slave trade.

In 1807, in apparent hot haste, they passed the law, nearly a year in advance to take effect the first day of 1808—the very first day the constitution would permit—

prohibiting the African slave trade by heavy pecuniary and corporal penalties.

In 1820, finding these provisions ineffectual, they declared the trade piracy, and annexed to it, the extreme penalty of death. While all this was passing in the general government, five or six of the original slave States had adopted systems of gradual emancipation; and by which the institution was rapidly becoming extinct within these limits.

Thus we see, the plain unmistakable spirit of that age, towards slavery, was hostility to the PRINCIPLE, and toleration, ONLY BY NECESSITY.

But NOW it is to be transformed into a "sacred right." Nebraska brings it forth, places it on the high road to extension and perpetuity; and, with a pat on its back, says to it, "Go, and God speed you." Henceforth it is to be the chief jewel of the nation—the very figure-head of the ship of State. Little by little, but steadily as man's march to the grave, we have been giving up the OLD for the NEW faith. Near eighty years ago we began by declaring that all men are created equal; but now from that beginning we have run down to the other declaration, that for SOME men to enslave OTHERS is a "sacred right of self-government." These principles can not stand together. They are as opposite as God and mammon; and whoever holds to the one, must despise the other. When [Sen. John] Pettit, in connection with his support of the Nebraska bill, called the Declaration of Independence "a self-evident lie" he only did what consistency and candor require all other Nebraska men to do. Of the forty odd Nebraska Senators who sat present and heard him, no one rebuked him. Nor am I apprized that any Nebraska newspaper, or any Nebraska orator, in the whole nation, has ever yet rebuked him. If this had been said among [Francis] Marion's men, Southerners though they were, what would have become of the man who said it? If this had been said to the men who captured [Maj. John] Andre, the man who said it, would probably have been hung sooner than Andre was.

If it had been said in old Independence Hall, seventy-eight years ago, the very door-keeper would have throttled the man, and thrust him into the street.

Let no one be deceived. The spirit of seventy-six and the spirit of Nebraska, are utter antagonisms; and the former is being rapidly displaced by the latter.

Fellow countrymen—Americans south, as well as north, shall we make no effort to arrest this? Already the liberal party throughout the world, express the apprehension "that the one retrograde institution in America, is undermining the principles of progress, and fatally violating the noblest political system the world ever saw." This is not the taunt of enemies, but the warning of friends. Is it quite safe to disregard it—to despise it? Is there no danger to liberty itself, in discarding the earliest practice, and first precept of our ancient faith? In our greedy chase to make profit of the negro, let us beware, lest we "cancel and tear to pieces" even the white man's charter of freedom.

Our republican robe is soiled, and trailed in the dust. Let us repurify it. Let us turn and wash it white, in the spirit, if not the blood, of the Revolution. Let us turn slavery from its claims of "moral right," back upon its existing legal rights, and its arguments of "necessity." Let us return it to the position our fathers gave it; and there let it rest in peace. Let us re-adopt the Declaration of Independence, and with it, the practices, and policy, which harmonize with it. Let north and south—let all Americans—let all lovers of liberty everywhere—join in the great and good work. If we do this, we shall not only have saved the Union; but we shall have so saved it, as to make, and to keep it, forever worthy of the saving. We shall have so saved it, that the succeeding millions of free happy people, the world over, shall rise up, and call us blessed, to the latest generations. . . .

14

AL to Ichabod Codding
CW, 2:288

Ichabod Codding, a Congregational clergyman, temperance advocate, and peripatetic abolitionist, lectured throughout the Midwest. He spent most of his time in Illinois, helping to organize Anti-Nebraska Democrats, Whigs, and political abolitionists into what would become the Republican Party. On October 4 in Springfield, he heard Lincoln denounce Stephen A. Douglas's notion of popular sovereignty and defenders of slavery as "political hypocrites before the world." Codding became convinced that he had found a new leader for the Republicans. He and his fellow abolitionist Owen Lovejoy invited Lincoln to future Republican conventions and named him to their state central committee. Lincoln, however, remained committed to the Whig Party and did not want to be associated with the abolitionists, who he believed played too public a role in organizing the new party. He had shrewdly presented himself as a Unionist, rejecting Douglas's assertion that the Compromise of 1850 had abrogated the Compromise of 1820, which barred the expansion of slavery into the territories. But to Codding and Lovejoy, Lincoln appeared to have delivered a "glorious *abolition* speech" at Springfield. Mindful of the direction of state and national politics, Lincoln informed Codding that his opposition to slavery was as strong as anyone's in the new party, but he would never assert that opposition as strongly as did the clergyman and his associates. For Lincoln's desire to distance himself from abolitionists, see: David Herbert Donald, *Lincoln* (London: Jonathan Cape, 1995), 177–180.

I. Codding, Esq.   Springfield,
Dear Sir: *Novr 27, 1854*

Your note of the 13th. requesting my attendance of the
Republican State Central Committee, on the 17th. Inst. at
Chicago, was, owing to my absence from home, received
on the evening of that day (17th) only. While I have pen
in hand allow me to say I have been perplexed some to
understand why my name was placed on that committee.
I was not consulted on the subject; nor was I apprized of
the appointment, until I discovered it by accident two or
three weeks afterwards. I suppose my opposition to the
principle of slavery is as strong as that of any member of
the Republican party; but I had also supposed that the
extent to which I feel authorized to carry that opposition,
practically; was not at all satisfactory to that party. The
leading men who organized that party, were present, on
the 4th. of Oct. at the discussion between Douglas and
myself at Springfield, and had full oppertunity [*sic*] to not
misunderstand my position. Do I misunderstand theirs?
Please write, and inform me.

Yours truly
A. Lincoln—

15

AL to Owen Lovejoy
CW, 2:316–317

In 1846, Lincoln won election as a Whig to the U.S. House of Representatives but served only one term. As he readied himself for a return to electoral politics eight years later, he found his party disintegrating. Despite their differing positions on slavery, the abolitionist Owen Lovejoy sought to bring Lincoln into the fledgling Republican Party. Lincoln proved reluctant to abandon the party of his revered mentor Henry Clay, wary of joining a party containing a strong antislavery faction. Lovejoy had long roots in abolitionist politics that culminated in four consecutive terms in the U.S. House of Representatives beginning in 1856. In 1840—three years after a proslavery mob murdered his brother Elijah, the editor of an antislavery newspaper—Lovejoy had co-founded the abolitionist Liberty Party, the first political party to run African Americans as political candidates. Though it never gained traction, the Liberty Party represented one influential precedent to the new organization that Lovejoy helped create out of the diverse political elements that opposed the 1854 Kansas-Nebraska Act. A divided political landscape became further complicated by the rise of nativist parties like the anti-immigration Know Nothings. A large number of Whigs, themselves leery of foreigners, had defected to the Know Nothings after the Whig Party tried to recruit immigrants away from the Democratic Party. In early 1856, with the dissolution of the Whig Party all but complete, Lincoln led a group of Anti-Nebraska editors in drafting a declaration announcing the intentions of the Republican Party in the coming presidential election. It contained compromises that would allow a "fusion" party to form, incorporating the divergent platforms of antislavery advocates, immigrants, and Know Nothings. On May 29, 1856, Lincoln publicly broke with the Whigs and joined the Illinois Republican Party. For Lincoln's slow progress toward the Republicans, see: David Herbert Donald, *Lincoln* (New York: Simon & Schuster, 1995).

Hon. Owen Lovejoy: Springfield,
My dear Sir: *August 11—1855*

Yours of the 7th. was received the day before yesterday. Not even *you* are more anxious to prevent the extension of slavery than I; and yet the political atmosphere is such, just now, that I fear to do any thing, lest I do wrong. Knownothingism has not yet entirely tumbled to pieces—nay, it is even a little encouraged by the late elections in Tennessee, Kentucky & Alabama. Until we can get the elements of this organization, there is not sufficient materials to successfully combat the Nebraska democracy with. We can not get them so long as they cling to a hope of success under their own organization; and I fear an open push by us now, may offend them, and tend to prevent our ever getting them. About us here, they are mostly my old political and personal friends; and I have hoped their organization would die out without the painful necessity of my taking an open stand against them. Of their principles I think little better than I do of those of the slavery extensionists. Indeed I do not perceive how any one professing to be sensitive to the wrongs of the negroes, can join in a league to degrade a class of white men.

I have no objection to "fuse" with any body provided I can fuse on ground which I think is right; and I believe the opponents of slavery extension could now do this, if it were not for this K. N. ism. In many speeches last summer I advised those who did me the honor of a hearing to "stand with any body who stands right"—and I am still quite willing to follow my own advice. I lately saw, in the Quincy Whig, the report of a preamble and resolutions, made by Mr. Williams, as chairman of a committee, to a public meeting and adopted by the meeting. I saw them but once, and have them not now at command; but so far as I can remember them, they occupy about the ground I should be willing to "fuse" upon. . . .

Yours truly
A. Lincoln—

16

AL to George Robertson
CW, 2:317–318

In Congress on February 18, 1819, Kentucky representative George Robertson argued against allowing slavery in Arkansas, the newest Southern territory. He invoked slavery as the "most delicate and formidable of all the vexatious subjects" that threatened to ruin the fledging Union in 1787. By the 1850s, the Kentuckian had become a college professor and befriended Lincoln as a legal adviser. When visiting Springfield, the retired congressman left Lincoln his book, *Scrap Book on Law and Politics, Men and Times*, a collection of his speeches and essays. Lincoln responded in this letter and referenced Robertson's 1819 speech that had helped generate the Missouri Compromise, forged by Henry Clay to preserve the Union and threatened by Stephen A. Douglas's Kansas-Nebraska Act. Lincoln's position regarding the 1820 Compromise is reminiscent of Robertson's, focusing on the Founding Fathers' intention to place the institution of slavery on a gradual road to extinction. But Lincoln expressed uncharacteristic pessimism on the current generation's willingness to fulfill the Founders' intentions. The "peaceful extinction of slavery" now appeared all but impossible to Lincoln, and he believed that the nation must decide whether it could endure half slave and half free. This question, which Lincoln posed at the end of his letter, became the foundation for his famous "House Divided" speech delivered three years later. George Robertson, *Scrap Book on Law and Politics, Men and Times* (Lexington: A. W. Elder, 1855), 21–25.

A STARTLING FACT!!

A COINCIDENCE.

In the year 1819 a bill passed the House of Representatives in Congress, providing that all slaves which should hereafter be born in Arkansas, should become free on arriving at the age of twenty-five. The vote, however, was reconsidered, and the provision finally rejected by the

Casting Vote of the Speaker, HENRY CLAY!

Had the bill become a law, the first slaves born under its provisions in 1819, would have become free in 1844. Those men and women, native-born Americans, who are this year arriving at the age of twenty-five, and looking forward to interminable servitude, both for themselves AND THEIR POSTERITY,

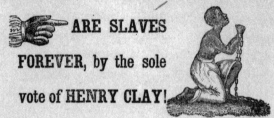

ARE SLAVES

FOREVER, by the sole

vote of HENRY CLAY!

And the very year that this vote first becomes thus diabolically operative upon the actual condition of men, he is a candidate for the Presidency, and Abolitionists are called upon to reward him for that vote, and are told that voting for him is the only way to prove the sincerity of their opposition to Slavery! Says the Christian Citizen :—" It is a fact most singular and painfully significant, that the very year in which he is set up for the highest office in the nation, would have been a year of jubilee to thousands now held in hopeless slavery, had it not been for his successful resistance to the principles of freedom. It is a bitter thought—would that it might reach his heart—that, had it not been for his single vote, every slave born in Arkansas in 1819, would have been unchained from his gloomy destiny in 1844. That vote! it doomed generations of human beings to remediless bondage."

A Startling Fact! *Broadside [1844?]. Antislavery effort to expose Henry Clay's 1819 congressional vote to scuttle efforts to end slavery in Arkansas. The broadside quotes Elihu Burritt's reform newspaper the* Christian Citizen *to prove that Clay "doomed generations of human beings to remediless bondage."*

Hon: Geo. Robertson   Springfield, Ills.
Lexington, Ky.   *Aug. 15, 1855*

My dear Sir: The volume you left for me has been received. I am really grateful for the honor of your kind
remembrance, as well as for the book. The partial reading
I have already given it, has afforded me much of both
pleasure and instruction. It was new to me that the exact
question which led to the Missouri compromise, had
arisen before it arose in regard to Missouri; and that you
had taken so prominent a part in it. Your short, but able
and patriotic speech upon that occasion, has not been improved upon since, by those holding the same views; and,
with all the lights you then had, the views you took appear
to me as very reasonable.

You are not a friend of slavery in the abstract. In that
speech you spoke of *"the peaceful extinction of slavery"*
and used other expressions indicating your belief that the
thing was, at some time, to have an end[.] Since then we
have had thirty six years of experience; and this experience has demonstrated, I think, that there is no peaceful
extinction of slavery in prospect for us. The signal failure
of Henry Clay, and other good and great men, in 1849,
to effect any thing in favor of gradual emancipation in
Kentucky, together with a thousand other signs, extin-
guishes that hope utterly. On the question of liberty, as a
principle, we are not what we have been. When we were
the political slaves of King George, and wanted to be free,
we called the maxim that "all men are created equal" a self
evident truth; but now when we have grown fat, and have
lost all dread of being slaves ourselves, we have become so
greedy to be *masters* that we call the same maxim "a self-
evident lie[.]" The fourth of July has not quite dwindled
away; it is still a great day—*for burning fire-crackers*!!!

That spirit which desired the peaceful extinction of
slavery, has itself become extinct, with the *occasion*, and

the *men* of the Revolution. Under the impulse of that occasion, nearly half the states adopted systems of emancipation at once; and it is a significant fact, that not a single state has done the like since. So far as peaceful, voluntary emancipation is concerned, the condition of the negro slave in America, scarcely less terrible to the contemplation of a free mind, is now as fixed, and hopeless of change for the better, as that of the lost souls of the finally impenitent. The Autocrat of all the Russias will resign his crown, and proclaim his subjects free republicans sooner than will our American masters voluntarily give up their slaves.

Our political problem now is "Can we, as a nation, continue together *permanently—forever—*half slave, and half free?" The problem is too mighty for me. May God, in his mercy, superintend the solution. Your much obliged friend, and humble servant

A. Lincoln—

17

AL to Joshua F. Speed
CW, 2:320–323

Lincoln first met Joshua Fry Speed, the son of wealthy Kentucky slaveowners, in 1837 in Springfield, Illinois, where the fellow Kentuckian operated a store. The two became fast friends and even shared a bed for almost four years in a room over Speed's store. They often exchanged intimate details of their lives, discussed women and wedding plans, and worked hard to build the town's Whig Party. By the time Lincoln had penned this private letter to his trusted friend, civil war had broken out in Kansas over slavery, and the North had become inflamed over enforcement of the Fugitive Slave Law. This remarkable letter to Speed was one of the only times that Lincoln freely expressed his personal views on the institution of slavery, and he did so without fear that his words would end up on the front page of a newspaper. Clearly, the sight of shackled slaves pained Lincoln considerably, but he assured his slaveholding friend that he and others like him in the North were willing to suppress their resentment of so terrible a system for the sake of the Union. While Speed was prepared to execute proslavery terrorists in Kansas, like the Stringfellow brothers, to satisfy the North, Lincoln viewed such sentiments as irrelevant to the national crisis since his good friend and others like him inflexibly insisted on their right to take their "property" into the territories. Moreover, as Lincoln would reiterate in his many debates with "Judge" Douglas, the failure to accept the Founding Fathers' view of equality—which still encompassed racial discrimination—would lead to the destruction of true liberty. "When it comes to this," Lincoln wrote, "I should prefer emigrating to some country where they make no pretence of loving liberty—to Russia, for instance, where despotism can be taken pure, and without the base alloy of hypocracy."

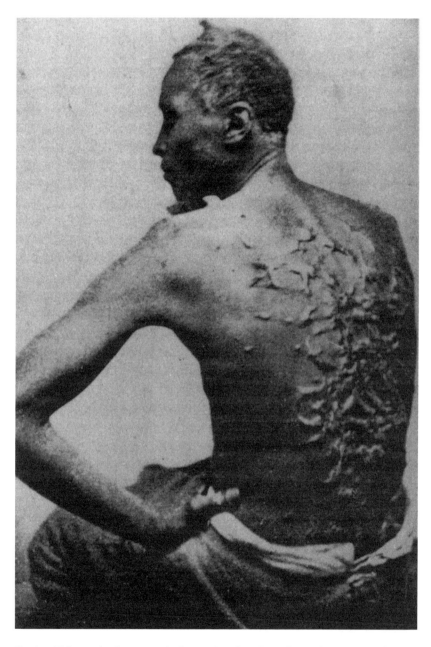

Gordon. *Taken on April 2, 1863, of a former slave from Baton Rouge, Louisiana. The image, which came to symbolize the cruelty of slavery, was sent home by a surgeon from the Forty-seventh Massachusetts Regiment who found many more slaves similarly abused. MOLLUS—Massachusetts Collection, U.S. Army Military History Institute, Carlisle, Pennsylvania.*

Springfield, *Aug. 24, 1855*

Dear Speed:

You know what a poor correspondent I am. Ever since I received your very agreeable letter of the 22ⁿᵈ. Of May I have been intending to write you in answer to it. You suggest that in political action now, you and I would differ. I suppose we would; not quite as much, however, as you may think. You know I dislike slavery; and you fully admit the abstract wrong of it. So far there is no cause of difference. But you say that sooner than yield your legal right to the slave—especially at the bidding of those who are not themselves interested, you would see the Union dissolved. I am not aware that *any one* is bidding you to yield that right; very certainly *I* am not. I leave that matter entirely to yourself. I also acknowledge *your* rights and *my* obligations, under the constitution, in regard to your slaves. I confess I hate to see the poor creatures hunted down, and caught, and carried back to their stripes, and unrewarded toils; but I bite my lip and keep quiet. In 1841 you and I had together a tedious low-water trip, on a Steam Boat from Louisville to St. Louis. You may remember, as I well do, that from Louisville to the mouth of the Ohio there were, on board, ten or a dozen slaves, shackled together with irons. That sight was a continual torment to me; and I see something like it every time I touch the Ohio, or any other slave-border. It is hardly fair for you to assume, that I have no interest in a thing which has, and continually exercises, the power of making me miserable. You ought rather to appreciate how much the great body of the Northern people do crucify their feelings, in order to maintain their loyalty to the constitution and the Union.

I do oppose the extension of slavery, because my judgment and feelings so prompt me; and I am under no obligation to the contrary. If for this you and I must differ, differ we must. You say if you were President, you would send an army and hang the leaders of the Missouri outrages upon the Kansas elections; still, if Kansas fairly votes herself a slave state, she must be admitted, or the Union must be dissolved. But how if she votes herself a slave state *unfairly*—that is, by the very means for which you say you would hang men? Must she still be admitted, or the Union be dissolved? That will be the phase of the question when it first becomes a practical one. In your assumption that there may be a *fair* decision of the slavery question in Kansas, I plainly see you and I would differ about the Nebraska-law. I look upon that enactment not as a *law*, but as *violence* from the beginning. It was conceived in violence, passed in violence, is maintained in violence, and is being executed in violence. I say it was *conceived* in violence, because the destruction of the Missouri Compromise, under the circumstances, was nothing less than violence. It was *passed* in violence, because it could not have passed at all but for the votes of many members, in violent disregard of the known will of their constituents. It is *maintained* in violence because the elections since, clearly demand it's repeal, and this demand is openly disregarded. *You* say men ought to be hung for the way they are executing that law; and *I* say the way it is being executed is quite as good as any of its antecedents. It is being executed in the precise way which was intended from the first; else why does no Nebraska man express astonishment or condemnation? Poor [Gov. Andrew H.] Reeder is the only public man who has been silly enough to believe that any thing like fairness was ever intended; and he has been bravely undeceived.

That Kansas will form a Slave constitution, and, with it, will ask to be admitted into the Union, I take to be an already settled question; and so settled by the very means you so pointedly condemn. By every principle of law, ever held by any court, North or South, every negro taken to Kansas is free; yet in utter disregard of this—in the spirit of violence merely—that beautiful Legislature gravely passes a law to hang men who shall venture to inform a negro of his legal rights. This is the substance, and real object of the law. If, like Haman, they should hang upon the gallows of their own building, I shall not be among the mourners for their fate.

In my humble sphere, I shall advocate the restoration of the Missouri Compromise, so long as Kansas remains a territory; and when, by all these foul means, it seeks to come into the Union as a Slave-state, I shall oppose it. I am very loth, [*sic*] in any case, to withhold my assent to the enjoyment of property *acquired*, or *located*, in good faith; but I do not admit that *good faith*, in taking a negro to Kansas, to be held in slavery, is a *possibility* with any man. Any man who has sense enough to be the controller of his own property, has too much sense to misunderstand the outrageous character of this whole Nebraska business. But I digress. In my opposition to the admission of Kansas I shall have some company; but we may be beaten. If we are, I shall not, on that account, attempt to dissolve the Union. On the contrary, if we succeed, there will be enough of us to take care of the Union. I think it probable, however, we shall be beaten. Standing as a unit among yourselves, you can, directly, and indirectly, bribe enough of our men to carry the day—as you could on an open proposition to establish monarchy. Get hold of some man in the North, whose position and ability is such, that he can make the support of your measure—whatever it may be—a *democratic party necessity*, and the thing is done. *Appropos* of this, let me tell you an anecdote. Douglas introduced the Nebraska bill in January. In February afterwards, there was a call session of the Illinois Legislature. Of the one hundred members composing the two branches of that body, about seventy were democrats. These latter held a caucus, in which the Nebraska bill was talked of, if not formally discussed. It was thereby discovered that just three, and no more, were in favor of the measure. In a day or two Douglas' orders came on to have resolutions passed approving the bill; and they were passed by large majorities!!! The truth of this is vouched for by a bolting democratic member. The masses too, democratic as well as whig, were even, nearer unanimous against it; but as soon as the party necessity of supporting it, became apparent, the way the democracy began to see the *wisdom* and *justice* of it, was perfectly astonishing.

You say if Kansas fairly votes herself a free state, as a Christian you will rather rejoice at it. All decent slave-holders *talk* that way; and I do not doubt their candor. But they never *vote* that way. Although in a private letter, or conversation, you will express your preference that Kansas shall be free, you would vote for no man for Congress who would say the same thing publicly. No such man could be elected from any district in any slave-state. You think [Benjamin F. & John H.] Stringfellow & Co ought to be hung; and yet, at the next presidential election you will vote for the exact type and representative of Stringfellow. The slave-breeders and slave-traders, are a small, odious and detested class, among you; and yet in politics, they dictate the course of all of you, and are as completely your masters, as you are the masters of your own negroes.

You enquire where I now stand. That is a disputed point. I think I am a whig; but others say there are no whigs, and that I am an abolitionist. When I was at Washington I voted for the Wilmot Proviso as good as forty times, and I never heard of any one attempting to unwhig me for that. I now do no more than oppose the *extension* of slavery.

I am not a Know-Nothing. That is certain. How could I be? How can any one who abhors the oppression of negroes, be in favor of degrading classes of white people? Our progress in degeneracy appears to me to be pretty rapid. As a nation, we began by declaring that "*all men are created equal.*" We now practically read it "all men are created equal, *except negroes.*" When the Know-Nothings get control, it will read "all men are created equal, except negroes, *and foreigners, and catholics*." When it comes to this I should prefer emigrating to some country where they make no pretence of loving liberty—to Russia, for instance, where despotism can be taken pure, and without the base alloy of hypocracy [*sic*].

Mary will probably pass a day or two in Louisville in October. My kindest regards to Mrs. Speed. On the leading subject of this letter, I have more of her sympathy than I have of yours.

And yet let [me] say I am

Your friend forever

A. Lincoln.—

18

Speech at Kalamazoo, Michigan
CW, 2:361–366

Roughly two months after the first Republican National Convention, Lincoln campaigned in Kalamazoo, Michigan, for the newly nominated John C. Frémont against the Democratic nominee, James Buchanan. "The question of slavery," explained Lincoln, "should be not only the greatest question, but very nearly the sole question." He sought to focus public attention on one fundamental issue: should slavery be permitted to expand into the territories as allowed by Senator Douglas's Kansas-Nebraska Act? "This is the naked question." But for Lincoln and his fellow Republicans, who carefully distanced themselves from abolitionism, the real issue appeared to be how to keep the territories open for "the homes of free white people." Lincoln also singled out the *Richmond Enquirer,* a highly influential semiweekly newspaper founded by Democratic activist Thomas Ritchie in 1804. From 1855 to 1857, the *Enquirer* featured several editorials by the proslavery ideologue George Fitzhugh, some unsigned, justifying the institution of slavery regardless of color and suggesting that Southern slaves lived better than working-class whites in the North. Lincoln used Fitzhugh's writings as a warning to the North of "the Southern view of the Free States" and the ultimate tendency of a slave society.

August 27, 1856

Fellow countrymen:—Under the Constitution of the U.S. another Presidential contest approaches us. All over this land—that portion at least, of which I know much—the people are assembling to consider the proper course to be adopted by them. One of the first considerations is to learn what the people differ about. If we ascertain what we differ about, we shall be better able to decide. The

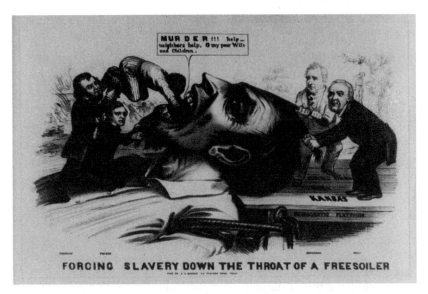

Forcing Slavery Down the Throat of a Freesoiler, *lithograph by John L. Magee, 1856. In this anti-Kansas-Nebraska cartoon, Democrats James Buchanan and Lewis Cass, standing on an expansionist platform, are assisting Stephan A. Douglas and Franklin Pierce in their attempt to spread slavery into the West. Rare Book and Special Collections Division, Stern Collection, Library of Congress. LC-USZ62-92043.*

question of slavery, at the present day, should be not only the greatest question, but very nearly the sole question. Our opponents, however, prefer that this should not be the case. To get at this question, I will occupy your attention but a single moment. The question is simply this:—Shall slavery be spread into the new Territories, or not? This is the naked question. If we should support Fremont successfully in this, it may be charged that we will not be content with restricting slavery in the new territories. If we should charge that James Buchanan, by his platform, is bound to extend slavery into the territories, and that he is in favor of its being thus spread, we should be puzzled to prove it. We believe it, nevertheless. By taking the issue as I present it, whether it shall be permitted as an issue, is made up between the parties. Each takes his own stand. This is the question: Shall the Government of the United States prohibit slavery in the United States.

We have been in the habit of deploring the fact that slavery exists amongst us. We have ever deplored it. Our forefathers did, and they declared, as we have done in later years, the blame rested on the mother Government of Great Britain. We constantly condemn Great Britain for not preventing slavery from coming amongst us. She would not interfere to prevent it, and so individuals were enabled to introduce the institution without opposition. I have alluded to this, to ask you if this is not exactly the policy of Buchanan and his friends, to place this government in the attitude then occupied by the government of Great Britain—placing the nation in the position to authorize the territories to reproach it, for refusing to allow them to hold slaves. I would like to ask your attention, any gentleman to tell me when the people of Kansas are going to decide. When are they to do it? How are they to do it? . . . The Southerners say there is no power in the people, whatever. . . . We know our Southern friends say that the General Government cannot interfere. The people, say they, have no right to interfere. They could as truly say,—"It is amongst us—we cannot get rid of it. . . ."

By our Constitution we are represented in Congress in proportion to numbers, and in counting the numbers that give us our representatives, three slaves are counted as two people. The State of Maine has six representatives in the lower house of Congress. In strength South Carolina is equal to her. But stop! Maine has *twice as many* white people, and 32,000 to boot! And is that fair? I don't complain of it. This regulation was put in force when the exigencies of the times demanded it, and could not have been avoided. Now, one man in South Carolina is the same as two men here. Maine should have twice as many men in Congress as South Carolina. It is a fact that any man in South Carolina has more influence and power in Congress today than any two now before me. The same thing is true of all slave States, though it may not be in the same proportion. It is a truth that cannot be denied, that in all the free States no white man is the equal of the white man of the slave States. But this is in the Constitution, and we must stand up to it. The question, then is, "Have we no interest as to whether the white man of the North shall be the equal of the white man of the South?" Once when I used this argument in the presence of Douglas, he answered that in the North the black man was counted as a full man, and had an equal vote with the white, while at the South they were counted at but three-fifths. And Douglas, when he had made this reply, doubtless thought he had forever silenced the objection.

Have we no interest in the free Territories of the United States—that they should be kept open for the homes of free white people? As our Northern States are growing more and more in wealth and population, we are continually in want of an outlet, through which it may pass out to enrich our country. In this we have an interest—a deep and abiding interest. There is another thing, and that is the mature knowledge we have—the greatest interest of all. It is the doctrine, that the people are to be driven from the maxims of our free Government, that despises the spirit which for eighty years has celebrated the anniversary of our national independence. . . .

I have noticed in Southern newspapers, particularly the Richmond *Enquirer*, the Southern view of the Free States. They insist that slavery has a right to spread. They defend it upon principle. They insist that their slaves are far better off than Northern freemen. What a mistaken view do these men have of Northern laborers! They think that men are always to remain laborers here—but there is no such class. The man who labored for another last year, this year labors for himself, and next year he will hire others to labor for him. These men don't understand when they think in this manner of Northern free labor. When these reasons can be introduced, tell me not that we have no interest in keeping the Territories free for the settlement of free laborers. . . .

Our adversaries charge Fremont with being an abolitionist. When pressed to show proof, they frankly confess
that they can show no such thing. They then run off upon
the assertion that his supporters are abolitionists. But this
they have never attempted to prove. I know of no word
in the language that has been used so much as that one
"abolitionist," having no definition. It has no meaning
unless taken as designating a person who is abolishing
something. If that be its signification, the supporters of
Fremont are not abolitionists. In Kansas all who come
there are perfectly free to regulate their own social relations. There has never been a man there who was an
abolitionist—for what was there to be abolished? People
there had perfect freedom to express what they wished
on the subject, when the Nebraska bill was first passed.
. . . This government is sought to be put on a new track.
Slavery is to be made a ruling element in our government.
The question can be avoided in but two ways. By the one,
we must submit, and allow slavery to triumph, or, by the
other, we must triumph over the black demon. We have
chosen the latter manner. If you of the North wish to get
rid of this question, you must decide between these two
ways—submit and vote for Buchanan, submit and vote
that slavery is a just and good thing and immediately
get rid of the question; or unite with us, and help us to
triumph. We would all like to have the question done
away with, but we cannot submit.

They tell us that we are in company with men who
have long been known as abolitionists. What care we how
many may feel disposed to labor for our cause? Why do
not you, Buchanan men, come in and use your influence
to make our party respectable? (Laughter.) . . . When
this Nebraska bill was first introduced into Congress, the
sense of the Democratic party was outraged. That party
has ever prided itself, that it was the friend of individual,
universal freedom. It was that principle upon which
they carried their measures. When the Kansas scheme

was conceived, it was natural that this respect and sense should have been outraged. Now I make this appeal to the Democratic citizens here. Don't you find yourself making arguments in support of these measures, which you never would have made before? Did you ever do it before this Nebraska bill compelled you to do it? If you answer this in the affirmative, see how a whole party have been turned away from their love of liberty! And now, my Democratic friends, come forward. Throw off these things, and come to the rescue of this great principle of equality. Don't interfere with anything in the Constitution. That must be maintained, for it is the only safeguard of our liberties. And not to Democrats alone do I make this appeal, but to all who love these great and true principles. Come, and keep coming! Strike, and strike again! So sure as God lives, the victory shall be yours. (Great cheering.)

19

AL to Newton Deming and George P. Strong

CW, 2:[online edition only]

While traveling on the Ohio River in May of 1854, a flat-bottom cargo boat carrying sixty railroad cars was engulfed by the waves of a passing steamboat and sank. Between 1855 and 1858, a series of trials took place—*Eads & Nelson v. Ohio & Mississippi RR*—first in Missouri and later in Illinois, to determine the correct compensation for the salvage company's work on the sunken cars. In 1857, Eads & Nelson and its representatives, Benjamin F. Hickman, John T. Stuart, and Benjamin S. Edwards, appealed to the U.S. Circuit Court for the Southern District of Illinois to increase the compensation settlement awarded in Missouri. Lincoln, a prominent corporate lawyer who had successfully handled railroad disputes in the past, at the request of the law firm Page & Bacon, became the third representative for the railroad company. Lincoln corresponded with the two lawyers who originally represented the railroad, Newton D. Strong and George P. Strong, and in May 1857 advised them to arrange a court date for the upcoming appeal. Two months earlier, the U.S. Supreme Court had infamously ruled against the appeal of Dred Scott for his freedom, thus helping to nationalize the institution of slavery and establishing as constitutional principle the idea that African Americans had no rights. Lincoln mocked the court's questionable ruling. However, his casual use of the term "nigger," written with quotation marks, is well worth noting in what was otherwise a standard note to his colleagues. Lincoln rarely used such language until he campaigned for the Illinois U.S. Senate seat in 1858. For further information about these cases, see: *Eads & Nelson v. Ohio & Mississippi Railroad*, in *The Papers of Abraham Lincoln: Legal Documents and Cases*, ed. Daniel W. Stowell (Charlottesville: University of Virginia Press, 2008), 3:205–224.

Springfield,   *May 25, 1857.*
Messrs. N.D. & G.P. Strong
Gentlemen . . .

. . . I have just been to see Stuart & Edwards and they
suggest that you see the plantiff's [*sic*] lawyer in St. Louis
(I forget his name) and make an arrangement with him as
to a day of taking up the case, and notify us.

I do not think any defence has been presented based on
the fact of Messrs Page & Bacon having purchased under
the Deed of Trust. Quere. Does not the Libellants right,
attach to the specific thing—this case—regardless of who
may own them?

There is no longer any difficult question of jurisdiction
in the Federal courts; they have jurisdiction in all possible
cases, except such as might redound to the benefit of a
"nigger" in some way.

Seriously, I wish you to prepare, on the question jurisdiction as well as you can; for I fear the later decisions are
against us. I understand they have some new Admiralty
Books here, but I have not examined them.

Yours truly
A. Lincoln

20

Speech at Springfield, Illinois
CW, 2:403–409

The U.S. Supreme Court handed down its Dred Scott decision on March 6, 1857. Scott, a Missouri slave, claimed that since his owner had taken him to Illinois and to the Minnesota Territory where slavery did not exist, his status as a slave had ended. Chief Justice Roger B. Taney concluded that Scott had no right to sue for his freedom because as a "Negro" he was not a U.S. citizen and, thus, did not enjoy benefits deriving from the Declaration of Independence and the Constitution. Neither the plaintiff nor any other African American, Taney explained in his famous dictum, had any "rights that white men were bound to respect." The Court's decision not only rejected the idea of black citizenship but asserted that Congress possessed no right to ban slavery in the territories, voiding the 1820 Missouri Compromise. Nearly four months passed before Lincoln responded publicly to it. When he did so, the fighting in Kansas-Nebraska had just been put down by federal troops, and enraged Republicans across the North were denouncing the decision as a coup d'état aimed at expanding slavery *and* destroying their party. If the Supreme Court ruled that all property—including slaves—could be taken into the territories, how could anyone halt slavery's expansion? Ultimately, according to Lincoln, the Taney Court's decision would authorize slaveowners to take their "property" anywhere in the country, invalidating all state laws and constitutions banning slavery. The threat to American freedom, Lincoln believed, could not be greater. On June 7, Senator Douglas spoke in Springfield, praising the Court's decision as a vindication of his own stand and his controversial 1854 Kansas-Nebraska Act. He then damned the Republicans as promoters of miscegenation. Lincoln could not let Douglas's dangerous opinions and salacious charges stand. His June 26 response repudiated the Taney Court's decision and unwaveringly defended the principle that all of humanity was embraced by the Declaration of Independence's assertion of equality. He parsed the words of the sacrosanct documents to prove his point—that the Founding Fathers ensured the freedom (though not the complete equality) of all—and blasted Taney and Douglas for making a mockery of them. Lincoln further developed the implications of Taney's decision in his famous "House Divided" speech a year later. But his principled stand on the equality of "all men" remained marred by his assertion of the racial inferiority of African Americans: "There is a natural disgust in the minds of nearly all white people, to the idea of an indiscriminate amalgamation of the white and black races." Only racial separation and colonization could, Lincoln maintained, answer the nation's race problem. As for Douglas's accusation that Republicans promoted miscegenation, he showed through census statistics that racial mixing thrived in slavery, not freedom, and that by defending slavery Douglas, not Lincoln, promoted it.

June 26, 1857

. . . I have said, in substance, that the Dred Scott decision was, in part, based on assumed historical facts which were not really true; and I ought not to leave the subject without giving some reasons for saying this; I therefore give an instance or two, which I think fully sustain me. Chief Justice [Roger B.] Taney, in delivering the opinion of the majority of the Court, insists at great length that negroes were no part of the people who made, or for whom was made, the Declaration of Independence, or the Constitution of the United States.

On the contrary, Judge [Benjamin R.] Curtis, in his dissenting opinion, shows that in five of the then thirteen states, to wit, New Hampshire, Massachusetts, New York, New Jersey and North Carolina, free negroes were voters, and, in proportion to their numbers, had the same part in making the Constitution that the white people had. He shows this with so much particularity as to leave no doubt of its truth; and, as a sort of conclusion on that point, holds the following language:

"The Constitution was ordained and established by the people of the United States, through the action, in each State, of those persons who were qualified by its laws to act thereon in behalf of themselves and all other citizens of the State. In some of the States, as we have seen, colored persons were among those qualified by law to act on the subject. These colored persons were not only included in the body of 'the people of the United States,' by whom the Constitution was ordained and established; but in at least five of the States they had the power to act, and, doubtless, did act, by their suffrages, upon the question of its adoption."

Again, Chief Justice Taney says: "It is difficult, at this day to realize the state of public opinion in relation to that unfortunate race, which prevailed in the civilized and enlightened portions of the world at the time of the Declaration of Independence, and when the Constitution of the United States was framed and adopted." And again, after quoting from the Declaration, he says: "The general words above quoted would seem to include the whole human family, and if they were used in a similar instrument at this day, would be so understood."

In these the Chief Justice does not directly assert, but plainly assumes, as a fact, that the public estimate of the black man is more favorable *now* than it was in the days of the Revolution. This assumption is a mistake. In some trifling particulars, the condition of that race has been ameliorated; but, as a whole, in this country, the change between then and now is decidedly the other way; and their ultimate destiny has never appeared so hopeless as in the last three or four years. In two of the five States—New Jersey and North Carolina—that then gave the free negro the right of voting, the right has since been taken away; and in a third—New York—it has been greatly abridged; while it has not been extended, so far as I know, to a single additional State, though the number of the States has more than doubled. In those days, as I understand, masters could, at their own pleasure, emancipate their slaves; but since then, such legal restraints have been made upon emancipation, as to amount almost to prohibition. In those days, Legislatures held the unquestioned power to abolish slavery in their respective States; but now it is becoming quite fashionable for State Constitutions to withhold that power from the Legislatures. In those days, by common consent, the spread of the black man's bondage to new countries was prohibited; but now, Congress decides that it *will* not continue the prohibition, and the Supreme Court decides that it *could* not if it would. In those days, our Declaration of Independence was held sacred by all, and thought to include all; but now, to aid in making the bondage of the negro universal and eternal, it is assailed, and sneered at, and construed, and hawked at, and torn, till, if its framers could rise from their graves, they could not at all recognize it. All the powers of earth seem rapidly combining against him. Mammon is after him; ambition follows, and philosophy follows, and the Theology of the day is fast joining the cry. They have him in his prison house; they have searched his person, and left no prying instrument with him. One after another they have closed the heavy iron doors upon him, and now they have him, as it were, bolted in with a lock of a hundred keys, which can never be unlocked without the concurrence of every key; the keys in the hands of a hundred different men, and they scattered to a hundred different and distant places; and they stand musing as to what invention, in all the dominions of mind and matter, can be produced to make the impossibility of his escape more complete than it is. . . .

There is a natural disgust in the minds of nearly all white people, to the idea of an indiscriminate amalgamation of the white and black races; and Judge Douglas evidently is basing his chief hope, upon the chances of being able to appropriate the benefit of this disgust to himself. If he can, by much drumming and repeating, fasten the odium of that idea upon his adversaries, he thinks he can struggle through the storm. He therefore clings to this hope, as a drowning man to the last plank. He makes an occasion for lugging it in from the opposition to the Dred Scott decision. He finds the Republicans insisting that the Declaration of Independence includes ALL men, black as well as white; and forth-with he boldly denies that it includes negroes at all, and proceeds to argue gravely that all who contend it does, do so only because they want to vote, and eat, and sleep, and marry with negroes! He will have it that they cannot be consistent else. Now I protest against that counterfeit logic which concludes that, because I do not want a black woman for a *slave* I must necessarily want her for a *wife*. I need not have her for either, I can just leave her alone. In some respects she certainly is not my equal; but in her natural right to eat the bread she earns with her own hands without asking leave of any one else, she is my equal, and the equal of all others.

Chief Justice Taney, in his opinion in the Dred Scott case, admits that the language of the Declaration is broad enough to include the whole human family, but he and Judge Douglas argue that the authors of that instrument did not intend to include negroes, by the fact that they did not at once, actually place them on an equality with the whites. Now this grave argument comes to just nothing at all, by the other fact, that they did not at once, *or ever afterwards*, actually place all white people on an equality with one or another. And this is the staple argument of both the Chief Justice and the Senator, for doing this obvious violence to the plain unmistakable language of the Declaration. I think the authors of that notable instrument intended to include *all* men, but they did not intend to declare all men equal *in all respects*. They did not mean to say all were equal in color, size, intellect, moral developments, or social capacity. They defined with tolerable distinctness, in what respects they did consider all men created equal—equal in "certain inalienable rights, among which are life, liberty, and the pursuit of happiness." This they said, and this meant. They did not mean to assert the obvious untruth, that all were then actually enjoying that equality, nor yet, that they were about to confer it immediately upon them. In fact they had no power to confer such a boon. They meant simply to declare the *right*, so that the *enforcement* of it might follow as fast as circumstances should permit. They meant to set up a standard maxim for free society, which should be familiar to all, and revered by all; constantly looked to, constantly labored for, and even though never perfectly attained, constantly approximated, and thereby constantly spreading and deepening its influence, and augmenting the happiness and value of life to all people of all colors everywhere. The assertion that "all men are created equal" was of no practical use in effecting our separation from Great Britain; and it was placed in the Declaration, no[t] for that, but for future use. Its authors meant it to be, thank God, it is now proving itself, a stumbling block to those who in after times might seek to turn a free people back into the hateful paths of despotism. They knew the proneness of prosperity to breed tyrants, and they meant when such should re-appear in this fair land and commence their vocation they should find left for them at least one hard nut to crack.

I have now briefly expressed my view of the *meaning* and *objects* of that part of the Declaration of Independence which declares that "all men are created equal."

Now let us hear Judge Douglas' view of the same subject, as I find it in the printed report of his late speech. Here it is:

"No man can vindicate the character, motives and conduct of the signers of the Declaration of Independence except upon the hypothesis that they referred to the white race alone, and not to the African, when they declared all men to have been created equal—that they were speaking of British subjects on this continent being equal to British subjects born and residing in Great Britain—that they were entitled to the same inalienable rights, and among them were enumerated life, liberty and the pursuit of happiness. The Declaration was adopted for the purpose of justifying the colonists in the eyes of the civilized world in withdrawing their allegiance from the British crown, and dissolving their connection with the mother country."

My good friends, read that carefully over some leisure hour, and ponder well upon it—see what a mere wreck—mangled ruin—it makes of our once glorious Declaration.

"They were speaking of British subjects on this continent being equal to British subjects born and residing in Great Britain!" Why, according to this, not only negroes but white people outside of Great Britain and America are not spoken of in that instrument. The English, Irish and Scotch, along with white Americans, were included to be sure, but the French, Germans and other white people of the world are all gone to pot along with the Judge's inferior races.

I had thought the Declaration promised something better than the condition of British subjects; but no, it only meant that we should be *equal* to them in their own oppressed and *unequal* condition. According to that, it gave no promise that having kicked off the King and Lords of Great Britain, we should not at once be saddled with a King and Lords of our own.

I had thought the Declaration contemplated the progressive improvement in the condition of all men everywhere; but no, it merely "was adopted for the purpose of justifying the colonists in the eyes of the civilized world in withdrawing their allegiance from the British crown, and dissolving their connection with the mother country." Why, that object having been effected some eighty years ago, the Declaration is of no practical use now—mere rubbish—old wadding left to rot on the battle-field after the victory is won.

I understand you are preparing to celebrate the "Fourth," tomorrow week. What for? The doings of that day had no reference to the present; and quite half of you are not even descendants of those who were referred to at that day. But I suppose you will celebrate; and will even go so far as to read the Declaration. Suppose after you read it once in the old fashioned way, you read it once more with Judge Douglas' version. It will then run thus: "We hold these truths to be self-evident that all British subjects who were on this continent eighty-one years ago, were created equal to all British subjects born and *then* residing in Great Britain."

And now I appeal to all—to Democrats as well as others,—are you really willing that the Declaration shall be thus frittered away?—thus left no more at most, than an interesting memorial of the dead past? thus shorn of its vitality, and practical value; and left without the *germ* or even the *suggestion* of the individual rights of man in it?

But Judge Douglas is especially horrified at the thought of the mixing blood by the white and black races: agreed for once—a thousand times agreed. There are white men enough to marry all the white women, and black men enough to marry all the black women; and so let them be married. On this point we fully agree with the Judge; and when he shall show that his policy is better adapted to prevent amalgamation than ours we shall drop ours, and adopt his. Let us see. In 1850 there were in the United States, 405,751, mulattoes. Very few of these are the off-spring of whites and *free* blacks; nearly all have sprung from black *slaves* and white masters. A separation of the races is the only perfect preventive of amalgamation but as an immediate separation is impossible the next best thing is to *keep* them apart *where* they are not already together. If white and black people never get together in Kansas, they will never mix blood in Kansas. That is at least one self-evident truth. A few free colored persons may get into the free States, in any event; but their number is too insignificant to amount to much in the way of mixing blood. In 1850 there were in the free states, 56,649 mulattoes; but for the most part they were not born there—they came from the slave States, ready made up. In the same year the slave States had 348,874 mulattoes all of home production. The proportion of free mulattoes to free blacks—the only colored classes in the free states—is much greater in the slave than in the free states. It is worthy of note too, that among the free states those which make the colored man the nearest to equal the white, have, proportionably the fewest mulattoes the least of amalgamation. In New Hampshire, the State which goes farthest towards equality between the races, there are just 184 Mulattoes while there are in Virginia—how many do you think? 79,775, being 23,126 more than in all the free States together.

These statistics show that slavery is the greatest source of amalgamation; and next to it, not the elevation, but the degeneration of the free blacks. Yet Judge Douglas dreads the slightest restraints on the spread of slavery, and the slightest human recognition of the negro, as tending horribly to amalgamation.

This very Dred Scott case affords a strong test as to which party most favors amalgamation, the Republicans or the dear Union-saving Democracy. Dred Scott, his wife and two daughters were all involved in the suit. We desired the court to have held that they were citizens so far at least as to entitle them to a hearing as to whether they were free or not; and then, also, that they were in fact and in law really free. Could we have had our way, the chances of these black girls, ever mixing their blood with that of white people, would have been diminished at least to the extent that it could not have been without their consent. But Judge Douglas is delighted to have them decided to be slaves, and not human enough to have a hearing, even if they were free, and thus left subject to the forced concubinage of their masters, and liable to

become the mothers of mulattoes in spite of themselves—
the very state of case that produces nine tenths of all the
mulattoes—all the mixing of blood in the nation.

Of course, I state this case as an illustration only, not
meaning to say or intimate that the master of Dred Scott
and his family, or any more than a per centage of masters
generally, are inclined to exercise this particular power
which they hold over their female slaves.

I have said that the separation of the races is the only
perfect preventive of amalgamation. I have no right to
say all the members of the Republican party are in favor
of this, nor to say that as a party they are in favor of it.
There is nothing in their platform directly on the subject.
But I can say a very large proportion of its members are
for it, and that the chief plank in their platform—opposition to the spread of slavery—is most favorable to that
separation.

Such separation, if ever effected at all, must be effected
by colonization; and no political party, as such, is now
doing anything directly for colonization. Party operations
at present only favor or retard colonization incidentally.
The enterprise is a difficult one; but "when there is a will
there is a way;" and what colonization needs most is a
hearty will. Will springs from the two elements of moral
sense and self-interest. Let us be brought to believe it is
morally right, and, at the same time, favorable to, or, at
least, not against, our interest, to transfer the African to
his native clime, and we shall find a way to do it, however
great the task may be. The children of Israel, to such
numbers as to include four hundred thousand fighting
men, went out of Egyptian bondage in a body.

How differently the respective courses of the Democratic and Republican parties incidentally bear on the
question of forming a will—a public sentiment—for
colonization, is easy to see. The Republicans inculcate,
with whatever of ability they can, that the negro is a
man; that his bondage is cruelly wrong, and that the

field of his oppression ought not to be enlarged. The Democrats deny his manhood; deny, or dwarf to insignificance, the wrong of his bondage; so far as possible, crush all sympathy for him, and cultivate and excite hatred and disgust against him; compliment themselves as Union-savers for doing so; and call the indefinite outspreading of his bondage "a sacred right of self-government. . . ."

21

A House Divided, Speech at Springfield, Illinois
CW, 2:461–462, 464–465, 466–468

On the evening of June 16, 1858, Lincoln accepted the state Republican Party's nomination to challenge incumbent U.S. senator Stephen A. Douglas. For weeks he worked furiously on his acceptance speech and delivered it from memory. His oration drew upon a popular biblical metaphor, "a house divided," that abolitionists and proslavery advocates like George Fitzhugh had used to dramatize the challenge slavery posed to the nation. Lincoln, however, employed it to draw out the starkest, most fateful choice facing the nation. For years he had warned of the dangers posed by Douglas's Kansas-Nebraska Act, and he denounced the Supreme Court's Dred Scott decision the previous year as a blatant attempt to nationalize the institution of slavery. By 1858, he spoke of a conspiracy of proslavery advocates in the three branches of the nation's government to extend slavery throughout the country, not just in the West. Because of what Douglas and his allies had done, he warned, the compromises that had kept the nation together had been destroyed. Americans now had to choose: "'A house divided against itself cannot stand.' I believe this government cannot endure, permanently half *slave* and half *free*. I do not expect the Union to be *dissolved*—I do not expect the house to *fall*—but I *do* expect it will cease to be divided. It will become *all* one thing, or *all* the other. Either the *opponents* of slavery, will arrest the further spread of it, and place it where the public mind shall rest in the belief that it is in course of ultimate extinction; or its *advocates* will push it forward, till it shall become alike lawful in *all* the States, *old* as well as *new—North* as well as *South*." Heightening the tension and sense of foreboding, Lincoln declared that a single Supreme Court decision would spell the end of every state statute and constitution that had outlawed slavery since the Revolution. Under Douglas and his Southern allies, the country had regressed to a point never imagined by the Founding

Fathers. Soon the slave trade would resume, and the enslavement of blacks outside the territorial limits of the United States would expand. Lincoln avoided discussing race, which suffused nearly all of his other political speeches, and focused both more abstractly and more concretely on slavery, heightening the sense of national crisis.

June 16, 1858

. . . Mr. PRESIDENT and Gentlemen of the Convention.

If we could first know *where* we are, and *whither* we are tending, we could then better judge *what* to do, and *how* to do it.

We are now far into the *fifth* year, since a policy was initiated, with the *avowed* object, and *confident* promise, of putting an end to slavery agitation.

Under the operation of that policy, that agitation has not only, *not ceased*, but has constantly *augmented*.

In *my* opinion, it *will* not cease, until a *crisis* shall have been reached, and passed.

"A house divided against itself cannot stand."

I believe this government cannot endure, permanently half *slave* and half *free*.

I do not expect the Union to be *dissolved*—I do not expect the house to *fall*—but I *do* expect it will cease to be divided.

It will become *all* one thing, or *all* the other.

Either the *opponents* of slavery, will arrest the further spread of it, and place it where the public mind shall rest in the belief that it is in course of ultimate extinction; or its *advocates* will push it forward, till it shall become alike lawful in *all* the States, *old* as well as *new*—*North* as well as *South*. . . .

The several points of the Dred Scott decision, in connection with Senator Douglas' "care not" policy, constitute the piece of machinery, in its *present* state of advancement. This was the third point gained.

The *working* points of that machinery are:

First, that no negro slave, imported as such from Africa, and no descendant of such slave can ever be a *citizen* of any State, in the sense of that term as used in the Constitution of the United States.

This point is made in order to deprive the negro, in every possible event, of the benefit of this provision of the United States Constitution, which declares that—

"The citizens of each State shall be entitled to all privileges and immunities of citizens in the several States."

Secondly, that "subject to the Constitution of the United States," neither *Congress* nor a *Territorial Legislature* can exclude slavery from any United States territory.

This point is made in order that individual men may *fill up* the territories with slaves, without danger of losing them as property, and thus to enhance the chances of *permanency* to the institution through all the future.

Thirdly, that whether the holding a negro in actual slavery in a free State, makes him free, as against the holder, the United States courts will not decide, but will leave to be decided by the courts of any slave State the negro may be forced into by the master.

This point is made, not to be pressed *immediately*; but, if acquiesced in for a while, and apparently *indorsed* by the people at an election, *then* to sustain the logical conclusion that what Dred Scott's master might lawfully do with Dred Scott, in the free State of Illinois, every other master may lawfully do with any other *one*, or one *thousand* slaves, in Illinois, or in any other free State.

Auxiliary to all this, and working hand in hand with it, the Nebraska doctrine, or what is left of it, is to *educate* and *mould* public opinion, at least *Northern* public opinion, to not *care* whether slavery is voted *down* or voted *up*.

This shows exactly where we now *are*; and *partially* also, whither we are tending. . . .

In what cases the power of the *states* is so restrained by the U.S. Constitution, is left an *open* question, precisely as the same question, as to the restraint on the power of the *territories* was left open in the Nebraska act. Put *that* and *that* together, and we have another nice little niche, which we may, ere long, see filled with another Supreme Court decision, declaring that the Constitution of the United States does not permit a *state* to exclude slavery from its limits.

And this may especially be expected if the doctrine of "care not whether slavery be voted *down* or voted *up*," shall gain upon the public mind sufficiently to give promise that such a decision can be maintained when made.

Such a decision is all that slavery now lacks of being alike lawful in all the States.

Welcome or unwelcome, such decision *is* probably coming, and will soon be upon us, unless the power of the present political dynasty shall be met and overthrown.

We shall *lie down* pleasantly dreaming that the people of *Missouri* are on the verge of making their State *free*; and we shall *awake* to the *reality*, instead, that the *Supreme Court* has made *Illinois* a *slave* State. . . .

A leading Douglas Democratic newspaper thinks Douglas' superior talent will be needed to resist the revival of the African slave trade.

Does Douglas believe an effort to revive that trade is approaching? He has not said so. Does he *really* think so? But if it is, how can he resist it? For years he has labored to prove it a *sacred right* of white men to take negro slaves into the new territories. Can he possibly show that it is *less* a sacred right to *buy* them where they can be bought cheapest? And, unquestionably they can be bought *cheaper* in *Africa* than in *Virginia*. . . .

22

AL to John L. Scripps
CW, 2:471

John Locke Scripps, the prominent Chicago publisher and a co-founder of the *Chicago Tribune*, wrote to Lincoln in response to his "House Divided" speech. Like many supporters of Lincoln's bid for a seat in the U.S. Senate, Scripps felt that the speech endorsed a far too radical stance on the abolition of slavery. Lincoln reacted with alarm at Scripps's interpretation of his remarks. He clarified his position, asserting that his speech revealed no intention of interfering with the institution of slavery in the Southern states. Instead, he reiterated his belief—and the Republican Party's founding principle—that Congress could only prevent slavery's expansion and indeed was obligated to do so. Although Lincoln claimed that he did not intend that Scripps publish his letter, he wished to exploit the editor's considerable clout and use him to help blunt any misconstruction of his remarks. Given Senator Douglas's penchant for describing his opponents as "Black Republicans," Lincoln worked throughout his campaign to carefully trace the limits of Republicanism.

Jno. L. Scripps, Esq   Springfield,
My dear Sir   *June 23, 1858*

Your kind note of yesterday is duly received. I am much flattered by the estimate you place on my late speech; and yet I am much mortified that any part of it should be construed so differently from any thing intended by me. The language, "place it where the public mind shall rest in the belief that it is in course of ultimate extinction," I used deliberately, not dreaming then, nor believing now, that it asserts, or intimates, any power or purpose, to interfere with slavery in the States where it exists. But, to not cavil about language, I declare that whether the clause used by me, will bear such construction or not, I never so intended it. I have declared a thousand times, and now repeat that, in my opinion, neither the General Government, nor any other power outside of the slave states, can constitutionally or rightfully interfere with slaves or slavery where it already exists. I believe that whenever the effort to spread slavery into the new territories, by whatever means, and into the free states themselves, by Supreme court decisions, shall be fairly headed off, the institution will then be in course of ultimate extinction; and by the language used I meant only this.

I do not intend this for publication; but still you may show it to any one you think fit. I think I shall, as you suggest, take some early occasion to publicly repeat the declaration I have already so often made as before stated.

Yours very truly
A. Lincoln

23

Fragment on the Struggle Against Slavery
CW, 2:482

In this fragment from an unknown speech, Lincoln evoked the storied accomplishments of the British antislavery movement in order to underscore his own views on the abolition of slavery. The rhetorical tone of the text and the opening statement concerning public office clearly establish its context within the series of speeches delivered during Lincoln's unsuccessful bid for a seat in the U.S. Senate in the summer and fall of 1858. In this text, Lincoln spoke of a higher cause for the nation's political leaders. He used the word "republican" to refer, if not solely to the recently founded Republican Party itself, then in the more general sense to a polity based on universal principles of liberty. His reference to the British antislavery movement, which had successfully banned the slave trade fifty years earlier, embodied Lincoln's support for the abolition of slavery. It recalled the political context of the British precedent, referring to William Wilberforce as the major power in Parliament behind the antislavery bill and to Granville Sharp, a lawyer—like Lincoln—and popular antislavery leader. Lincoln positioned himself as the ardent follower of these pioneer opponents of slavery and recalled that history remembered their noble actions but forgot their proslavery opponents. His mention of the "don't care" opponents refers to Stephen A. Douglas, who professed not to care whether slavery "was voted up or down" by residents of the territories. Lincoln underscored the transcendent nature of abolition, which surpassed the usual scope of human affairs. In closing, he used the rhetorical device of self-abnegation to stress the magnitude of the issue.

I have never professed an indifference to the honors of official station; and were I to do so now, I should only make myself ridiculous. Yet I have never failed—do not now fail—to remember that in the republican cause there is a higher aim than that of mere office. I have not allowed myself to forget that the abolition of the Slave-trade by Great Brittain, [*sic*] was agitated a hundred years before it was a final success; that the measure had it's open fire-eating opponents; it's stealthy "dont care" opponents; it's dollar and cent opponents; it's inferior race opponents; its negro equality opponents; and its religion and good order opponents; that all these opponents got offices, and their adversaries got none. But I have also remembered that though they blazed, like tallow-candles for a century, at last they flickered in the socket, died out, stank in the dark for a brief season, and were remembered no more, even by the smell. School-boys know that Wilbe[r]force, and Granville Sharpe [*sic*], helped that cause forward; but who can now name a single man who labored to retard it? Remembering these things I can not but regard it as possible that the higher object of this contest may not be completely attained within the term of my natural life. But I can not doubt either that it will come in due time. Even in this view, I am proud, in my passing speck of time, to contribute an humble mite to that glorious consummation, which my own poor eyes may not last to see.

24

Speech at Chicago, Illinois
CW, 2:491–494, 497–502

Lincoln delivered the following speech in response to Senator Stephen A. Douglas's much-anticipated oration of the previous evening. On that occasion, Douglas repudiated Lincoln's famed "House Divided" speech. The result of this exchange would define the major issues of the campaign. Later in the month, he challenged Douglas to the first of seven debates that would continue into October. They would make Lincoln the subject of national attention and put him at center stage for the Republican candidacy for president in 1860. At Chicago, Lincoln reiterated the well-known phrases of that Springfield speech, words which Douglas had subjected to caustic review, and focused national attention on the defining question of his generation: should slavery be allowed into the territories acquired as a result of the Mexican War? In his full address, Lincoln lampooned Douglas's principle of "popular sovereignty," denounced the proslavery coup in Kansas and the bogus Lecompton Constitution it devised, and outlined the fatal ramifications of the U.S. Supreme Court's 1857 Dred Scott decision. He deflected Douglas's charge that his views were indistinguishable from those of radical abolitionists who schemed to force emancipation upon the South. He fought off the senator's attempt to stigmatize him as out of touch with his constituents and a threat to national peace. Douglas had asserted that no reason existed why the country could not continue to exist half slave and half free as it had been for eighty-two years. But Lincoln would not be disarmed and went directly after his opponent. The nation could no longer endure as it had been because of Douglas and the fundamental changes wrought by his Kansas-Nebraska Act and the nationalization of slavery in *Dred Scott*. While Douglas reiterated his stand that he didn't care whether slavery was voted up or down by those in the territories, Lincoln asserted that the Supreme Court had rendered the "don't care" attitude irrelevant at best. Alongside his argument against the spread of slavery and for the right of all men to liberty, Lincoln also took care to assure his audience that the Republican Party represented the only bulwark for white men "who want the land [in the West] to bring up their families upon."

July 10, 1858

. . . I am not, in the first place, unaware that this Government has endured eight-two [*sic*] years, half slave and half free. I know that. I am tolerably well acquainted with the history of the country, and I know that it has endured eighty-two years, half slave and half free. I *believe*—and that is what I meant to allude to there—I *believe* it has endured because, during all that time, until the introduction of the Nebraska Bill, the public mind did rest, all the time, in the belief that slavery was in course of ultimate extinction. ["Good!" "Good!" and applause.] That was what gave us the rest that we had through that period of eight-two [*sic*] years; at least, so I believe. I have always hated slavery, I think as much as any Abolitionist. [Applause.] I have been an Old Line Whig. I have always hated it, but I have always been quiet about it until this new era of the introduction of the Nebraska Bill began. I always believed that everybody was against it, and that it was in course of ultimate extinction. . . .

I have said a hundred times, and I have now no inclination to take it back, that I believe there is no right, and ought to be no inclination in the people of the free States to enter into the slave States, and interfere with the question of slavery at all. I have said that always. Judge Douglas has heard me say it—if not quite a hundred times, at least as good as a hundred times; and when it is said that I am in favor of interfering with slavery where it exists, I know it is unwarranted by anything I have ever *intended,* and, as I believe, by anything I have ever *said.* If, by any means, I have ever used language which could fairly be so construed, (as, however, I believe I never have,) I now correct it. . . .

How is it, then, that Judge Douglas infers, because I hope to see slavery put where the public mind shall rest in the belief that it is in the course of ultimate extinction, that I am in favor of Illinois going over and interfering with the cranberry laws of Indiana? What can authorize him to draw any such *inference*? I suppose there might be one thing that at least enabled *him* to draw such an inference that would not be true with me or with many others, that is, because he looks upon all this matter of slavery as an exceedingly little thing—this matter of keeping one-sixth of the population of the whole nation in a state of oppression and tyranny unequalled in the world. He looks upon it as being an exceedingly little thing—only equal to the question of the cranberry laws of Indiana—as something having no moral question in it—as something on a par with the question of whether a man shall pasture his land with cattle, or plant it with tobacco—so little and so small a thing, that he concludes, if I could desire that anything should be done to bring about the ultimate extinction of that little thing, I must be in favor of bringing about an amalgamation of all the other little things in the Union. Now, it so happens—and there, I presume, is the foundation of this mistake—that the Judge thinks thus; and it so happens that there is a vast portion of the American people that do *not* look upon that matter as being this very little thing. They look upon it as a vast moral evil; they can prove it is such by the writings of those who gave us the blessings of liberty which we enjoy, and that they so looked upon it, and not as an evil merely confining itself to the States where it is situated; and while we agree that, by the Constitution we assented to, in the States where it exists we have no right to interfere with it because it is in the Constitution and we are by both duty and inclination to stick by that

Constitution in all its letter and spirit from beginning to end. [Great applause.] . . .

I do not claim, gentlemen, to be unselfish, I do not pretend that I would not like to go to the United States Senate, (laughter), I make no such hypocritical pretense, but I do say to you that in this mighty issue, it is nothing to you—nothing to the mass of the people of the nation, whether or not Judge Douglas or myself shall ever be heard of after this night, it may be a trifle to either of us, but in connection with this mighty question, upon which hang the destinies of the nation, perhaps, it is absolutely nothing; but where will you be placed if you re-endorse Judge Douglas? Don't you know how apt he is—how exceedingly anxious he is at all times to seize upon anything and everything to persuade you that something *he* has done *you* did yourselves? Why, he tried to persuade you last night that our Illinois Legislature instructed him to introduce the Nebraska bill. There was nobody in that legislature ever thought of such a thing; and when he first introduced the bill, he never thought of it; but still he fights furiously for the proposition, and that he did it because there was a standing instruction to our Senators to be always introducing Nebraska bills. [Laughter and applause]. . . . Now I could ask the Republican party after all the hard names that Judge Douglas has called them by—all his repeated charges of their inclination to marry with and hug negroes—all his declarations of Black Republicanism—by the way we are improving, the black has got rubbed off—but with all that, if he be endorsed by Republican votes where do you stand? Plainly you stand ready saddled, bridled and harnessed and waiting to be driven over to the slavery extension camp of the nation [a voice "we will hang ourselves first"]—just ready to be driven over tied together in a lot—to be driven over, every man with a rope around his neck, that halter being held by Judge Douglas. That is the question. If Republican men have been in earnest in what they have done, I think they had better not do it, but I think that the Republican party is made up of those who, as far as they can peaceably, will oppose the extension of slavery, and who will hope for its ultimate extinction. If they believe it is wrong in grasping up the new lands of the continent, and keeping them from the settlement of free white laborers, who want the land to bring up their families upon. . . .

We were often—more than once at least—in the course of Judge Douglas' speech last night, reminded that this government was made for white men—that he believed it was made for white men. Well, that is putting it into a shape in which no one wants to deny it, but the Judge then goes into his passion for drawing inferences that are not warranted. I protest, now and forever, against that counterfeit logic which presumes that because I do not want a negro woman for a slave, I do necessarily want her for a wife. [Laughter and cheers.] My understanding is that I need not have her for either, but as God made us separate, we can leave one another alone and do one another much good thereby. There are white men enough to marry all the white women, and enough black men to marry all the black women, and in God's name let them be so married. The Judge regales us with the terrible enormities that take place by the mixture of races; that the inferior race bears the superior down. Why, Judge, if we do not let them get together in the Territories they won't mix there. [Immense applause.] . . .

We find a race of men living in that day whom we claim as our fathers and grandfathers; they were iron men, they fought for the principle that they were contending for; and we understood that by what they then did it has followed that the degree of prosperity that we now enjoy has come to us. We hold this annual celebration to remind ourselves of all the good done in this process of time of how it was done and who did it, and how we are historically connected with it; and we go from these meetings in better humor with ourselves—we feel more attached the one to the other, and more firmly bound to the country we inhabit. In every way we are better men in the age, and race, and country in which we live for these celebrations. But after we have done all this we have not yet reached the whole. There is something else connected with it. We have besides these men—descended by blood from our ancestors—among us perhaps half our people who are not descendants at all of these men, they are men who have come from Europe—German, Irish, French and Scandinavian—men that have come from Europe themselves, or whose ancestors have come hither and settled here, finding themselves our equals in all things. If they look back through this history to trace their connection with those days by blood, they find they have none, they cannot carry themselves back into that glorious epoch and make themselves feel that they are part of us, but when they look through that old Declaration of Independence they find that those old men say that "We hold these truths to be self-evident, that all men are created equal," and then they feel that that moral sentiment taught in that day evidences their relation to those men, that it is the father of all moral principle in them, and that they have a right to claim it as though they were blood of the blood, and flesh of the flesh of the men who wrote that Declaration, (loud and long continued applause) and so they are. That is the electric cord in that Declaration that links the hearts of patriotic and liberty-loving men together, that will link those patriotic hearts as long as the love of freedom exists in the minds of men throughout the world. [Applause.]

Now, sirs, for the purpose of squaring things with this idea of "don't care if slavery is voted up or voted down," for sustaining the Dred Scott decision [A voice—"Hit him again"], for holding that the Declaration of Independence did not mean anything at all, we have Judge Douglas giving his exposition of what the Declaration of Independence means, and we have him saying that the people of America are equal to the people of England. According to his construction, you Germans are not connected with it. Now I ask you in all soberness, if all these things, if indulged in, if ratified, if confirmed and endorsed, if taught to our children, and repeated to them, do not tend to rub out the sentiment of liberty in the country, and to transform this Government into a government of some other form. Those arguments that are made, that the inferior race are to be treated with as much allowance as they are capable of enjoying; that as much is to be done for them as their condition will allow. What are these arguments? They are the arguments that kings have made for enslaving the people in all ages of the world. You will find that all the arguments in favor of king-craft were of this class; they always bestrode the necks of the people, not that they wanted to do it, but because the people were better off for being ridden. That is their argument, and this argument of the Judge is the same old serpent that says you work and I eat, you toil and I will enjoy the fruits of it. Turn in whatever way you will—whether it come from the mouth of a King, an excuse for enslaving the people of his country, or from the mouth of men of one race as a reason for enslaving the men of another race, it is all the same old serpent, and I hold if that course of argumentation that is made for the purpose of convincing the public mind that we should not care about this, should be granted, it does not stop with the negro. I should like to know if taking this old Declaration of Independence, which declares that all men are equal upon principle and making exceptions to it where will it stop. If one man says it does not mean a negro, why not another say it does not mean some other man? If that declaration is not the truth, let us get the Statute book, in which we find it and tear it out! Who is so bold as to do it! [Voices "me" "no one," &c.] If it is not true let us tear it out! [cries of "no, no,"] let us stick to it then, [cheers] let us stand firmly by it then. [Applause.] . . .

It may be argued that there are certain conditions that make necessities and impose them upon us, and to the extent that a necessity is imposed upon a man he must submit to it. I think that was the condition in which we found ourselves when we established this government. We had slavery among us, we could not get our constitution unless we permitted them to remain in slavery, we could not secure the good we did secure if we grasped for more, and having by necessity submitted to that much, it does not destroy the principle that is the charter of our liberties. Let that charter stand as our standard. . . .

My friends, I have detained you about as long as I desired to do, and I have only to say, let us discard all this quibbling about this man and the other man—this race and that race and the other race being inferior, and therefore they must be placed in an inferior position—discarding our standard that we have left us. Let us discard all these things, and unite as one people throughout this land, until we shall once more stand up declaring that all men are created equal. . . .

I leave you, hoping that the lamp of liberty will burn in your bosoms until there shall no longer be a doubt that all men are created free and equal.

Mr. Lincoln retired amid a perfect torrent of applause and cheers.

Speech at Springfield, Illinois

CW, 2:514–516, 518–521

A week after his response to Douglas in Chicago, Lincoln and his opponent traveled south to Springfield. The "Little Giant" rode in an elaborate railcar festooned with banners and ribbons, accompanied by his wife, secretaries, and a host of minions and cronies. Lincoln went as an ordinary passenger. After arriving in the capital, Douglas spoke in the afternoon, Lincoln in the evening, sparking the Douglas press corps to claim that following their leader was the only way Lincoln could get up a crowd. Just before the start of the famed debates across the state, Lincoln reiterated his warning against the "nationalization of slavery." Restricting its growth, as intended by the Founding Fathers, he held, would hasten the institution toward its "ultimate extinction." Lincoln concluded his address reminding his audience about his stand on the equality of blacks and whites. He ridiculed Douglas's attempt to stigmatize him as an "amalgamator" and pointed up his contradictions regarding race and nationality. Douglas appeared to believe that the Declaration of Independence meant only that white Americans were the equal of white Englishmen. But what about "the Germans, the Irish, the Portuguese, and all the other people who have come amongst us since the Revolution. . . [?] I press him a little further, and ask if it meant to include the Russians in Asia?" In the end, Lincoln asserted, the Declaration's statement of equality must include all men, or it could not protect any men. But the fact that all men are entitled to "life, liberty and the pursuit of happiness," he held, did not imply social and political equality. "What I would most desire," he reasserted, "would be the separation of the white and black races." He confessed that his views were often misrepresented, but they should not be misunderstood. "I have said that I do not understand the Declaration to mean that all men were created equal in all respects. They are not our equal in color.

... Certainly the negro is not our equal in color—perhaps not in many other respects; still, in the right to put into his mouth the bread that his own hands have earned, he is the equal of every other man, white or black. . . . All I ask for the negro is that if you do not like him, let him alone. If God gave him but little, that little let him enjoy."

July 17, 1858

... Although I have ever been opposed to slavery, so far I rested in the hope and belief that it was in course of ultimate extinction. For that reason, it had been a minor question with me. I might have been mistaken; but I had believed, and now believe, that the whole public mind, that is the mind of the great majority, had rested in that belief up to the repeal of the Missouri Compromise. But upon that event, I became convinced that either I had been resting in a delusion, or the institution was being placed on a new basis—a basis for making it perpetual, national and universal. Subsequent events have greatly confirmed me in that belief. I believe that bill to be the beginning of a conspiracy for that purpose. So believing, I have since then considered that question a paramount one. So believing, I have thought the public mind will never rest till the power of Congress to restrict the spread of it, shall again be acknowledged and exercised on the one hand, or on the other, all resistance be entirely crushed out. I have expressed that opinion, and I entertain it to-night. It is denied that there is any tendency to the nationalization of slavery in these States.

Mr. [Preston] Brooks, of South Carolina, in one of his speeches, when they were presenting him with canes, silver plate, gold pitchers and the like, for assaulting Senator [Charles] Sumner, distinctly affirmed his opinion that when this Constitution was formed, it was the belief of no man that slavery would last to the present day.

He said, what I think, that the framers of our Constitution placed the institution of slavery where the public mind rested in the hope that it was in course of ultimate extinction. But he went on to say that the men of the present age, by their experience, have become wiser than the framers of the Constitution; and the invention of the cotton gin had made the perpetuity of slavery a necessity in this country.

As another piece of evidence tending to the same point:—Quite recently in Virginia, a man—the owner of slaves—made a will providing that after his death certain of his slaves should have their freedom if they should so choose, and go to Liberia, rather than remain in slavery. They chose to be liberated. But the persons to whom they would descend as property, claimed them as slaves. A suit was instituted, which finally came to the Supreme Court of Virginia, and was therein decided against the slaves, upon the ground that a negro cannot make a choice—that they had no legal power to choose—could not perform the condition upon which their freedom depended. . . .

He says this Dred Scott case is a very small matter at most—that it has no practical effect; that at best, or rather, I suppose, at worst, it is but an abstraction. I submit that the proposition that the thing which determines whether a man is free or a slave, is rather *concrete* than *abstract*. I think you would conclude that it was, if your liberty depended upon it, and so would Judge Douglas if his liberty depended upon it. But suppose it was on the question of spreading slavery over the new territories that he considers it as being merely an abstract matter, and one of no practical importance. How has the planting of slavery in new countries always been effected? It has now been decided that slavery cannot be kept out of our new territories by any legal means. In what does our new territories now differ in this respect, from the old colonies when slavery was first planted within them? It was planted as Mr. Clay once declared, and as history proves true, by individual men in spite of the wishes of the people; the mother government refusing to prohibit it, and withholding from the people of the colonies the authority to prohibit it for themselves. Mr. Clay says this was one of the great and just causes of complaint against Great Britain by the colonies, and the best apology we can now make for having the institution amongst us. In that precise condition our Nebraska politicians have at last succeeded in placing our own new territories; the government will not prohibit slavery within them, nor allow the people to prohibit it. . . .

Last night Judge Douglas tormented himself with horrors about my disposition to make negroes perfectly equal with white men in social and political relations. He did not stop to show that I have said any such thing, or that it legitimately follows from any thing I have said, but he rushes on with his assertions. I adhere to the Declaration of Independence. If Judge Douglas and his friends are not willing to stand by it, let them come up and amend it. Let them make it read that all men are created equal except negroes. Let us have it decided, whether the Declaration of Independence, in this blessed year of 1858, shall be thus amended. In his construction of the Declaration last year he said it only meant that Americans in America were equal to Englishmen in England. Then, when I pointed out to him that by that rule he excludes the Germans, the Irish, the Portuguese, and all the other people who have come amongst us since the Revolution, he reconstructs his construction. In his last speech he tells us it meant Europeans.

I press him a little further, and ask if it meant to include the Russians in Asia? or does he mean to exclude that vast population from the principles of our Declaration of Independence? I expect ere long he will introduce another amendment to his definition. He is not at all particular. He is satisfied with any thing which does not endanger the nationalizing of negro slavery. It may draw white men down, but it must not lift negroes up. Who shall say, "I am the superior, and you are the inferior?"

My declarations upon this subject of negro slavery may be misrepresented, but can not be misunderstood. I have said that I do not understand the Declaration to mean that all men were created equal in all respects. They are not our equal in color; but I suppose that it does mean to declare that all men are equal in some respects; they are equal in their right to "life, liberty, and the pursuit of happiness." Certainly the negro is not our equal in color—perhaps not in many other respects; still, in the right to put into his mouth the bread that his own hands have earned, he is the equal of every other man, white or black. In pointing out that more has been given you, you can not be justified in taking away the little which has been given him. All I ask for the negro is that if you do not like him, let him alone. If God gave him but little, that little let him enjoy. . . .

What I would most desire would be the separation of the white and black races. . . .

26

Speech at Lewistown, Illinois
CW, 2:546–547

This address was delivered on the porch of the Fulton County courthouse, where Stephen A. Douglas had served as a circuit court judge. The elevated moral tone of the speech made it a favorite of Lincoln supporters, and the oft-quoted address became known as the "Return to the Fountain" speech. In tribute to its historical importance, the event was re-created on its 150th anniversary. Lincoln condemned the false, morally neutral stand of his opponent and tried to corner him politically by compelling Douglas to state his personal view of slavery. Douglas, Lincoln charged, "never said that he regarded it either as an evil or a good, morally right or morally wrong." Such a choice would have proven fatal to the senator's presidential aspirations. Lincoln then returned to his central belief in the inalienable rights of man, "Yes, gentlemen, to *all* His creatures, to the whole great family of man." Such principles offered the only protection from "the doctrine that none but rich men, or none but white men, were entitled to life, liberty and the pursuit of happiness." The soaring rhetoric did not contradict his belief in racial segregation but, rather, established a level below which no one should tread in American society. Nowhere else did Lincoln offer such eloquence in defense of Jefferson's words in the Declaration of Independence. He concentrated squarely on the noble goal of liberty and equality for all men, and implored all who have strayed from this ideal to "return to the fountain." He concluded his address by elevating his argument from the sphere of worldly governance to the level of divine authority. In the ultimate validity of this context, he declared that all other interests, including his own political ambition (and that of his opponent as well), are inconsequential beside this sanctified cause.

August 17, 1858

... * * * The Declaration of Independence (said Mr. L.) was formed by the representatives of American liberty from thirteen States of the confederacy—twelve of which were slaveholding communities. We need not discuss the way or the reason of their becoming slaveholding communities. It is sufficient for our purpose that all of them greatly deplored the evil and that they placed a provision in the Constitution which they supposed would gradually remove the disease by cutting off its source. This was the abolition of the slave trade. So general was conviction—the public determination—to abolish the African slave trade, that the provision which I have referred to as being placed in the Constitution, declared that it should *not* be abolished prior to the year 1808. A constitutional provision was necessary to prevent the people, through Congress, from putting a stop to the traffic immediately at the close of the war. Now, if slavery had been a good thing, would the Fathers of the Republic have taken a step calculated to diminish its beneficent influences among themselves, and snatch the boon wholly from their posterity? These communities, by their representatives in old Independence Hall, said to the whole world of men: "We hold these truths to be self evident: that all men are created equal; that they are endowed by their Creator with certain unalienable rights; that among these are life, liberty and the pursuit of happiness." This was their majestic interpretation of the economy of the Universe. This was their lofty, and wise, and noble understanding of the justice of the Creator to His creatures. [Applause.] Yes, gentlemen, to *all* His creatures, to the whole great family of man. In their enlightened belief, nothing stamped with the Divine image and likeness was sent into the world to be trodden on, and degraded, and imbruted by its fellows. They grasped not only the whole race of man then living, but they reached forward and seized upon the farthest posterity. They erected a beacon to guide their children and their children's children, and the countless myriads who should inhabit the earth in other ages. Wise statesmen as they were, they knew the tendency of prosperity to breed tyrants, and so they established these great self-evident truths, that when in the distant future some man, some faction, some interest, should set up the doctrine that none but rich men, or none but white men, were entitled to life, liberty and the pursuit of happiness, their posterity might look up again to the Declaration of Independence and take courage to renew the battle which their fathers began—so that truth, and justice, and mercy, and all the humane and Christian virtues might not be extinguished from the land; so that no man would hereafter dare to limit and circumscribe the great principles on which the temple of liberty was being built. [Loud cheers.]

Now, my countrymen (Mr. Lincoln continued with great earnestness,) if you have been taught doctrines conflicting with the great landmarks of the Declaration of Independence; if you have listened to suggestions which would take away from its grandeur, and mutilate the fair symmetry of its proportions; if you have been inclined to believe that all men are *not* created equal in those inalienable rights enumerated by our chart of liberty, let me entreat you to come back. Return to the fountain whose waters spring close by the blood of the Revolution. Think nothing of me—take no thought for the political fate of any man whomsoever—but come back to the truths that are in the Declaration of Independence. You may do anything with me you choose, if you will but heed these sacred principles. You may not only defeat me for the Senate, but you may take me and put me to death. While pretending no indifference to earthly honors, I *do claim* to be actuated in this contest by something higher than an anxiety for office. I charge you to drop every paltry and insignificant thought for any man's success. It is nothing; I am nothing; Judge Douglas is nothing. *But do not destroy that immortal emblem of Humanity—the Declaration of American Independence.*

27

First Debate with Stephen A. Douglas at Ottawa, Illinois
CW, 3:14–18, 27–30

On July 24, 1858, Abraham Lincoln challenged Stephen A. Douglas to a series of debates. Douglas reluctantly accepted and insisted that they appear in each of the state's nine congressional districts—excepting Chicago and Springfield, where each candidate recently had delivered speeches. Douglas also named the towns for each event, and by July 31 the two had settled on the format. The first debate took place in the small north-central Illinois town of Ottawa, attended by a crowd of several thousand people. The historic debates, focusing on slavery and race, revisited the positions Lincoln had taken since adoption of the 1854 Kansas-Nebraska Act. By 1858, however, civil war in Kansas and especially the 1857 Dred Scott decision had changed the political landscape. Lincoln always condemned slavery as a "monstrous injustice," but he insisted that only by adhering to the intentions of the Founding Fathers could the nation preserve democracy and safely rid itself of slavery and the unwanted slave. Lincoln singled out the 1820 Compromise as necessary to recognize the interests of slaveholders *and* the Fathers' intention of placing slavery on the road to extinction. Douglas's policies, Lincoln asserted, abandoned the legacy of the Founders. With a conciliatory tone, he carefully avoided holding Southerners responsible for the existence of slavery and reaffirmed his preference for emancipation and black resettlement in Liberia. He shared Douglas's popular racial attitudes: "There is a physical difference between the two, which in my judgment will probably forever forbid their living together upon the footing of perfect equality." He did not hesitate to refer to blacks as niggers. He also marked out a fundamental difference with his Democratic opponent on the race issue. While Douglas believed that blacks were best kept in slavery, Lincoln insisted that African Americans always had been included in the definition of equality offered by the Declaration of Independence.

While blacks would never be the equal of whites, Lincoln insisted that they had a basic right to enjoy the fruit of their own labor "without leave of anybody else, which his own hand earns." In that way, and only in that way, did Lincoln consider blacks as *"my equal and the equal of Judge Douglas, and the equal of every living man."*

August 21, 1858

. . . I think, and shall try to show, that it is wrong; wrong in its direct effect, letting slavery into Kansas and Nebraska—and wrong in its prospective principle, allowing it to spread to every other part of the wide world, where men can be found inclined to take it.

This *declared* indifference, but as I must think, covert *real* zeal for the spread of slavery, I can not but hate. I hate it because of the monstrous injustice of slavery itself. I hate it because it deprives our republican example of its just influence in the world—enables the enemies of free institutions, with plausibility, to taunt us as hypocrites— causes the real friends of freedom to doubt our sincerity, and especially because it forces so many really good men amongst ourselves into an open war with the very fundamental principles of civil liberty—criticising the Declaration of Independence, and insisting that there is no right principle of action but *self-interest.*

Before proceeding, let me say I think I have no prejudice against the Southern people. They are just what we would be in their situation. If slavery did not now exist amongst them, they would not introduce it. If it did now exist amongst us, we should not instantly give it up. This I believe of the masses north and south. Doubtless there are individuals, on both sides, who would not hold slaves under any circumstances; and others who would gladly introduce slavery anew, if it were out of existence. We know that some southern men do free their slaves, go north, and become tip-top abolitionists; while some northern ones go south, and become most cruel slave-masters.

When southern people tell us they are no more responsible for the origin of slavery, than we; I acknowledge the fact. When it is said that the institution exists, and that it is very difficult to get rid of it, in any satisfactory way, I can understand and appreciate the saying. I surely will not blame them for not doing what I should not know how to do myself. If all earthly power were given me, I should not know what to do, as to the existing institution. My first impulse would be to free all the slaves, and send them to Liberia,—to their own native land. But a moment's reflection would convince me, that whatever of high hope, (as I think there is) there may be in this, in the long run, its sudden execution is impossible. If they were all landed there in a day, they would all perish in the next ten days; and there are not surplus shipping and surplus money enough in the world to carry them there in many times ten days. What then? Free them all, and keep them among us as underlings? Is it quite certain that this betters their condition? I think I would not hold one in slavery, at any rate; yet the point is not clear enough to me to denounce people upon. What next? Free them, and make them politically and socially, our equals? My own feelings will not admit of this; and if mine would, we well know that those of the great mass of white people will not. Whether this feeling accords with justice and sound judgment, is not the sole question, if indeed, it is any part of it. A universal feeling, whether well or ill-founded, can not be safely disregarded. We can not, then, make them equals. It does seem to me that systems of gradual emancipation might be adopted; but for their tardiness in this, I will not undertake to judge our brethren of the south.

When they remind us of their constitutional rights, I acknowledge them, not grudgingly, but fully, and fairly; and I would give them any legislation for the reclaiming of their fugitives, which should not, in its stringency, be

more likely to carry a free man into slavery, than our ordinary criminal laws are to hang an innocent one. . . .

Now gentlemen, I don't want to read at any greater
length, but this is the true complexion of all I have ever
said in regard to the institution of slavery and the black
race. This is the whole of it, and anything that argues me
into his idea of perfect social and political equality with
the negro, is but a specious and fantastic arrangement of
words, by which a man can prove a horse chestnut to be
a chestnut horse. [Laughter.] I will say here, while upon
this subject, that I have no purpose directly or indirectly
to interfere with the institution of slavery in the States
where it exists. I believe I have no lawful right to do so,
and I have no inclination to do so. I have no purpose to introduce political and social equality between the white and
the black races. There is a physical difference between the
two, which in my judgment will probably forever forbid
their living together upon the footing of perfect equality,
and inasmuch as it becomes a necessity that there must be
a difference, I, as well as Judge Douglas, am in favor of
the race to which I belong, having the superior position.
I have never said anything to the contrary, but I hold that
notwithstanding all this, there is no reason in the world
why the negro is not entitled to all the natural rights enumerated in the Declaration of Independence, the right to
life, liberty and the pursuit of happiness. [Loud cheers.] I
hold that he is as much entitled to these as the white man.
I agree with Judge Douglas he is not my equal in many
respects—certainly not in color, perhaps not in moral or
intellectual endowment. But in the right to eat the bread,
without leave of anybody else, which his own hand earns,
*he is my equal and the equal of Judge Douglas, and the
equal of every living man.* [Great applause.] . . .

Now, my friends, I ask your attention to this matter for
the purpose of saying something seriously. I know that
the Judge may readily enough agree with me that the
maxim which was put forth by the Saviour is true, but he

may allege that I misapply it; and the Judge has a right
to urge that, in my application, I do misapply it, and then
I have a right to show that I do not misapply it. When he
undertakes to say that because I think this nation, so far
as the question of Slavery is concerned, will all become
one thing or all the other, I am in favor of bringing about
a dead uniformity in the various States, in all their institutions, he argues erroneously. The great variety of the
local institutions in the States, springing from differences
in the soil, differences in the face of the country, and in the
climate, are bonds of Union. They do not make "a house
divided against itself," but they make a house united. If
they produce in one section of the country what is called
for by the wants of another section, and this other section
can supply the wants of the first, they are not matters of
discord but bonds of union, true bonds of union. But can
this question of slavery be considered as among *these* va-
rieties in the institutions of the country? I leave it to you
to say whether, in the history of our government, this institution of slavery has not always failed to be a bond of
union, and, on the contrary, been an apple of discord and
an element of division in the house. [Cries of "Yes, yes,"
and applause.] I ask you to consider whether, so long as
the moral constitution of men's minds shall continue to be
the same, after this generation and assemblage shall sink
into the grave, and another race shall arise, with the same
moral and intellectual development we have—whether, if
that institution is standing in the same irritating position
in which it now is, it will not continue an element of division? [Cries of "Yes, yes."] If so, then I have a right to
say that in regard to this question, the Union is a house
divided against itself, and when the Judge reminds me
that I have often said to him that the institution of slavery
has existed for eighty years in some States, and yet it does
not exist in some others, I agree to the fact, and I account for
it by looking at the position in which our fathers originally
placed it—restricting it from the new Territories where it

had not gone, and legislating to cut off its source by the abrogation of the slave trade, thus putting the seal of legislation *against its spread*. The public mind *did* rest in the belief that it was in the course of ultimate extinction. [Cries of "Yes, yes."] But lately, I think—and in this I charge nothing on the Judge's motives—lately, I think, that he, and those acting with him, have placed that institution on a new basis, which looks to the *perpetuity and nationalization* of slavery. [Loud cheers.] And while it is placed upon this new basis, I say, and I have said, that I believe we shall not have peace upon the question until the opponents of slavery arrest the further spread of it, and place it where the public mind shall rest in the belief that it is in the course of ultimate extinction; or, on the other hand, that its advocates will push it forward until it shall become alike lawful in all the States, old as well as new, North as well as South. Now, I believe if we could arrest the spread, and place it where Washington, and Jefferson, and Madison placed it, it *would* be in the course of ultimate extinction, and the public mind *would*, as for eighty years past, believe that it was in the course of ultimate extinction. The crisis would be past and the institution might be let alone for a hundred years, if it should live so long, in the States where it exists, yet it would be going out of existence in the way best for both the black and the white races. [Great cheering.] . . .

When my friend, Judge Douglas, came to Chicago, on the 9th of July, this speech having been delivered on the 16th of June, he made an harangue there, in which he took hold of this speech of mine, showing that he had carefully read it; and while he paid no attention to *this* matter at all, but complimented me as being a "kind, amiable, and intelligent gentleman," notwithstanding I had said this; he goes on and eliminates, or draws out, from my speech this tendency of mine to set the States at war with one another, to make all the institutions uniform, and set the niggers and white people to marrying together. [Laughter.]

Then, as the Judge had complimented me with these pleasant titles, (I must confess to my weakness,) I was a little "taken," [laughter] for it came from a great man. I was not very much accustomed to flattery, and it came the sweeter to me. I was rather like the Hoosier, with the gingerbread, when he said he reckoned he loved it better than any other man, and got less of it. [Roars of laughter.] As the Judge had so flattered me, I could not make up my mind that he meant to deal unfairly with me; so I went to work to show him that he misunderstood the whole scope of my speech, and that I really never intended to set the people at war with one another. As an illustration, the next time I met him, which was at Springfield, I used this expression, that I claimed no right under the Constitution, nor had I any inclination, to enter into the Slave States and interfere with the institutions of slavery. He says upon that: Lincoln will not enter into the Slave States, but will go to the banks of the Ohio, on this side, and shoot over! [Laughter.] He runs on, step by step, in the horse-chestnut style of argument, until in the Springfield speech, he says, "Unless he shall be successful in firing his batteries until he shall have extinguished slavery in all the States, the Union shall be dissolved." Now I don't think that was exactly the way to treat a kind, amiable, intelligent gentleman. [Roars of laughter.] I know if I had asked the Judge to show when or where it was I had said that, if I didn't succeed in firing into the Slave States until slavery should be extinguished, the Union should be dissolved, he could not have shown it. I understand what he would do. He would say, "I don't mean to quote from you, but this was the *result* of what you say." But I have the right to ask, and I do ask now, Did you not put it in such a form that an ordinary reader or listener would take it as an expression *from me*? [Laughter.] . . .

I ask the attention of the people here assembled and elsewhere, to the course that Judge Douglas is pursuing every day as bearing upon this question of making slavery national. Not going back to the records but taking the speeches he makes, the speeches he made yesterday and day before and makes constantly all over the country—I ask your attention to them. In the first place what is necessary to make the institution national? Not war. There is no danger that the people of Kentucky will shoulder their muskets and with a young nigger stuck on every bayonet march into Illinois and force them upon us. There is no danger of our going over there and making war upon them. Then what is necessary for the nationalization of slavery? It is simply the next Dred Scott decision. It is merely for the Supreme Court to decide that no *State* under the Constitution can exclude it, just as they have already decided that under the Constitution neither Congress nor the Territorial Legislature can do it. When that is decided and acquiesced in, the whole thing is done. This being true, and this being the way as I think that slavery is to be made national, let us consider what Judge Douglas is doing every day to that end. In the first place, let us see what influence he is exerting on public sentiment. In this and like communities, public sentiment is everything. With public sentiment, nothing can fail; without it nothing can succeed. Consequently he who moulds public sentiment, goes deeper than he who enacts statutes or pronounces decisions. He makes statutes and decisions possible or impossible to be executed. This must be borne in mind, as also the additional fact that Judge Douglas is a man of vast influence, so great that it is enough for many men to profess to believe anything, when they once find out that Judge Douglas professes to believe it. Consider also the attitude he occupies at the head of a large party—a party which he claims has a majority of all the voters in the country. . . . But I cannot shake Judge Douglas' teeth loose from the Dred Scott decision. Like some obstinate animal (I mean no disrespect,) that will hang on when he has once got his teeth fixed, you may cut off a leg, or you may tear away an arm, still he will not relax his hold. And so I may point out

to the Judge, and say that he is bespattered all over, from
the beginning of his political life to the present time, with
attacks upon judicial decisions—I may cut off limb after
limb of his public record, and strive to wrench him from a
single dictum of the Court—yet I cannot divert him from
it. He hangs to the last, to the Dred Scott decision. [Loud
cheers.] These things show there is a purpose *strong as
death and eternity* for which he adheres to this decision,
and for which he will adhere to *all other decisions* of the
same Court. [Vociferous applause.]

A HIBERNIAN.
—Give us something besides Dred Scott.

MR. LINCOLN.
—Yes; no doubt you want to hear something that don't
hurt. [Laughter and applause.] Now, having spoken of
the Dred Scott decision, one more word and I am done.
Henry Clay, my beau ideal of a statesman, the man for
whom I fought all my humble life—Henry Clay once
said of a class of men who would repress all tendencies to
liberty and ultimate emancipation, that they must, if they
would do this, go back to the era of our Independence,
and muzzle the cannon which thunders its annual joyous
return; they must blow out the moral lights around us;
they must penetrate the human soul, and eradicate there
the love of liberty; and then and not till then, could they
perpetuate slavery in this country! [Loud cheers.] To my
thinking, Judge Douglas is, by his example and vast influence, doing that very thing in this community, [cheers,]
when he says that the negro has nothing in the Declaration of Independence. Henry Clay plainly understood
the contrary. Judge Douglas is going back to the era of
our Revolution, and to the extent of his ability, muzzling
the cannon which thunders its annual joyous return.
When he invites any people willing to have slavery, to
establish it, he is blowing out the moral lights around us.

[Cheers.] When he says he "cares not whether slavery is voted down or voted up,"—that it is a sacred right of self government—he is in my judgment penetrating the human soul and eradicating the light of reason and the love of liberty in this American people. [Enthusiastic and continued applause.] And now I will only say that when, by all these means and appliances, Judge Douglas shall succeed in bringing public sentiment to an exact accordance with his own views—when these vast assemblages shall echo back all these sentiments—when they shall come to repeat his views and to avow his principles, and to say all that he says on these mighty questions—then it needs only the formality of the second Dred Scott decision, which he endorses in advance, to make Slavery alike lawful in all the States—old as well as new, North as well as South. . . .

28

Second Debate with Stephen A. Douglas
at Freeport, Illinois
CW, 3:39–42

Lincoln sought to dispel charges that he supported abolitionism by responding to questions on seven controversial slavery issues that Senator Douglas posed soon after their first debate. The provocatively phrased questions intended to trap Lincoln and either expose his radicalism, making him unpopular with the electorate, or depict him as endorsing Democratic positions and, thus, undercut support in his own party. Indeed, his steadfast insistence that the federal government must enforce the 1850 Fugitive Slave Law led the great abolitionist leader Wendell Phillips to label Lincoln the "slave-hound of Illinois." Nevertheless, Lincoln remained consistent with his previously held views and unwavering in his support even for the most controversial aspects of the 1850 Compromise. After these brief responses, he elaborated upon his answers to emphasize his belief in the constitutional power of the Congress to legislate on slavery for the District of Columbia and the territories, but without ignoring white opinion. He avoided saying anything meaningful about the interstate slave trade. The most important consequence of the second debate, however, remains Lincoln's selection of a key issue related to the Dred Scott decision, the theoretical right of territories to exclude slavery, as a stratagem to ensnare his opponent. Lincoln had been told by key advisers that Douglas had put him on the defensive during the first debate. At Freeport, he attempted to reverse this posture and pin Douglas down on his well-known advocacy of "popular sovereignty." Did the people of a territory have the right, he asked, to vote down slavery before that territory adopted a state constitution? Douglas answered, with qualification, in the affirmative. The Kansas-Nebraska Act, he stated, permitted the status of slavery in territories to be settled by the inhabitants and not through any decision of the judiciary, referring to the Supreme Court's verdict in the Dred Scott case. In the latter, the Court denied the territories or Congress any role in the determination of slavery's spread there. His defense of the Kansas-Nebraska Act alienated extreme proslavery advocates, subsequently became known as the "Freeport Doctrine," and came up time and again during the ensuing debates.

August 27, 1858

. . . Having said thus much, I will take up the Judge's interrogatories as I find them printed in the Chicago *Times*, and answer them *seriatim*. In order that there may be no mistake about it, I have copied the interrogatories in writing, and also my answers to them. The first one of these interrogatories is in these words:

QUESTION 1.
"I desire to know whether Lincoln to-day stands, as he did in 1854, in favor of the unconditional repeal of the fugitive slave law?"
ANSWER.
I do not now, nor ever did, stand in favor of the unconditional repeal of the fugitive slave law. [Cries of "Good," "Good."]

Q. 2.
"I desire him to answer whether he stands pledged to-day, as he did in 1854, against the admission of any more slave States into the Union, even if the people want them?"
A.
I do not now, nor ever did, stand pledged against the admission of any more slave States into the Union.

Q. 3.
"I want to know whether he stands pledged against the admission of a new State into the Union with such a

Constitution as the people of that State may see fit to make."

A.

I do not stand pledged against the admission of a new State into the Union, with such a Constitution as the people of that State may see fit to make. [Cries of "good," "good."]

Q. 4.

"I want to know whether he stands to-day pledged to the abolition of slavery in the District of Columbia?"

A.

I do not stand to-day pledged to the abolition of slavery in the District of Columbia.

Q. 5.

"I desire him to answer whether he stands pledged to the prohibition of the slave trade between the different States?"

A.

I do not stand pledged to the prohibition of the slave trade between the different States.

Q. 6.

"I desire to know whether he stands pledged to prohibit slavery in all the Territories of the United States, North as well as South of the Missouri Compromise line."

A.

I am impliedly, if not expressly, pledged to a belief in the right and duty of Congress to prohibit slavery in all the United States Territories. [Great applause.]

Q. 7.

"I desire him to answer whether he is opposed to the acquisition of any new territory unless slavery is first prohibited therein."

A.

I am not generally opposed to honest acquisition of territory; and, in any given case, I would or would not oppose

such acquisition, accordingly as I might think such acquisition would or would not agravate [*sic*] the slavery
question among ourselves. [Cries of good, good.] . . .

As to the first one, in regard to the Fugitive Slave Law,
I have never hesitated to say, and I do not now hesitate
to say, that I think, under the Constitution of the United
States, the people of the Southern States are entitled to
a Congressional Fugitive Slave Law. Having said that,
I have had nothing to say in regard to the existing Fugitive Slave Law further than that I think it should have
been framed so as to be free from some of the objections
that pertain to it, without lessening its efficiency. And inasmuch as we are not now in an agitation in regard to an
alteration or modification of that law, I would not be the
man to introduce it as a new subject of agitation upon the
general question of slavery.

In regard to the other question of whether I am pledged
to the admission of any more slave States into the Union,
I state to you very frankly that I would be exceedingly
sorry ever to be put in a position of having to pass upon
that question. I should be exceedingly glad to know that
there would never be another slave State admitted into
the Union; [applause]; but I must add, that if slavery
shall be kept out of the Territories during the territorial
existence of any one given Territory, and then the people
shall, having a fair chance and a clear field, when they
come to adopt the Constitution, do such an extraordinary
thing as to adopt a Slave Constitution, uninfluenced by
the actual presence of the institution among them, I see
no alternative, if we own the country, but to admit them
into the Union. [Applause.]

The third interrogatory is answered by the answer to the
second, it being, as I conceive, the same as the second.

The fourth one is in regard to the abolition of slavery
in the District of Columbia. In relation to that, I have my
mind very distinctly made up. I should be exceedingly
glad to see slavery abolished in the District of Columbia.

[Cries of "good, good."] I believe that Congress possesses the constitutional power to abolish it. Yet as a member of Congress, I should not with my present views, be in favor of *endeavoring* to abolish slavery in the District of Columbia, unless it would be upon these conditions. *First*, that the abolition should be gradual. *Second*, that it should be on a vote of the majority of qualified voters in the District, and *third*, that compensation should be made to unwilling owners. With these three conditions, I confess I would be exceedingly glad to see Congress abolish slavery in the District of Columbia, and, in the language of Henry Clay, "sweep from our Capital that foul blot upon our nation." [Loud applause.]

In regard to the fifth interrogatory, I must say here, that as to the question of the abolition of the Slave Trade between the different States, I can truly answer, as I have, that I am *pledged* to nothing about it. It is a subject to which I have not given that mature consideration that would make me feel authorized to state a position so as to hold myself entirely bound by it. In other words, that question has never been prominently enough before me to induce me to investigate whether we really have the Constitutional power to do it. I could investigate it if I had sufficient time, to bring myself to a conclusion upon that subject, but I have not done so, and I say so frankly to you here, and to Judge Douglas. I must say, however, that if I should be of opinion that Congress does possess the Constitutional power to abolish the slave trade among the different States, I should still not be in favor of the exercise of that power unless upon some conservative principle as I conceive it, akin to what I have said in relation to the abolition of slavery in the District of Columbia.

My answer as to whether I desire that slavery should be prohibited in all the Territories of the United States is full and explicit within itself, and cannot be made clearer by any comments of mine. So I suppose in regard to the question whether I am opposed to the acquisition of any more territory unless slavery is first prohibited therein, my answer is such that I could add nothing by way of illustration, or making myself better understood, than the answer which I have placed in writing.

Now in all this, the Judge has me and he has me on the record. I suppose he had flattered himself that I was really entertaining one set of opinions for one place and another set for another place—that I was afraid to say at one place what I uttered at another. What I am saying here I suppose I say to a vast audience as strongly tending to Abolitionism as any audience in the State of Illinois, and I believe I am saying that which, if it would be offensive to any persons and render them enemies to myself, would be offensive to persons in this audience. . . .

29

Speech at Carlinville, Illinois
CW, 3:77–81

The address at Carlinville, delivered at the invitation of John M. Palmer, a Sangamon County lawyer and Republican activist, occurred between the second and third debates with Senator Douglas. Lincoln opened with the sobering declaration that the crisis over slavery had been ignited in 1854, ironically, by Douglas's attempt to halt the agitation over slavery with the Kansas-Nebraska Act. As he would throughout his political career, Lincoln invoked the intention of the Founding Fathers to gradually eliminate slavery, and even cited the example of Laurence M. Keitt, a fire-eating, proslavery congressman from South Carolina, who once expressed the belief that slavery could not last. Lincoln emphasized his conservative Whig credentials and ridiculed his opponent's attempt to wrap himself in the legacy of Henry Clay. More pointedly, Lincoln took the opportunity to repudiate Douglas's characterizations of his racial views and stood irrevocably on the ground of racial segregation. He quoted from his own important speech at Peoria to guarantee that he would not be mistaken: "'Shall we free them and make them politically and socially our equals? MY OWN FEELINGS WILL NOT ADMIT OF THIS.'" Douglas constantly taunted Lincoln's party with the label of "Black Republicans" and charged that it secretly promoted "amalgamation." Lincoln, however, reminded his audience that racial mixing took place precisely where slavery was the *strongest*. Slavery, not freedom, promoted race mixing; thus, according to Lincoln, the best way to halt amalgamation was to stop the spread of slavery. Focusing on the racial implications of the Supreme Court's decision in *Dred Scott*, President James Buchanan's subservience to the South, and Douglas's views, Lincoln warned that slavery's expansion meant white men would lose jobs. "Sustain these men," Lincoln warned, "and negro equality will be abundant, as every white laborer will have occasion to regret when he is elbowed from his plow or his anvil by slave niggers."

... The measures of '50 settled it for a time, only to be reopened in '54 in a worse and more malignant form in a territory where it had been previously at rest. [Henry] Clay, [Daniel] Webster, [John C.] Calhoun and [Thomas Hart] Benton have gone but we still have the slavery agitation, and will have it till a more conservative and less aggressive party gains power. The north is not alone to blame—for churches and families divided upon this question—is it then a little thing?

In view of its importance and aggressive nature, I think it must come to a crisis—that it will become national by court verdicts or local by the popular voice. We have no idea of interfering with it in any manner. I am standing up to our bargain for its maintenance where it lawfully exists. Our fathers restricted its spread and stopped the importation of negroes, with the hope that it would remain in a dormant condition till the people saw fit to emancipate the negroes. There is no allusion to slavery in the constitution—and Madison says it was omitted that future generations might not know such a thing ever existed—and that the constitution might yet be a "national charter of freedom." And [Laurence M.] Keitt of S.C., once admitted that nobody ever thought it would exist to this day.

If placed in the former attitude we should have peace. But it is now advancing to become lawful everywhere. The Nebraska bill introduced this era—and it was gotten up by a man who twice voted for the Wilmot Proviso and the extension of the Missouri Compromise line to the Pacific. This change in our national policy is decided to be constitutional—although the court would not decide the only question before them—whether Dred Scott was a slave or not—and did decide, too, that a territorial legislature cannot exclude slavery in behalf of the people, and if their premises be correct a state cannot exclude it—for they tell us that the negro is property anywhere in the light that horses are property, and if the constitution gives the master a right of property in negroes above the jurisdiction of the territorial laws, enacted in the sovereignty of the people—it only requires another case and another favorable decision from the same court to make the rights of property alike in states as well as territories, and that by virtue of the constitution and in disregard of local laws to the contrary—[Pres. James] Buchanan takes this position now. Sustain these men and negro equality will be abundant, as every white laborer will have occasion to regret when he is elbowed from his plow or his anvil by slave niggers. . . .

Douglas tries to make capital by charges of negro equality against me. My speeches have been printed and before the country for some time on this question, and Douglas knows the utter falsity of such a charge. To prove it Mr. L. read from a speech of his at Peoria in '54 in reply to Douglas as follows:

"Shall we free them and make them politically and socially our equals? MY OWN FEELINGS WILL NOT ADMIT OF THIS, and if they would the feelings of the great mass of white people would not. Whether this accords with strict justice or not is not the sole question. A universal feeling, whether well or ill-founded, cannot safely be disregarded. We cannot then make them our equals. . . . When they remind us of their constitutional rights I acknowledge them fully and freely, and I would give them any legislation for the recovery of their fugitives, which would not be more likely, in the stringency of its provisions, to take a man into slavery than our ordinary criminal laws are to hang an innocent man."

There is no reason in favor of sending slavery to Kansas that might not be adduced in support of the African slave trade. Each are demanded by the profitableness of the traffic thus made in opening a new slave mart, and not from the rightfulness of it. They are upon a common basis, and should be alike condemned. The compromises of the constitution we must all stand by, but where is the justness of extending the institution to compete with white labor and thus to degrade it? Is it not rather our duty to make labor more respectable by preventing all black competition, especially in the territories? Mr. L. then read from another speech of his in '54, showing that Douglas there attempted to gain the public favor by pandering to the prejudices of the masses, in disregard of truth. Negroes have natural rights however, as other men have, although they cannot enjoy them here, and even Taney once said that "the Declaration of Independence was broad enough for all men." But though it does not declare that all men are equal in their attainments or social position, yet no sane man will attempt to deny that the African upon his own soil has all the natural rights that instrument vouchsafes to all mankind. It has proved a stumbling block to tyrants, and ever will, unless brought into contempt by its pretended friends. Douglas says no man can defend it except on the hypothesis that it only referred to British white subjects, and that no other white men are included—that it does not speak alike to the down trodden of all nations— German, French, Spanish, etc., but simply meant that the English were born equal and endowed by their Creator with certain natural or equal rights among which are life, liberty and the pursuit of happiness, and that it meant nobody else. Are Jeffersonian Democrats willing to have the gem taken from the magna charta of human liberty in this shameful way? Or will they maintain that its declaration of equality of natural rights among all nations is correct?

Douglas pretends to be horrified at amalgamation, yet had he not opened the way for slavery in Kansas, could there have been any amalgamation there? If you keep the two races separate is there any danger of amalgamation? Is not slavery the great source of it? You know that Virginia has more mulattoes than all the northern states! Douglas says he does not care whether they vote slavery up or down in Kansas; then I submit it to this audience which is the most favorable to amalgamation, he who would not raise his finger to keep it out, or I who would give my vote and use my lawful means to prevent its extension. Clay and other great men were ever ready to express their abhorrence of slavery—but we of the north dare not use his noble language when he said, to force its perpetuation and extension you must muzzle the cannon that annually proclaims liberty, and repress all tendencies in the human heart to justice and mercy. We can no longer express our admiration for the Declaration of Independence without their petty sneers. And it is thus they are fast bringing that sacred instrument into contempt. These men desire that slavery should be perpetual and that we should not foster all lawful moves toward emancipation, and to gain their end they will endeavor to impress upon the public mind that the negro is not human, and even upon his own soil he has no rights which white men are bound to respect. Douglas demands that we shall bow to all decisions. If the courts are to decide upon political subjects, how long will it be till Jefferson's fears of a political despotism are realized? He denounces all opposed to the Dred Scott opinions, in disregard to his former opposition to real decisions and the fact that he got his title of Judge by breaking down a decision of our supreme court. He has an object in these denunciations, and is it not to prepare our minds for acquiescence in the next decision declaring slavery to exist in the states? If Douglas can make you believe that slavery is a sacred right—if we are to swallow Dred Scottism that the right of property in negroes is not confined to those states where it is established by local law—if by special sophisms he can make you believe that no nation except the English are born equal and are en-titled to life, liberty, and the pursuit of happiness, upon their own soil, or when they are not constitutionally di-vested of the God-given rights to enjoy the fruits of their own labor, then may we truly despair of the universality of freedom, or the efficacy of those sacred principles enunciated by our fathers—and give in our adhesion to the perpetuation and unlimited extension of slavery.

30

Speech at Clinton, Illinois
CW, 3:81–84

Clinton, Illinois, lay in the center of the state and was the home of Clifton H. Moore, a lawyer with whom Lincoln had worked on a number of railroad cases during the 1840s. The town already had played a role in the campaign—on July 27, both Lincoln and Douglas spoke there. Lincoln gave this September speech, like those at Carlinville and Edwardsville, between the second and third of the formal Lincoln-Douglas debates. He opened, as he had done at Carlinville, with the rhetorical question "What is all this fuss that is being made about negroes?" He rehearsed his stands on the question of slavery and the territories, emphasizing the enormity of the slave question and dismissing his opponent's attempt to belittle Republican principles as merely a smokescreen for the party's attempt to promote racial intermarriage and black office holding. "He knows that we advocate no such doctrines as those, but he cares not how much he misrepresents us if he can gain a few votes by so doing." Lincoln then cited his own speeches, including the pivotal one at Peoria in October 1854, to dismiss yet again any idea that either he or his party advocated racial equality—"where I always stood," he exclaimed. Slavery, not freedom, caused racial mixing, he maintained, and without it the races would remain separate. To support his case, Lincoln cited census statistics recording the far greater number of mulattos in the slaveholding South than in the free states of the North.

September 2, 1858

. . . The questions are sometimes asked. "What is all this fuss that is being made about negroes?—what does it amount to?—and where will it end?" These questions imply that those who ask them consider the slavery question a very insignificant matter—they think that it amounts to little or nothing, and that those who agitate it are extremely foolish. Now it must be admitted that if the great question which has caused so much trouble *is* insignificant, we are very foolish to have anything to do with it—if it is of no importance we had better throw it aside and busy ourselves about something else. But let us inquire a little into this *insignificant* matter, as it is called by some, and see if it is not important enough to demand the close attention of every well-wisher of the Union. . . .

And now let me say a few words in regard to Douglas' great hobby of negro equality. He thinks—he says at least—that the Republican party is in favor of allowing whites and blacks to intermarry, and that a man can't be a good Republican unless he is willing to elevate black men to office and to associate with them on terms of perfect equality. He knows that we advocate no such doctrines as those, but he cares not how much he misrepresents us if he can gain a few votes by so doing. . . .

Slavery, continued Mr. Lincoln, is not a matter of little importance: it overshadows every other question in which we are interested. It has divided the Methodist and Presbyterian Churches, and has sown discord in the American Tract Society. The churches have split, and the Society will follow their example before long. So it will be seen that slavery is agitated in the religious as well as in the political world.

Judge Douglas is very much afraid that the triumph of the Republican party will lead to a general mixture of the white and black races. Perhaps I am wrong in saying that he *is* afraid; so I will correct myself by saying that he *pretends* to fear that the success of our party will result in the amalgamation of blacks and whites. I think I can show plainly, from documents now before me, that Judge Douglas' fears are groundless. The census of 1850 tells us that in that year there were over four hundred thousand mulattoes in the United States. Now let us take what is called an Abolition State—the Republican, slavery-hating

State of New Hampshire—and see how many mulattoes we can find within her borders. The number amounts to just one hundred and eighty-four. In the Old Dominion— in the Democratic and aristocratic State of Virginia—there were a few more mulattoes than the census-takers found in New Hampshire. How many do you suppose there were? Seventy-nine thousand seven hundred and seventy-five— twenty-three thousand more than there were in all the free States! In the slave States there were, in 1850, three hundred and forty-eight thousand mulattoes—all of home production; and in the free States there were less than sixty thousand mulattoes—and a large number of them were imported from the South.

31

Speech at Edwardsville, Illinois
CW, 3:92–95

Edwardsville, where Lincoln had previously spoken on May 18, lay near the Missouri border in the southern portion of Illinois. He began this address as an impromptu response to a question from a man in the crowd who had asked him to distinguish between Republicans and Democrats on key issues of the campaign. Fundamentally, Lincoln explained, Republicans felt that slavery was "a moral, social and political wrong," while Democrats did not; all other positions taken by the two contending parties derived from those positions. He rehearsed his positions on Kansas-Nebraska, Dred Scott, popular sovereignty, and the wisdom of Henry Clay. Primarily, however, he wished to establish the fact that Republicans considered slavery to be "an unqualified evil to the negro, to the white man, to the soil, and to the State." Given his rural audience, which would have included Missourians familiar with the institution of slavery, Lincoln felt free to use the language of denigration to impress those who might otherwise find Senator Douglas appealing. He cited his usual defense of the Declaration of Independence but failed to link it to the basic humanity of African Americans as he had done as a matter of course in the past. Instead, he ridiculed the corrupt version of "Popular Sovereignty" that Douglas sought to pedal. "He [Douglas] had not the *impudence* to say that the *right of people to govern niggers* was the *right of people to govern themselves*. His notions of the fitness of things were not moulded to the brazen degree of calling the right to put a hundred niggers through under the lash in Nebraska, a '*sacred right of self-government.*'" Perhaps having gained a measure of trust with his audience, Lincoln warned against following Douglas and the Democrats into the complete dehumanization of African Americans: "when you have extinguished his soul, and placed him where the ray of hope is blown out in darkness like that which broods over the spirits of the damned;

are you quite sure the demon which you have roused *will not turn and rend you?*"

. . . "POPULAR SOVEREIGNTY," WHAT DID DOUGLAS REALLY INVENT?

Let us inquire, what Douglas really invented, when he introduced, and drove through Congress, the Nebraska bill. He called it "Popular Sovereignty." What does Popular Sovereignty mean? Strictly and literally it means the sovereignty of the people over their own affairs—in other words, the right of the people of every nation and community to govern themselves. Did Mr. Douglas invent this? Not quite. The idea of Popular Sovereignty was floating about the world several ages before the author of the Nebraska bill saw daylight—indeed before Columbus set foot on the American continent. In the year 1776 it took tangible form in the noble words which you are all familiar with: "We hold these truths to be self-evident: That all men are created equal; That they are endowed by their Creator with certain inalienable rights; That among these are life, liberty and the pursuit of happiness; That to secure these rights governments are instituted among men, *deriving their just powers from the consent of the governed.*" Was not this the origin of Popular Sovereignty as applied to the American people? Here we are told that Governments are instituted among men to secure certain rights, and that they derive their just powers *from the consent of the governed.* If that is not Popular Sovereignty, then I have no conception of the meaning of words.

Then, if Mr. Douglas did not invent *this* kind of sovereignty, let us pursue the inquiry and find out what the invention really was. Was it the right of emigrants in Kansas and Nebraska to govern themselves and a gang of niggers too, if they wanted them? Clearly this was no invention of his, because Gen. [Lewis] Cass put forth the same doctrine in 1848, in his so-called Nicholson letter— six whole years before Douglas thought of such a thing. Gen. Cass could have taken out a patent for the idea, if he had chosen to do so, and have prevented his Illinois rival from reaping a particle of benefit from it. Then what was it, I ask again, that this "Little Giant" invented? It never occurred to Gen. Cass to call his discovery by the odd name of "Popular Sovereignty." He had not the *impudence* to say that the *right of people to govern niggers* was the *right of people to govern themselves*. His notions of the fitness of things were not moulded to the brazen degree of calling the right to put a hundred niggers through under the lash in Nebraska, a *"sacred right of self-government."* And here, I submit to this intelligent audience and the whole world, was Judge Douglas' discovery, and the whole of it. He invented a *name* for Gen. [Lewis] Cass' old Nicholson letter dogma. He discovered that the right of the white man to breed and flog niggers in Nebraska was POPULAR SOVEREIGNTY!—[Great applause and laughter.]

WHAT MAY WE LOOK FOR AFTER THE NEXT DRED SCOTT DECISION?

My friends, I have endeavored to show you the logical consequences of the Dred Scott decision, which holds that the people of a Territory cannot prevent the establishment of Slavery in their midst. I have stated what cannot be gainsayed—that the grounds upon which this decision is made are equally applicable to the Free States as to the Free Territories, and that the peculiar reasons put forth by Judge Douglas for endorsing this decision, commit him in advance to the next decision, and to all other decisions emanating from the same source. Now, when by all these means you have succeeded in dehumanizing the negro; when you have put him down, and made it forever impossible for him to be but as the beasts of the field; when you have extinguished his soul, and placed him where the ray of hope is blown out in darkness like that which broods over the spirits of the damned; are you quite sure the demon which you have roused *will not turn and rend you?* What constitutes the bulwark of our own liberty and independence? It is not our frowning battlements, our bristling sea coasts, the guns of our war steamers, or the strength of our gallant and disciplined army. These are not our reliance against a resumption of tyranny in our fair land. All of them may be turned against our liberties, without making us stronger or weaker for the struggle. Our reliance is in the *love of liberty* which God has planted in our bosoms. Our defense is in the preservation of the spirit which prizes liberty as the heritage of all men, in all lands, every where. Destroy this spirit, and you have planted the seeds of despotism around your own doors. Familiarize yourselves with the chains of bondage, and you are preparing your own limbs to wear them. Accustomed to trample on the rights of those around you, you have lost the genius of your own independence, and become the fit subjects of the first cunning tyrant who rises. And let me tell you, all these things are prepared for you with the logic of history, if the elections shall promise that the next Dred Scott decision and all future decisions will be quietly acquiesced in by the people. — [Loud applause.]

32

Fourth Debate with Stephen A. Douglas
CW, 3:145–146, 179, 181

When Lincoln arrived to debate the "Little Giant" in the east-central Illinois town of Charleston, his supporters had hung an eighty-foot banner featuring a young Abraham Lincoln driving a team of oxen into the county back in 1828. They plastered posters of their hero throughout the town, one showing "Old Abe" clubbing Douglas into the ground. Democrats, on the other hand, waited until just before the start of the debate to raise their own banner, one emblazoned with the image of a white man, a black woman, and their mixed-race child. The slogan read, "Negro equality." Nearly fifteen thousand spectators choked the fairgrounds just outside of town to hear the two men repeat their stands on race and the impact of the Kansas-Nebraska Act. Lincoln reiterated his belief that the Declaration of Independence recognized the basic humanity of blacks, *and* his opposition to black citizenship. "Now my opinion is that the different States have the power to make a negro a citizen under the Constitution of the United States if they choose," he explained. "The Dred Scott decision," however, "decides that they have not that power. If the State of Illinois had that power I should be opposed to the exercise of it. [Cries of "good," "good," and applause.] That is all I have to say about it." To underscore his stand against racial integration and social and political equality, Lincoln tarred his opponent with the inflammatory case of Kentuckian Richard M. Johnson, whom he referred to as "Judge Douglas' old friend." Johnson had served as the ninth vice president of the United States and had run for a seat in Congress. During the 1820s, he had entered into a common-law relationship with his octoroon slave, Julie Chinn. Kentucky law would not recognize such a relationship, but the couple defied racial practices and lived openly as man and wife. Lincoln, defending his honor as an opponent of amalgamation, explained that the only case of miscegenation known to him was fostered by the institution of Southern slavery, not Northern freedom. For conditions at the time of the debate, see: Harold Holzer, ed., *The Lincoln-Douglas Debates* (New York: HarperCollins, 1993), 184–233.

September 18, 1858

. . . While I was at the hotel to-day an elderly gentleman called upon me to know whether I was really in favor of producing a perfect equality between the negroes and white people. [Great laughter.] While I had not proposed to myself on this occasion to say much on that subject, yet as the question was asked me I thought I would occupy perhaps five minutes in saying something in regard to it. I will say then that I am not, nor ever have been in favor of bringing about in any way the social and political equality of the white and black races, [applause]—that I am not nor ever have been in favor of making voters or jurors of negroes, nor of qualifying them to hold office, nor to intermarry with white people; and I will say in addition to this that there is a physical difference between the white and black races which I believe will for ever forbid the two races living together on terms of social and political equality. And inasmuch as they cannot so live, while they do remain together there must be the position of superior and inferior, and I as much as any other man am in favor of having the superior position assigned to the white race. I say upon this occasion I do not perceive that because the white man is to have the superior position the negro should be denied everything. I do not understand that because I do not want a negro woman for a slave I must necessarily want her for a wife. [Cheers and laughter.] My understanding is that I can just let her alone. I am now in my fiftieth year, and I certainly never have had a black woman for either a slave or a wife. So it seems to me quite possible for us to get along without making either slaves or wives of negroes. I will add to this that I have never seen to my knowledge a man, woman or child who was in favor of producing a perfect equality, social and political, between negroes and white men. I recollect of but one distinguished instance that I ever heard of so frequently as to be entirely satisfied of its correctness—and that is the case of Judge Douglas' old friend Col. Richard M. Johnson. [Laughter.] I will also add to the remarks I have made, (for I am not going to enter at large upon this subject,) that I have never had the least apprehension that I or my friends would marry negroes if there was no law to keep them from it, [laughter] but as Judge Douglas and his friends seem to be in great apprehension that they might, if there were no law to keep them from it, [roars of laughter] I give him the most solemn pledge that I will to the very last stand by the law of this State, which forbids the marrying of white people with negroes. [Continued laughter and applause.] I will add one further word, which is this, that I do not understand there is any place where an alteration of the social and political relations of the negro and the white man can be made except in the State Legislature—not in the Congress of the United States—and as I do not really apprehend the approach of any such thing myself, and as Judge Douglas seems to be in constant horror that some such danger is rapidly approaching, I propose as the best means to prevent it that the Judge be kept at home and placed in the State Legislature to fight the measure. [Uproarious laughter and applause.] I do not propose dwelling longer at this time on this subject. . . .

Judge Douglas has said to you that he has not been able to get from me an answer to the question whether I am in favor of negro-citizenship. So far as I know, the Judge never asked me the question before. [Applause.] He shall have no occasion to ever ask it again, for I tell him very frankly that I am not in favor of negro citizenship. [Renewed applause.] This furnishes me an occasion for saying a few words upon the subject.

I mentioned in a certain speech of mine which has been printed, that the Supreme Court had decided that a negro could not possibly be made a citizen, and without saying what was my ground of complaint in regard to that, or whether I had any ground of complaint, Judge Douglas has from that thing manufactured nearly every thing that he ever says about my disposition to produce an equality between the negroes and the white people. [Laughter and applause.] If any one will read my speech, he will find I mentioned that as one of the points decided in the course of the Supreme Court opinions, but I did not state what objection I had to it. But Judge Douglas tells the people what my objection was when I did not tell them myself. [Loud applause and laughter.] Now my opinion is that the different States have the power to make a negro a citizen under the Constitution of the United States if they choose. The Dred Scott decision decides that they have not that power. If the State of Illinois had that power I should be opposed to the exercise of it. [Cries of "good," "good," and applause.] That is all I have to say about it. . . .

The other way is for us to surrender and let Judge Douglas and his friends have their way and plant slavery over all the States—cease speaking of it as in any way a wrong—regard slavery as one of the common matters of property, and speak of negroes as we do of our horses and cattle. But while it drives on in its state of progress as it is now driving, and as it has driven for the last five years, I have ventured the opinion, and I say to-day, that we will have no end to the slavery agitation until it takes one turn or the other. [Applause.] I do not mean that when it takes a turn towards ultimate extinction it will be in a day, nor in a year, nor in two years. I do not suppose that in the most peaceful way ultimate extinction would occur in less than a hundred years at the least; but that it will occur in the best way for both races in God's own good time, I have no doubt. [Applause.] But, my friends, I have used up more of my time than I intended on this point. . . .

33

Fragment on Pro-slavery Theology
CW, 3:204–205

The idea that the Bible and God's will justified slavery held a central place in proslavery ideology, especially after the 1830s. A prime example of this trend is the 1857 book *Slavery Ordained of God* by the Alabama Presbyterian minister and doctor of divinity Frederick A. Ross. In a series of speeches and letters, some addressed to the Northern antislavery minister Albert Barnes, Ross—who, ironically, had freed his own slaves—offered common ground that both Northern and Southern Christians could occupy to maintain "the union of this great people." In short, he asserted, "*slavery is of God*," and should be continued "for the good of the slave, the good of the master, the good of the whole American family, until another and better destiny may be unfolded." Slavery may be an evil, even a curse, he asserted, but it "has its corresponding and greater good" such that an enslaved man "is elevated and ennobled compared with his brethren in Africa." In this 1858 fragment, Lincoln deepened his objection to the institution of slavery, challenging those who claimed to know best what God ordained. While Lincoln rarely attended church and scorned evangelicalism, he had great familiarity with the Bible and had fashioned his own fatalistic belief in God. The confidence that Ross and his ilk showed in their belief that God approved of and willed slavery, to Lincoln, represented a "perversion of the Bible." He expressed his revulsion for those who lived off the labor of others and claimed that God had ordained such an arrangement. As he would repeatedly assert, if slavery was such a divine and positive institution, why did its advocates not suggest it for themselves? Quotations in Frederick A. Ross, *Slavery Ordained of God* (Philadelphia: J. B. Lippincott & Co., 1857), 1, 6.

Suppose it is true, that the negro is inferior to the white, in the gifts of nature; is it not the exact reverse justice that the white should, for that reason, take from the negro, any part of the little which has been given him? "*Give* to him that is needy" is the christian rule of charity; but "Take from him that is needy" is the rule of slavery.

PRO-SLAVERY THEOLOGY.

The sum of pro-slavery theology seems to be this: "Slavery is not universally *right*, nor yet universally *wrong*; it is better for some people to be slaves; and, in such cases, it is the Will of God that they be such."

Certainly there is no contending against the Will of God; but still there is some difficulty in ascertaining, and applying it, to particular cases. For instance we will suppose the Rev. Dr. Ross has a slave named Sambo, and the question is "Is it the Will of God that Sambo shall remain a slave, or be set free?" The Almighty gives no audable [*sic*] answer to the question, and his revelation— the Bible—gives none—or, at most, none but such as admits of a squabble, as to it's meaning. No one thinks of asking Sambo's opinion on it. So, at last, it comes to this, that *Dr. Ross* is to decide the question. And while he consider[s] it, he sits in the shade, with gloves on his hands, and subsists on the bread that Sambo is earning in the burning sun. If he decides that God Wills Sambo to continue a slave, he thereby retains his own comfortable position; but if he decides that God will's Sambo to be free, he thereby has to walk out of the shade, throw off his gloves, and delve for his own bread. Will Dr. Ross be actuated by that perfect impartiality, which has ever been considered most favorable to correct decisions?

But, slavery is good for some people!!! As a *good* thing, slavery is strikingly perculiar, [*sic*] in this, that it is the only good thing which no man ever seeks the good of, for *himself.*

Nonsense! Wolves devouring lambs, not because it is good for their own greedy maws, but because it [is] good for the lambs!!!

34

Seventh and Last Debate with
Stephen A. Douglas at Alton, Illinois
& AL to James N. Brown
CW, 3:298–305, 327–328

In 1837, Alton, Illinois, located across the Missouri River from St. Louis, witnessed the murder of the abolitionist editor Elijah P. Lovejoy. Proslavery feelings remained strong in the city, and Lincoln took care to assure whites in the region that he did not seek emancipation for Missouri slaves. He did, however, wish to make clear once again how profoundly he differed from Senator Douglas and the Democratic Party. By citing the revered statesman Henry Clay so frequently in his public addresses and private letters, Lincoln sought to place his party's limited antislavery principles on the incontestably safe ground of a Southerner, not on that of "radical" abolitionists. These words of Clay could have been spoken by Lincoln on the day before this address: "I desire no concealment of my opinions in regard to the institution of slavery. I look upon it as a great evil; and deeply lament that we have derived it from the parental government." Lincoln also countered Douglas's relentless attempt to paint him as an advocate of racial equality. "Judge Douglas," Lincoln declared, had twisted portions of several speeches and wove a "beautiful fabrication—of my purpose to introduce a perfect, social, and political equality between the white and black races." He assured his audience that nothing could be further from the truth. Lincoln repeated his guiding principle that the Founding Fathers had included African Americans in the Declaration of Independence's assertion of the equality of all men. Not that all men "were equal in color, size, intellect, moral development or social capacity," but equal before God and deserving of the right to govern their own fate—and do so away from whites. While at home in Springfield during a short stopover, Lincoln wrote to James N. Brown, a friend and prominent local politician from Sangamon County. Lincoln, amazed that anyone could misconstrue his position on race, sent some "foregoing extracts," a list of his own quotes on "negro equality" that came from a small notebook he kept during his campaign travels. Lincoln used the annotated clippings during his speeches, and Brown had used them in his campaign for the Illinois legislature in 1858. Aroused by reactions to his last debate with Senator Douglas, Lincoln offered a synopsis of his views on race and slavery for Brown's use.

October 15, 1858

. . . So far as Judge Douglas addressed his speech to me, or so far as it was about me, it is my business to pay some attention to it. I have heard the Judge state two or three times what he has stated to day—that in a speech which I made at Springfield, Illinois, I had in a very especial manner, complained that the Supreme Court in the Dred Scott case had decided that a negro could never be a citizen of the United States. I have omitted by some accident heretofore to analyze this statement, and it is required of me to notice it now. In point of fact it is untrue. I never have complained especially of the Dred Scott decision because it held that a negro could not be a citizen, and the Judge is always wrong when he says I ever did so complain of it. I have the speech here, and I will thank him or any of his friends to show where I said that a negro should be a citizen, and complained especially of the Dred Scott decision because it declared he could not be one. I have done no such thing, and Judge Douglas' so persistently insisting that I have done so, has strongly impressed me with the belief of a pre-determination on his part to misrepresent me. He could not get his foundation for insisting that I was in favor of this negro equality anywhere else as well as he could by assuming that untrue proposition. Let me tell this audience what is true in regard to that matter; and the means by which they may correct me if I do not tell them truly is by a recurrence to the speech itself. I spoke of the Dred Scott decision in my Springfield speech, and I was then endeavoring to prove that the Dred Scott decision was a portion of a system or scheme to make slavery national in this country. I pointed out what things had been decided by the court. I mentioned as a fact that they had decided that a negro could not be a citizen—that they had done so, as I supposed, to deprive the negro, under all circumstances, of the remotest possibility of ever becoming a citizen and claiming the rights of a citizen of the United States under a certain clause of the Constitution. I stated that, without making any complaint of it at all. I then went on and stated the other points decided in the case, namely: that the bringing of a negro into the State of Illinois and holding him in slavery for two years here was a matter in regard to which they would not decide whether it made him free or not; that they decided the further point that taking him into a United States Territory where slavery was prohibited by act of Congress, did not make him free because that act of Congress as they held was unconstitutional. I mentioned these three things as making up the points decided in that case. I mentioned them in a lump taken in connection with the introduction of the Nebraska bill, and the amendment of [Salmon P.] Chase, offered at the time, declaratory of the right of the people of the Territories to exclude slavery, which was voted down by the friends of the bill. I mentioned all these things together, as evidence tending to prove a combination and conspiracy to make the institution of slavery national. In that connection and in that way I mentioned the decision on the point that a negro could not be a citizen, and in no other connection.

Out of this, Judge Douglas builds up his beautiful fabrication—of my purpose to introduce a perfect, social, and political equality between the white and black races. His assertion that I made an "especial objection" (that is his exact language) to the decision on this account, is untrue in point of fact. . . .

Now I have upon all occasions declared as strongly as Judge Douglas against the disposition to interfere with the existing institution of slavery. You hear me read it from the same speech from which he takes garbled extracts for the purpose of proving upon me a disposition to interfere with the institution of slavery, and establish a perfect social and political equality between negroes and white people.

Allow me while upon this subject briefly to present one other extract from a speech of mine, more than a year ago, at Springfield, in discussing this very same question, soon after Judge Douglas took his ground that negroes were not included in the Declaration of Independence:

> I think the authors of that notable instrument intended to include all men, but they did not mean to declare all men equal in all respects. They did not mean to say all men were equal in color, size, intellect, moral development or social capacity. They defined with tolerable distinctness in what they did consider all men created equal—equal in certain inalienable rights, among which are life, liberty and the pursuit of happiness. This they said, and this they meant. They did not mean to assert the obvious untruth, that all were then actually enjoying that equality, nor yet, that they were about to confer it immediately upon them. In fact they had no power to confer such a boon. They meant simply to declare the right so that the enforcement of it might follow as fast as circumstances should permit.
>
> They meant to set up a standard maxim for free society which should be familiar to all: constantly looked to, constantly labored for, and even

though never perfectly attained, constantly approximated and thereby constantly spreading and deepening its influence and augmenting the happiness and value of life to all people, of all colors, everywhere. . . .

At Galesburg the other day, I said in answer to Judge Douglas, that three years ago there never had been a man, so far as I knew or believed, in the whole world, who had said that the Declaration of Independence did not include negroes in the term "all men." I re-assert it to-day. I assert that Judge Douglas and all his friends may search the whole records of the country, and it will be a matter of great astonishment to me if they shall be able to find that one human being three years ago had ever uttered the astounding sentiment that the term "all men" in the Declaration did not include the negro. Do not let me be misunderstood. I know that more than three years ago there were men who, finding this assertion constantly in the way of their schemes to bring about the ascendancy and perpetuation of slavery, *denied the truth of it*. I know that Mr. [John C.] Calhoun and all the politicians of his school denied the truth of the Declaration. I know that it ran along in the mouths of some Southern men for a period of years, ending at last in that shameful though rather forcible declaration of [John] Pettit of Indiana, upon the floor of the United States Senate, that the Declaration of Independence was in that respect "a self-evident lie," rather than a self-evident truth. But I say, with a perfect knowledge of all this hawking at the Declaration without directly attacking it, that three years ago there never had lived a man who had ventured to assail it in the sneaking way of pretending to believe it and then asserting it did not include the negro. [Cheers.] I believe the first man who ever said it was Chief Justice [Roger B.] Taney in the Dred Scott case, and the next to him was our friend Stephen A. Douglas. [Cheers and laughter.] And now it has become the catch-word of the entire party. I would like to call upon his friends everywhere to consider how they have come in so short a time to view this matter in a way so entirely different from their former belief? to ask whether they are not being borne along by an irresistible current—whither, they know not? [Great applause.]

In answer to my proposition at Galesburg last week, I see that some man in Chicago has got up a letter addressed to the Chicago Times, to show as he professes that somebody had said so before; and he signs himself "An Old Line Whig," if I remember correctly. In the first place I would say he was not an Old Line Whig. I am somewhat acquainted with Old Line Whigs. I was with the Old Line Whigs from the origin to the end of that party; I became pretty well acquainted with them, and I know they always had some sense, whatever else you could ascribe to them. [Great laughter.] I know there never was one who had not more sense than to try to show by the evidence he produces that some man had, prior to the time I named, said that negroes were not included in the term "all men" in the Declaration of Independence. What is the evidence he produces? I will bring forward his evidence and let you see what he offers by way of showing that somebody more than three years ago had said negroes were not included in the Declaration. He brings forward part of a speech from Henry Clay—the part of the speech of Henry Clay which I used to bring forward to prove precisely the contrary. [Laughter.] I guess we are surrounded to some extent to-day, by the old friends of Mr. Clay, and they will be glad to hear anything from that authority. While he was in Indiana a man presented him a petition to liberate his negroes, and he, (Mr. Clay) made a speech in answer to it, which I suppose he carefully wrote out himself and caused to be published. I have before me an extract from that speech which constitutes the evidence this pretended "Old Line Whig" at Chicago brought forward to show that Mr.

Clay didn't suppose the negro was included in the Declaration of Independence. Hear what Mr. Clay said:

And what is the foundation of this appeal to me in Indiana, to liberate the slaves under my care in Kentucky? It is a general declaration in the act announcing to the world the independence of the thirteen American colonies, that all men are created equal. Now, as an abstract principle, there is no doubt of the truth of that declaration; and it is desirable in the original construction of society, and in organized societies, to keep it in view as a great fundamental principle. But, then, I apprehend that in no society that ever did exist, or ever shall be formed, was or can the equality asserted among the members of the human race be practically enforced and carried out. There are portions, large portions, women, minors, insane, culprits, transient sojourners, that will always probably remain subject to the government of another portion of the community.

That declaration whatever may be the extent of its import, was made by the delegations of the thirteen States. In most of them slavery existed, and had long existed, and was established by law. It was introduced and forced upon the colonies by the paramount law of England. Do you believe, that in making that Declaration the States that concurred in it intended that it should be tortured into a virtual emancipation of all the slaves within their respective limits? Would Virginia and other Southern States have ever united in a declaration which was to be interpreted into an abolition of slavery among them? Did any one of the thirteen colonies entertain such a design or expectation? To impute such a secret and unavowed purpose would be to charge a political fraud upon the noblest band of patriots that ever assembled in council; a fraud upon the confederacy of the Revolution; a fraud upon the union of those States whose constitution not only recognized the lawfulness of slavery, but permitted the importation of slaves from Africa until the year 1808.

This is the entire quotation brought forward to prove that somebody previous to three years ago had said the negro was not included in the term "all men" in the Declaration. How does it do so? In what way has it a tendency to prove that? Mr. Clay says it is true as an abstract principle that all men are created equal, but that we cannot practically apply it in all cases. He illustrates this by bringing forward the cases of females, minors and insane persons with whom it cannot be enforced; but he says it is true as an abstract principle in the organization of society as well as in organized society, and it should be kept in view as a fundamental principle. Let me read a few words more before I add some comments of my own. Mr. Clay says a little further on:

> I desire no concealment of my opinions in regard to the institution of slavery. I look upon it as a great evil; and deeply lament that we have derived it from the parental government; and from our ancestors. But here they are and the question is, how can they be best dealt with?
> If a state of nature existed and we were about to lay the foundations of society, *no man would be more strongly opposed than I should be, to incorporating the institution of slavery among its elements. . . .*

And when this new principle—this new proposition that no human being ever thought of three years ago,—is brought forward, I combat it as having an evil tendency, if not an evil design; I combat it as having a tendency to dehumanize the negro—to take away from him the right of ever striving to be a man. I combat it as being one of the thousand things constantly done in these days to prepare the public mind to make property, and nothing but property of the *negro in all the States of this Union.* [Tremendous applause. "Hurrah for Lincoln." "Hurrah for (Lyman)Trumbull."]

But there is a point that I wish before leaving this part of the discussion to ask attention to. I have read, and I repeat the words of Henry Clay:

> I desire no concealment of my opinions in regard to the institution of slavery. I look upon it as a great evil and deeply lament that we have derived it from the parental government, and from our ancestors. I wish every slave in the United States was in the country of his ancestors. But here they are; the question is how they can best be dealt with? If a state of nature existed and we were about to lay the foundation of society, no man would be more strongly opposed than I should be to incorporate the institution of slavery among its elements.

The principle upon which I have insisted in this canvass, is in relation to laying the foundations of new societies. I have never sought to apply these principles to the old States for the purpose of abolishing slavery in those States. It is nothing but a miserable perversion of what I have said, to assume that I have declared Missouri, or any other slave State shall emancipate her slaves. I have proposed no such thing. But when Mr. Clay says that in laying the foundations of societies in our Territories where it does not exist he would be opposed to the introduction of slavery as an element, I insist that we have *his warrant*—his license for insisting upon the exclusion of that element, which he declared in such strong and emphatic language *was most hateful to him.* [Loud applause.] . . .

Hon. J. N. Brown   Springfield,
My dear Sir   *Oct. 18. 1858*

I do not perceive how I can express myself, more plainly, than I have done in the foregoing extracts. In four of them I have expressly disclaimed all intention to bring about social and political equality between the white and black races, and, in all the rest, I have done the same thing by clear implication

I have made it equally plain that I think the negro is included in the word "men" used in the Declaration of Independence.

I believe the declara[tion] that "all men are created equal" is the great fundamental principle upon which our free institutions rest; that negro slavery is violative of that principle; but that, by our frame of government, that principle has not been made one of legal obligation; that by our frame of government, the States which have slavery are to retain it, or surrender it at their own pleasure; and that all others—individuals, free-states and national government—are constitutionally bound to leave them alone about it.

I believe our government was thus framed because of the *necessity* springing from the actual presence of slavery, when it was framed.

That such necessity does not exist in the territories, where slavery is not present.

In his Mendenhall speech Mr. Clay says

"Now, as an abstract principle, there is no doubt of the truth of that declaration (all men created equal) and it is desireable, [*sic*] in the original construction of society, and in organized societies, to keep it in view, as a great fundamental principle"

Again, in the same speech Mr. Clay says:

"If a state of nature existed, and we were about to lay the foundations of society, no man would be more strongly opposed than I should to incorporate the institution of slavery among it's elements;"

Exactly so. In our new free teritories, [*sic*] a state of nature *does* exist. In them Congress lays the foundations of society; and, in laying those foundations, I say, with Mr. Clay, it is desireable [*sic*] that the declaration of the equality of all men shall be kept in view, as a great fundamental principle; and that Congress, which lays the foundations of society, should, like Mr. Clay, be strongly opposed to the incorporation of slavery among it's elements.

But it does not follow that social and political equality between whites and blacks, *must* be incorporated, because slavery must *not*. The declaration does not so require.

Yours as ever
A. Lincoln

35

AL to Salmon P. Chase
CW, 3:384

Organized resistance to the 1850 Fugitive Slave Law across the North crippled the federal government's attempt to enforce it. Even secretary of state Daniel Webster's threat—that anyone who failed to obey the law would be charged with treason—failed to quell the outrage. "Why did all manly gifts in Webster fail?" Ralph Waldo Emerson asked. "He wrote on nature's grandest brow, For Sale." Throughout the 1850s, in Boston, New York City, Syracuse, New York, and Christiana, Pennsylvania, across the Midwest, and on to California, black abolitionists and their white allies reenergized the underground railroad. If slave catchers happened to seize a runaway slave, rescue committees instantly swung into action, even if it meant raiding a federal courthouse. Salmon P. Chase had earned the sobriquet "Attorney General for Fugitive Slaves" for his legal work in Ohio defending black runaways. During the 1840s, Chase had joined the Liberty and Free Soil parties; he had served in the U.S. Senate from 1849 to 1855 and, at the time of this letter, was the Republican governor of Ohio. He became one of Lincoln's chief rivals for the presidential nomination in 1860 and later served as Lincoln's secretary of the treasury. Although Lincoln knew of Chase's antislavery principles, he warned him against the Ohio Republican Party's effort to fix a plank into its platform demanding repeal of the Fugitive Slave Law. "This is already damaging us here," Lincoln admonished. If such a move occurred at the national convention, Lincoln advised, "it will explode it." He wrote again to Chase on June 20, repeating his warning against opposing the controversial law. While he tried to avoid a debate with Chase, he asserted his belief that Congress had full authority "to enact a Fugitive Slave Law." Indeed, Lincoln believed that enforcing the law was essential to preservation of the Union. Chase did not accept Lincoln's dire warnings and expressed his hope that even Illinois Republicans would move to repeal the hated measure. For the Lincoln-Chase exchange, also see: *CW*, 3:386.

Caution!! Colored People of Boston. *Poster, April 24, 1851 (H.90.293). The Fugitive Slave Law of 1850, which threatened every African American, sparked organized resistance in many cities across the North. Courtesy of the Trustees of the Boston Public Library/Rare Books.*

Hon: S. P. Chase: Springfield, Ills.
Dear Sir   *June 9. 1859*

Please pardon the liberty I take in addressing you, as I
now do. It appears by the papers that the late Republican
State convention of Ohio adopted a Platform, of which the
following is one plank, "A repeal of the atrocious Fugitive
Slave Law."

This is already damaging us here. I have no doubt that
if that plank be even *introduced* into the next Republican
National convention, it will explode it. Once introduced,
its supporters and it's opponents will quarrel irrecon-
cilably. The latter believe the U.S. constitution declares
that a fugitive slave *"shall be delivered up";* and they look
upon the above plank as dictated by the spirit which declares a fugitive slave *"shall not be delivered up"*

I enter upon no argument one way or the other; but I
assure you the cause of Republicanism is hopeless in Illinois, if it be in any way made responsible for that plank.
I hope you can, and will, contribute something to relieve
us from it. Your Obt. Servt.

A. Lincoln

36

Speech at Columbus, Ohio
CW, 3:401–410, 417–425

In the September 1859 issue of *Harper's Magazine,* Senator Douglas published "The Dividing Line between Federal and Local Authority," his most complete argument in favor of popular sovereignty. To help spread the theme of his essay, Douglas accepted the invitation of Ohio Democrats to speak at Columbus on September 7, at Cincinnati on September 9, and then at Wooster on the 16th. Threatened by Douglas's appearance, state Republicans asked Lincoln to assist their campaign and counter the influence of the "Little Giant," thus extending the Lincoln-Douglas debates, which had formally ended eleven months earlier. At Columbus, Lincoln focused on Douglas's solution for avoiding the problem of slavery in the territories. He repeated his warnings that "popular sovereignty" masked the Democratic Party's secret attempt to expand slavery and, ultimately, legitimize it throughout the country. Lincoln distinguished genuine popular sovereignty — "a general government shall do all those things which pertain to it, and all the local governments shall do precisely as they please in respect to those matters which exclusively concern them" — from "Douglas Popular Sovereignty," which he defined as a principle that "if one man chooses to make a slave of another man, neither that other man or anybody else has a right to object." Lincoln began his remarks by addressing an editorial appearing that morning in the *Ohio Statesman*, claiming that Lincoln favored "negro suffrage." He rejected the accusation, and left no doubt in the minds of Ohio voters that he would never favor "the social and political equality of the white and black races." There remained, Lincoln reasserted, "a physical difference between the white and black races which I believe will forever forbid the two races living together on terms of social and political equality. . . . I do not understand that because I do not want a negro woman for a slave, I must necessarily want her for a wife." Having established his position on race, Lincoln went on to warn Ohioans of the fate that awaited the nation if Democrats prevailed.

September 16, 1859

Fellow-citizens of the State of Ohio:

... Appearing here for the first time in my life, I have been somewhat embarrassed for a topic by way of introduction to my speech; but I have been relieved from that embarrassment by an introduction which the Ohio *Statesman* newspaper gave me this morning. In this paper I have read an article, in which, among other statements, I find the following:

> In debating with Senator Douglas during the memorable contest of last fall, Mr. Lincoln declared in favor of negro suffrage, and attempted to defend that vile conception against the Little Giant.

I mention this now, at the opening of my remarks, for the purpose of making three comments upon it. The first I have already announced—it furnishes me an introductory topic; the second is to show that the gentleman is mistaken; thirdly, to give him an opportunity to correct it. (A voice—"That he won't do.")

In the first place, in regard to this matter being a mistake. I have found that it is not entirely safe, when one is misrepresented under his very nose, to allow the misrepresentation to go uncontradicted. I therefore purpose, here at the outset, not only to say that this is a misrepresentation, but to show conclusively that it is so. ...

Upon a subsequent occasion, when the reason for making a statement like this recurred, I said:

While I was at the hotel to-day an elderly gentleman called upon me to know whether I was really in favor of producing perfect equality between the negroes and white people. While I had not proposed to myself on this occasion to say much on that subject, yet as the question was asked me I thought I would occupy perhaps five minutes in saying something in regard to it. I will say then that I am not, nor ever have been in favor of bringing about in any way the social and political equality of the white and black races—that I am not, nor ever have been in favor of making voters or jurors of negroes, nor of qualifying them to hold office, or intermarry with white people; and I will say in addition to this that there is a physical difference between the white and black races which I believe will forever forbid the two races living together on terms of social and political equality. And inasmuch as they cannot so live, while they do remain together there must be the position of superior and inferior, and I as much as any other man am in favor of having the superior position assigned to the white race. I say upon this occasion I do not perceive that because the white man is to have the superior position, the negro should be denied everything. I do not understand that because I do not want a negro woman for a slave, I must necessarily want her for a wife. My understanding is that I can just let her alone. I am now in my fiftieth year, and I certainly never have had a black woman for either a slave or a wife. So it seems to me quite possible for us to get along without making either slaves or wives of negroes. I will add to this that I have never seen to my knowledge a man, woman or child, who was in favor of producing a perfect equality, social and political, between negroes and white men.

I recollect of but one distinguished instance that I ever heard of so frequently as to be satisfied of its correctness—and that is the case of Judge Douglas' old friend Col. Richard M. Johnson. I will also add to the remarks I have made, (for I am not going to enter at large upon this subject,) that I have never had the least apprehension that I or my friends would marry negroes, if there was no law to keep them from it; but as Judge Douglas and his friends seem to be in great apprehension that they might, if there were no law to keep them from it, I give him the most solemn pledge that I will to the very last stand by the law of the State, which forbids the marrying of white people with negroes.

There, my friends, you have briefly what I have, upon former occasions, said upon the subject to which this newspaper, to the extent of its ability, [laughter] has drawn the public attention. In it you not only perceive as a probability that in that contest I did not at any time say I was in favor of negro suffrage; but the absolute proof that twice—once substantially and once expressly—I declared against it. Having shown you this, there remains but a word of comment on that newspaper article. It is this: that I presume the editor of that paper is an honest and truth-loving man, [a voice—"that's a great mistake,"] and that he will be very greatly obliged to me for furnishing him thus early an opportunity to correct the misrepresentation he has made, before it has run so long that malicious people can call him a liar. [Laughter and applause.] . . .

The chief danger to this purpose of the Republican party is not just now the revival of the African slave trade, or the passage of a Congressional slave code, or the declaring of a second Dred Scott decision, making slavery lawful in all the States. These are not pressing us just now. They are not quite ready yet. The authors of these measures know that we are too strong for them; but they will be upon us in due time, and we will be grappling with them hand to hand, if they are not now headed off. They are not now the chief danger to the purpose of the Republican organization; but the most imminent danger that now threatens that purpose is that insidious Douglas Popular Sovereignty. This is the miner and sapper. While it does not propose to revive the African slave trade, nor to pass a slave code, nor to make a second Dred Scott decision, it is preparing us for the onslaught and charge of these ultimate enemies when they shall be ready to come on and the word of command for them to advance shall be given. I say this Douglas Popular Sovereignty—for there is a broad distinction, as I now understand it, between that article and a genuine popular sovereignty.

I believe there is a genuine popular sovereignty. I think a definition of genuine popular sovereignty, in the abstract, would be about this: That each man shall do precisely as he pleases with himself, and with all those things which exclusively concern him. Applied to government, this principle would be, that a general government shall do all those things which pertain to it, and all the local governments shall do precisely as they please in respect to those matters which exclusively concern them. I understand that this government of the United States, under which we live, is based upon this principle; and I am misunderstood if it is supposed that I have any war to make upon that principle.

Now, what is Judge Douglas' Popular Sovereignty? It is, as a principle, no other than that, if one man chooses to make a slave of another man, neither that other man nor anybody else has a right to object. [Cheers and laughter.] Applied in government, as he seeks to apply it, it is this: If, in a new territory into which a few people are beginning to enter for the purpose of making their homes, they choose to either exclude slavery from their limits, or to establish it there, however one or the other may affect the persons to be enslaved, or the infinitely greater number of persons who are afterward to inhabit that territory, or the other members of the families of communities, of which they are but an incipient member, or the general head of the family of States as parent of all—however their action may affect one or the other of these, there is no power or right to interfere. That is Douglas' popular sovereignty applied. . . .

Judge Douglas ought to remember when he is endeavoring to force this policy upon the American people that while he is put up in that way a good many are not. He ought to remember that there was once in this country a man by the name of Thomas Jefferson, supposed to be a Democrat—a man whose principles and policy are not very prevalent amongst Democrats to-day, it is true; but that man did not take exactly this view of the insignificance of the element of slavery which our friend Judge Douglas does. In contemplation of this thing, we all know he was led to exclaim, "I tremble for my country when I remember that God is just!" We know how he looked upon it when he thus expressed himself. There was danger to this country—danger of the avenging justice of God in that little unimportant popular sovereignty question of Judge Douglas. He supposed there was a question of God's eternal justice wrapped up in the enslaving of any race of men, or any man, and that those who did so braved the arm of Jehovah—that when a nation thus dared the Almighty every friend of that nation had cause to dread His wrath. Choose ye between Jefferson and Douglas as to what is the true view of this element among us. [Applause.] . . .

The Dred Scott decision expressly gives every citizen of the United States a right to carry his slaves into the United States' Territories. And now there was some inconsistency in saying that the decision was right, and saying too, that the people of the Territory could lawfully drive slavery out again. When all the trash, the words, the collateral matter was cleared away from it; all the chaff was fanned out of it, it was a bare absurdity—*no less than a thing may be lawfully driven away from where it has a lawful right to be.* [Cheers and laughter.] Clear it of all the verbiage, and that is the naked truth of his proposition— that a thing may be lawfully driven from the place where it has a lawful right to stay. Well, it was because the Judge couldn't help seeing this, that he has had so much trouble with it; and what I want to ask your especial attention to, just now, is to remind you, if you have not noticed the fact, that the Judge does not any longer say that the people cannot [can?] exclude slavery. He does not say so in the copyright essay; he did not say so in the speech that he made here, and so far as I know, since his re-election to the Senate, he has never said as he did at Freeport, that the people of the Territories can exclude slavery. He desires that you, who wish the Territories to remain free, should believe that he stands by that position, but he does not say it himself. He escapes to some extent the absurd position I have stated by changing his language entirely. What he says now is something different in language, and we will consider whether it is not different in sense too. It is now that the Dred Scott decision, or rather the Constitution under that decision, does not carry slavery into the Territories beyond the power of the people of the Territories *to control it as other property.* He does not say the people can drive it out, but they can control it as other property. The language is different, we should consider whether the sense is different. Driving a horse out of this lot, is too plain a proposition to be mistaken about; it is putting him on the other side of the fence. [Laughter.] Or it might be a sort of exclusion of him from the lot if you were to kill him and let the worms devour him; but neither of these things is the same as "controlling him as other property." That would be to feed him, to pamper him, to ride him, to use and abuse him, to make the most money out of him "as other property"; but, please you, what do the men who are in favor of slavery want more than this? [Laughter and applause.] What do they really want, other than that slavery being in the Territories, shall be controlled as other property. [Renewed applause.] . . .

. . . But I undertake to give the opinion, at least, that if the territories attempt by any direct legislation to drive the man with his slave out of the territory, or to decide that his slave is free because of his being taken in there, or to tax him to such an extent that he cannot keep him there, the Supreme Court will unhesitatingly decide all such legislation unconstitutional, as long as that Supreme Court is constructed as the Dred Scott Supreme Court is. . . .

What is that Dred Scott decision? Judge Douglas labors to show that it is one thing, while I think it is altogether different. It is a long opinion, but it is all embodied in this short statement: "The Constitution of the United States forbids Congress to deprive a man of his property, without due process of law; the right of property in slaves is distinctly and expressly affirmed in that Constitution; therefore, if Congress shall undertake to say that a man's slave is no longer his slave, when he crosses a certain line into a territory, that is depriving him of his property without due process of law, and is unconstitutional." There is the whole Dred Scott decision. . . .

The Judge says that the people of the territories have the right, by his principle, to have slaves, if they want them. Then I say that the people of Georgia have the right to buy slaves in Africa, if they want them, and I defy any man on earth to show any distinction between the two things—to show that the one is either more wicked or more unlawful; to show, on original principles, that one is better or worse than the other; or to show by the constitution, that one differs a whit from the other. He will tell me, doubtless, that there is no constitutional provision against people taking slaves into the new territories, and I tell him that there is equally no constitutional provision against buying slaves in Africa. He will tell you that a people, in the exercise of popular sovereignty, ought to do as they please about that thing, and have slaves if they want them; and I tell you that the people of Georgia are as much entitled to popular sovereignty and to buy slaves in Africa, if they want them, as the people of the territory are to have slaves if they want them. . . .

Then I say if this principle is established, that there is no wrong in slavery, and whoever wants it has a right to have it, is a matter of dollars and cents, a sort of question as to how they shall deal with brutes, that between us and the negro here there is no sort of question, but that at the South the question is between the negro and the crocodile. That is all. It is a mere matter of policy; there is a perfect right according to interest to do just as you please—when this is done, where this doctrine prevails, the miners and sappers will have formed public opinion for the slave trade. They will be ready for Jeff. Davis and [Alexander H.] Stephens and other leaders of that company, to sound the bugle for the revival of the slave trade, for the second Dred Scott decision, for the flood of slavery to be poured over the free States, while we shall be here tied down and helpless and run over like sheep. . . .

Now, if you are opposed to slavery honestly, as much as anybody I ask you to note that fact, and the like of which is to follow, to be plastered on, layer after layer, until very soon you are prepared to deal with the negro everywhere as with the brute. If public sentiment has not been debauched already to this point, a new turn of the screw in that direction is all that is wanting; and this is constantly being done by the teachers of this insidious popular sovereignty. You need but one or two turns further until your minds, now ripening under these teachings will be ready for all these things, and you will receive and support, or submit to, the slave trade; revived with all its horrors; a slave code enforced in our territories, and a new Dred Scott decision to bring slavery up into the very heart of the free North. This, I must say, is but carrying out those words prophetically spoken by Mr. Clay, many, many years ago. I believe more than thirty years when he told an audience that if they would repress all tendencies to liberty and ultimate emancipation, they must go back to the era of our independence and muzzle the cannon which thundered its annual joyous return on the Fourth of July; they must blow out the moral lights around us; they must penetrate the human soul and eradicate the love of liberty; but until they did these things, and others eloquently enumerated by him, they could not repress all tendencies to ultimate emancipation.

I ask attention to the fact that in a pre-eminent degree these popular sovereigns are at this work; blowing out the moral lights around us; teaching that the negro is no longer a man but a brute; that the Declaration has nothing to do with him; that he ranks with the crocodile and the reptile; that man, with body and soul, is a matter of dollars and cents. I suggest to this portion of the Ohio Republicans, or Democrats if there be any present, the serious consideration of this fact, that there is now going on among you a steady process of debauching public opinion on this subject. With this my friends, I bid you adieu.

37

Speech at Cincinnati, Ohio
CW, 3:445–446

In this excerpt from his speech at Cincinnati, Lincoln addressed members of the audience who may have crossed the Ohio River from his native Kentucky, a slave state. He argued against the idea that slavery could be justified by the Bible, a fallacy that would at best support only the enslavement of white people. Although proslavery authors such as George Fitzhugh endorsed nonracial servitude, Lincoln understood that Northern voters would be horrified by the idea. He also referred to Senator Douglas's frequently cited remark that "in all contests between the negro and the white man, he was for the white man, but that in all questions between the negro and the crocodile he was for the negro." In finding the sum ("rule of three") of white men, African Americans, and the crocodile, Douglas equated black people with beasts or reptiles, stripping them of their humanity. In this way they would be easily excluded from the elementary idea of equality embodied in the Declaration of Independence. Lincoln repeatedly asserted that if one group could be removed from the embrace of the Declaration, then any group could be similarly stripped of their humanity and basic rights. Finally, on the subject of free labor, which he increasingly focused upon in the days leading to his address before the Wisconsin State Agricultural Society on September 30, Lincoln maintained that slaves, not free blacks, inflicted economic distress upon the white working class. In words that he believed would resonate with Cincinnatians who lived so close to slavery, Lincoln contended that whites suffered "by the effect of slave labor in the vicinity of the fields of their own labor."

. . . THE BIBLE THEORY.

In Kentucky, perhaps, in many of the Slave States certainly, you are trying to establish the rightfulness of Slavery by reference to the Bible. You are trying to show that slavery existed in the Bible times by Divine ordinance. Now [Senator] Douglas is wiser than you, for your own benefit, upon that subject. Douglas knows that whenever you establish that Slavery was right by the Bible, it will occur that that Slavery was the Slavery of the *white* man—of men without reference to color—and he knows very well that you may entertain that idea in Kentucky as much as you please, but you will never win any Northern support upon it. He makes a wiser argument for you; he makes the argument that the slavery of the *black* man, the slavery of the man who has a skin of a different color from your own, is right. He thereby brings to your support Northern voters who could not for a moment be brought by your own argument of the Bible-right of slavery. Will you not give him credit for that? Will you not say that in this matter he is more wisely for you than you are for yourselves.

Now having established with his entire party this doctrine—having been entirely successful in that branch of his efforts in your behalf; he is ready for another.

A SUM IN THE RULE OF THREE.

At this same meeting at Memphis, he declared that while in all contests between the negro and the white man, he was for the white man, but that in all questions between the negro and the crocodile he was for the negro. (Laughter.) He did not make that declaration accidentally at Memphis. He made it a great many times in the canvass in Illinois last year, (though I don't know that it was reported in any of his speeches there,) but he frequently made it. I believe he repeated it at Columbus, and I should not wonder if he repeated it here. It is, then, a deliberate way of expressing himself upon that subject. It is a matter of mature deliberation with him thus to express himself upon that point of his case. It therefore requires some deliberate attention.

The first inference seems to be that if you do not enslave the negro you are wronging the white man in some way or other, and that whoever is opposed to the negro being enslaved is in some way or other against the white man. Is not that a falsehood? If there was a necessary conflict between the white man and the negro, I should be for the white man as much as Judge Douglas; but I say there is no such necessary conflict. I say that there is room enough for us all to be free, (loud manifestations of applause,) and that it not only does not wrong the white man that the negro should be free, but it positively wrongs the mass of the white men that the negro should be enslaved; that the mass of white men are really injured by the effect of slave labor in the vicinity of the fields of their own labor. (Applause.)

But I do not desire to dwell upon this branch of the question more than to say that this assumption of his is false, and I do hope that that fallacy will not long prevail in the minds of intelligent white men. At all events, you Kentuckians ought to thank Judge Douglas for it. It is for your benefit it is made.

The other branch of it is, that in a struggle between the negro and the crocodile, he is for the negro. Well, I don't know that there is any struggle between the negro and the crocodile, either. (Laughter.) I suppose that if a crocodile (or as we old Ohio river boatmen used to call them, alligators) should come across a white man, he would kill him if he could, and so he would a negro. But what, at last, is this proposition? I believe it is a sort of proposition in proportion, which may be stated thus: As the negro is to the white man, so is the crocodile as a beast or reptile, so the white man may rightfully treat the negro as a beast or a reptile. (Applause.) . . .

38

Fragment on Free Labor
CW, 3:462–463

The following fragment may have been intended for Lincoln's September 30, 1859, remarks at the Wisconsin State Agricultural Society, and also appears related to speeches on labor given in preceding weeks at Dayton and Cincinnati, Ohio. But whatever their origin, the ideas it expressed lay at the heart of Lincoln's political, moral, and economic world. His views on labor and capital in particular display the influence of Francis Wayland's 1837 *Elements of Political Economy*, which became the principal economics text in American colleges; according to Lincoln's law partner and good friend William Henry Herndon, Wayland's book had been one of Lincoln's favorites. It successfully simplified intricate economic principles in a way that could appeal to students and average Americans, and often employed moral arguments to elucidate economic ideas, a technique that Lincoln used throughout his career. Although a lawyer for major businesses, Lincoln nonetheless believed that the nation's political, economic, and social systems must encourage individual attainment. He cited his own rise from hired laborer to hirer of labor to illustrate what he saw as a fundamental democratic principle. His disgust with the institution of slavery and with Russian serfdom rested on the permanent and arbitrary economic and social subservience they imposed by force on a class—or race—of people. By exchanging incentives for force—"*hope*, for the *rod*"—such systems violated the moral order and common sense.

[September 17, 1859?]

---

change conditions with either Canada or South Carolina? *Equality*, in society, alike beats *inequality*, whether the lat[t]er be of the British aristocratic sort, or of the domestic slavery sort.

We know, Southern men declare that their slaves are better off than hired laborers amongst us. How little they *know*, whereof they *speak*! There is no permanent class of hired laborers amongst us. Twentyfive years ago, I was a hired laborer. The hired laborer of yesterday, labors on his own account to-day; and will hire others to labor for him to-morrow. Advancement—improvement in condition—is the order of things in a society of equals. As Labor is the common *burthen* of our race, so the effort of *some* to shift their share of the burthen on to the shoulders of others, is the great, durable, curse of the race. Originally a curse for transgression upon the whole race, when, as by slavery, it is concentrated on a part only, it becomes the double-refined curse of God upon his creatures.

Free labor has the inspiration of hope; pure slavery has no hope. The power of hope upon human exertion, and happiness, is wonderful. The slave-master himself has a conception of it; and hence the system of *tasks* among slaves. The slave whom you can not drive with the lash to break seventy-five pounds of hemp in a day, if you will task him to break a hundred, and promise him pay for all he does over, he will break you a hundred and fifty. You have substituted *hope*, for the *rod*. And yet perhaps it does not occur to you, that to the extent of your gain in the case, you have given up the slave system, and adopted the free system of labor.

39

Address at the Cooper Institute, New York City
CW, 3:522–550

In early 1860, following a string of successful speeches in the Midwest, Lincoln quietly initiated his campaign for president. Before he could openly challenge a party leader like William H. Seward, Lincoln began building momentum and expanding his influence. In December 1859, he published a brief autobiography. Then, in February 1860, he enthusiastically accepted an invitation to lecture at Henry Ward Beecher's Plymouth Church in Brooklyn, New York, a center of abolitionism. He purchased a new black suit (one hundred dollars at the local tailors, Woods & Heckle) and carefully researched and prepared what would become the speech of his career. However, upon arriving in New York, Lincoln learned that sponsorship of the event had been assumed by the Young Men's Central Republican Union, whose members included the not-so-young poet William Cullen Bryant and the graybeard abolitionist Horace Greeley, men intent on denying Seward the presidential nomination. They also moved the event from Brooklyn to the Cooper Union in Manhattan, the famed tuition-free school for adult education where conservative antislavery men Frank Blair from Missouri and Cassius Clay from Kentucky already had spoken. The speech proved a smashing success and appeared in the *New York Tribune*, the *Chicago Press and Tribune*, the *Detroit Tribune*, the *Albany Evening Journal*, and as a separate pamphlet. Lincoln had been well known in Republican circles, but national attention had focused largely on Seward, Salmon P. Chase, and Edward Bates as the party's possible presidential nominees. After the Cooper Institute address, Lincoln emerged as one of Seward's main rivals. The speech avoided the usual harsh racial commentary and focused entirely on the challenge posed by the South to the Union. The nationalist appeal proved effective and memorable. For the circumstances of Lincoln's famous address, see: David Herbert Donald, *Lincoln* (London: Jonathan Cape, 1995).

National Republican Chart / Presidential Campaign, 1860, *broadside, New York, 1860.*
A colorized, wood-engraving by H. H. Lloyd. The chart features images of Lincoln and his
running mate Hannibal Hamlin, quotes from Lincoln, the Republican Party platform, and
information about previous presidents.

Dividing the National Map. *Cincinnati (?), 1860. A lithograph showing the presidential candidates, Lincoln, Stephen A. Douglas, and John Breckinridge, tearing the nation apart, while John Bell of the Constitution-Union Party tries to repair it. Prints and Photographs Division, Library of Congress, LC-USZ62-10493.*

Stephen Finding His Mother. *Drawn by Louis Maurer (?), 1860, lithograph by Currier & Ives, criticizing Stephen A. Douglas, who explained a campaign swing through New England and New York as a trip to see his mother. The national image of Columbia is spanking Douglas with a switch symbolizing temperance (Douglas was often accused of overindulging in alcohol) while a Founding Father image urges Columbia to "lay it on." Prints and Photographs Division, Library of Congress, LC-USZ62-14832.*

. . . A few words now to Republicans. *It is exceedingly desirable that all parts of this great Confederacy shall be at peace, and in harmony, one with another. Let us Republicans do our part to have it so. Even though much provoked, let us do nothing through passion and ill temper. Even though the southern people will not so much as listen to us, let us calmly consider their demands, and yield to them if, in our deliberate view of our duty, we possibly can.* Judging by all they say and do, and by the subject and nature of their controversy with us, let us determine, if we can, what will satisfy them.

Will they be satisfied if the Territories be unconditionally surrendered to them? We know they will not. In all their present complaints against us, the Territories are scarcely mentioned. Invasions and insurrections are the rage now. Will it satisfy them, if, in the future, we have nothing to do with invasions and insurrections? We know it will not. We so know, because we know we never had anything to do with invasions and insurrections; and yet this total abstaining does not exempt us from the charge and the denunciation.

The question recurs, what will satisfy them? Simply this: We must not only let them alone, but we must, somehow, convince them that we do let them alone. This, we know by experience, is no easy task. We have been so trying to convince them from the very beginning of our organization, but with no success. In all our platforms and speeches we have constantly protested our purpose to let them alone; but this has had no tendency to convince them. Alike unavailing to convince them, is the fact that they have never detected a man of us in any attempt to disturb them.

These natural, and apparently adequate means all failing, what will convince them? This, and this only: cease to call slavery *wrong*, and join them in calling it *right.* And this must be done thoroughly—done in *acts* as well as in *words.* Silence will not be tolerated—we must place ourselves avowedly with them. Senator Douglas's new sedition law must be enacted and enforced, suppressing all declarations that slavery is wrong, whether made in politics, in presses, in pulpits, or in private. We must arrest and return their fugitive slaves with greedy pleasure. We must pull down our Free State constitutions. The whole atmosphere must be disinfected from all taint of opposition to slavery, before they will cease to believe that all their troubles proceed from us.

I am quite aware they do not state their case precisely in this way. Most of them would probably say to us, "Let us alone, *do* nothing to us, and *say* what you please about slavery." But we do let them alone—have never disturbed them—so that, after all, it is what we say, which dissatisfies them. They will continue to accuse us of doing, until we cease saying.

I am also aware they have not, as yet, in terms, demanded the overthrow of our Free-State Constitutions. Yet those Constitutions declare the wrong of slavery, with more solemn emphasis, than do all other sayings against it; and when all these other sayings shall have been silenced, the overthrow of these Constitutions will be demanded, and nothing be left to resist the demand. It is nothing to the contrary, that they do not demand the whole of this just now. Demanding what they do, and for the reason they do, they can voluntarily stop nowhere short of this consummation. Holding, as they do, that slavery is morally right, and socially elevating, they cannot cease to demand a full national recognition of it, as a legal right, and a social blessing.

Nor can we justifiably withhold this, on any ground save our conviction that slavery is wrong. If slavery is right, all words, acts, laws, and constitutions against it, are themselves wrong, and should be silenced, and swept away. If it is right, we cannot justly object to its nationality—its universality; if it is wrong, they cannot justly insist upon its extension—its enlargement. All they ask, we could readily grant, if we thought slavery right; all we ask, they could as readily grant, if they thought it wrong. Their thinking it right, and our thinking it wrong, is the precise fact upon which depends the whole controversy. Thinking it right, as they do, they are not to blame for desiring its full recognition, as being right; but, thinking it wrong, as we do, can we yield to them? Can we cast our votes with their view, and against our own? In view of our moral, social, and political responsibilities, can we do this?

Wrong as we think slavery is, we can yet afford to let it alone where it is, because that much is due to the necessity arising from its actual presence in the nation; but can we, while our votes will prevent it, allow it to spread into the National Territories, and to overrun us here in these Free States? If our sense of duty forbids this, then let us stand by our duty, fearlessly and effectively. Let us be diverted by none of those sophistical contrivances wherewith we are so industriously plied and belabored— contrivances such as groping for some middle ground between the right and the wrong, vain as the search for a man who should be neither a living man nor a dead man— such as a policy of "don't care" on a question about which all true men do care—such as Union appeals beseeching true Union men to yield to Disunionists, reversing the divine rule, and calling, not the sinners, but the righteous to repentance—such as invocations to Washington, imploring men to unsay what Washington said, and undo what Washington did.

Neither let us be slandered from our duty by false accusations against us, nor frightened from it by menaces of destruction to the Government nor of dungeons to ourselves. LET US HAVE FAITH THAT RIGHT MAKES MIGHT, AND IN THAT FAITH, LET US, TO THE END, DARE TO DO OUR DUTY AS WE UNDERSTAND IT.

The Undecided Political Prize Fight, *Cincinnati (?), 1860, boosts the candidacy of John C. Breckinridge of the southern wing of the Democratic Party by depicting Douglas as the candidate of the Irish and Lincoln as the stand-in for African Americans. Prints and Photographs Division, Library of Congress, LC-USZ62-7877.*

The Political Quadrille. Music by Dred Scott, *Cincinnati (?), 1860, places African Americans at the center of the presidential contest, with each candidate dancing to the tune played by the Supreme Court in the infamous 1857 Dred Scott decision. Following the charge repeated tirelessly by Senator Douglas, Lincoln is shown as the advocate of miscegenation. Prints and Photographs Division, Library of Congress, LC-USZ62-14827.*

Lincoln and Douglas in a presidential footrace, *a lithograph by J. Sage & Sons, Buffalo, New York, 1860. Image depicts a hurdle placed on the road to the White House by Abraham Lincoln that Stephen A. Douglas could not surmount. Prints and Photographs Division, Library of Congress, LC-USZ62-14834.*

"The Nigger" in the Woodpile, *lithograph, drawn by Louis Maurer (?), 1860, published by Currier & Ives, New York, promotes Democratic charges that abolitionists controlled the Republican Party, and that Lincoln's rise to party leadership rested upon antislavery support. Prints and Photographs Division, Library of Congress, LC-USZ62-8898.*

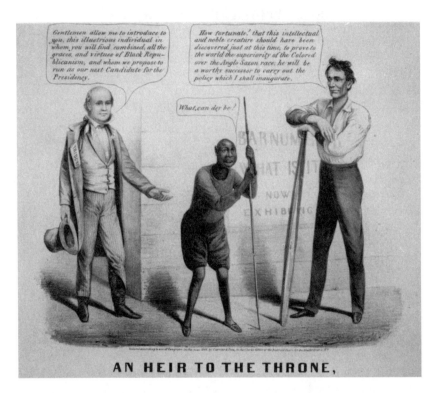

AN HEIR TO THE THRONE,

An Heir to the Throne, or the Next Republican Candidate, *lithograph drawn by Louis Maurer (?), 1860, published by Currier & Ives, New York. The image casts a black microcephalic who had appeared in P. T. Barnum's Broadway Museum as the next Republican candidate for president. Prints and Photographs Division, Library of Congress,* LC-USZ62-1997.

40

Speech at Hartford, Connecticut
CW, 4:2–13

In early March, Lincoln spoke almost daily to crowds in Rhode Island, New Hampshire, and Connecticut, avoiding Massachusetts because of Seward's popularity there. Away from the party's elite in New York and among the rougher-hewn folk of Connecticut, Lincoln delivered speeches more like those he had given in the Midwest but adapted to local circumstances. At the time of Lincoln's appearance in Hartford, city shoemakers had gone out on strike. "Now whether this is so or not, I know one thing—*there is a strike*! And I am glad to know that there is a system of labor where the laborer can strike if he wants to! I would to God that such a system prevailed all over the world." Connecting the white working class to the Republican Party's opposition to the expansion of slavery, Lincoln warned, "Why *slavery comes in upon you*! Public opinion against it gives way. The barriers which protected you from it are down; slavery comes in, and white free labor that *can* strike will give way to slave labor that *cannot*!" In the following excerpt, Lincoln inserted the metaphor of the rattlesnake to explain his policy of halting the extension of slavery but not eradicating it in the Southern states. Present in his speech is his oft-repeated response to Senator Stephen A. Douglas's statement about being for "the negro over the crocodile." Although Lincoln had addressed this statement many times before, using the term "negro" as Douglas had, here we see Lincoln repeatedly using the word "nigger." Conversely, the Cooper Institute speech did not contain "nigger" or "negro," and "black" appeared only in "Black Republicanism." For the circumstances in Hartford, see: Benjamin Thomas, *Abraham Lincoln: A Biography* (New York: Alfred A. Knopf, 1952), 204–205.

March 5, 1860

Whether we will have it so or not, the slave question is the prevailing question before the nation. Though it may be true, and probably *is* true, that all parties, factions and individuals desire it should be settled, it still goes on unsettled—the all-prevailing and all-pervading question of the day. Hardly any other great question, however important it may have appeared, has been before the country several years, that had the power so to excite the public mind as this question of slavery. It has been so for six years, and before this received considerable consideration. It is in reality, older. It was rife before the Revolution, even. But it was settled, apparently. It has been settled many times; but each time it has risen it has come higher and higher. It has been coming up and going down. Its last rise was in January, 1854; it rose then higher than any former time, but this has never subsided. Otherwise than this, it grows more and more in magnitude and importance. . . .

I think one great mistake is made by them all. I think our wisest men have made this mistake. They underrate its importance, and a settlement can never be effected until its magnitude is properly estimated. Until we do this, the means of settlement will never be properly estimated. Now what is the difficulty? One-sixth of the population of the United States is slave. One man of every six, one woman of every six, one child of every six, is a slave. Those who own them look upon them as property, and nothing else. They contemplate them as property, and speak of them as such. The slaves have the same "property quality," in the minds of their owners, as any other property. The entire value of the slave population of the United States, is, at a moderate estimate, not less than $2,000,000,000. This amount of *property* has a vast influence upon the minds of those who own it. The same amount of property owned by Northern men has the same influence upon *their* minds. In this we do not assume that we are better than the people of the South—neither do we admit that they are better than we. We are not better, barring circumstances, than they. Public opinion is formed relative to a property basis. Therefore, the slaveholders battle any policy which depreciates their slaves as property. What increases the value of this property, they favor. When you tell them that slavery is immoral, they rebel, because they do not like to be told they are interested in an institution which is not a moral one. When you enter into a defence of slavery, they seize upon it, for they like justification. The result is, that public opinion is formed among them which insists upon the encouragement or protection, the enlargement or perpetuation of slavery—and secures them property in the slave.

Now this comes in conflict with this proposition that we at the North view slavery as a wrong. We understand that the "equality of man" principle which actuated our forefathers in the establishment of the government is right; and that slavery, being directly opposed to this, is morally wrong. I think that if anything can be proved by natural theology, it is that slavery is morally wrong. God gave man a mouth to receive bread, hands to feed it, and his hand has a right to carry bread to his mouth without controversy.

We suppose slavery is wrong, and that it endangers the perpetuity of the Union. Nothing else menaces it. Its effect on free labor makes it what [Sen. William H.] Seward has been so roundly abused for calling, an irrepressible conflict. Almost every man has a sense of certain things being wrong, and at the same time, a sense of its pecuniary value. These conflict in the mind, and make a riddle of a man. If slavery is considered upon a property basis, public opinion must be forced to its support. The alternative is its settlement upon the basis of its being wrong. Some men think it is a question of neither right or wrong; that it is a question of dollars and cents, only; that the Almighty has drawn a line across the country,

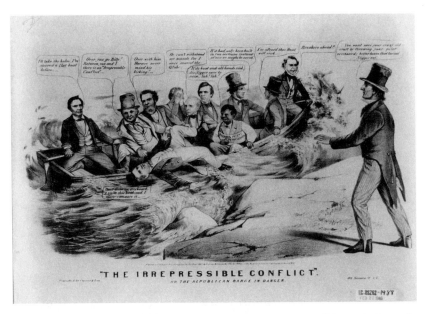

"The Irrepressible Conflict." Or the Republican Barge in Danger, *lithograph, drawn by Louis Maurer (?), 1860, published by Currier & Ives, New York. This cartoon appeared immediately after Abraham Lincoln's nomination and depicts Republican Party leaders throwing Senator William Henry Seward overboard because of his warnings against the dire influence of slavery on national politics and his support for blacks. The figure to the right suggests that to save the boat, the passengers should "heave that tarnal Nigger out." Prints and Photographs Division, Library of Congress, LC-USZ62-1988.*

south of which the land is always to be cultivated by slave labor; when the question is between the white man and the nigger, they go in for the white man; when it is between the nigger and the crocodile, they take sides with the nigger. There is effort to make this feeling of indifference prevalent [in] the country, and this is one of the things, perhaps, that prevents the sudden settlement of the question. Is it possible that a national policy can be sustained because nobody opposes or favors it? It may answer to serve the ends of politicians for a while, but it falls at last. There may be one way, however, to make it stand, and that is to make the opinion of the people conform to it; must be made to conclude that those who want slavery shall have it, and that it is simply a matter of dollars and cents. I do not believe a majority of the people of this nation can be made to take this view of it.

Is there any man of the Democratic party, especially the "Douglas wing," but will say that in his opinion the Declaration of Independence has no application to the negro? I have asked this question many times during the past three years, and no Democrat has yet denied that this was his belief, though I have asked it always where people are in the habit of answering their speakers when they please. So I assume this to be their belief to-day; and I tell you, you are safe to offer a premium to any man who will show you a Democrat who said so five years ago. I avow I never heard it from any man until I heard it from the lips of Judge Douglas. I had, to be sure, in certain portions of the country, heard men say something to this effect, but they didn't sneak around it with any statement like this. *They* took the bull by the horns, and said the Declaration of Independence wasn't true! Judge Taney might have first broached the doctrine. Perhaps he did; but I heard it first from Judge Douglas, though it was after Taney's Dred Scott decision. If so, Douglas possibly got it from him. Here's half the people of this nation saying what they would not have said five years ago; taking man from his kind and placing him among the brutes. This is a long stride towards bringing about this feeling of indifference in the minds of the people of this country. One more such stride and the object would be reached.

The proposition that there is a struggle between the white man and the negro contains a falsehood. There is *no* struggle between them. It assumes that unless the white man enslaves the negro, the negro will enslave the white man. In that case, I think I would go for enslaving the black man, in preference to being enslaved myself. As the learned Judge of a certain Court is said to have decided— "When a ship is wrecked at sea, and two men seize upon one plank which is capable of sustaining but one of them, either of them can rightfully push the other off!" There is, however, no such controversy here. They say that between the nigger and the crocodile they go for the nigger. The proportion, therefore, is, that as the crocodile to the nigger so is the nigger to the white man. . . .

If, then, we of the Republican party who think slavery is a wrong, and would mould public opinion to the fact that it is wrong, should get the control of the general government, I do not say we would or should meddle with it where it exists; but we could inaugurate a policy which would treat it as a wrong, and prevent its extension.

For instance, out in the street, or in the field, or on the prairie I find a rattlesnake. I take a stake and kill him. Everybody would applaud the act and say I did right. But suppose the snake was in a bed where children were sleeping. Would I do right to strike him there? I might hurt the children; or I might not kill, but only arouse and exasperate the snake, and he might bite the children. Thus, by meddling with him here, I would do more hurt than good. Slavery is like this. We dare not strike at it where it is. The manner in which our constitution is framed constrains us from making war upon it where it already exists. The question that we now have to deal with is, "Shall we be acting right to take this snake and carry it to a bed where there are children?" The Republican party insists upon keeping it out of the bed.

Again: I met Mr. Cassius M. Clay in the cars at New Haven one day last week, and it was my first opportunity to take him by the hand. There was an old gentleman in the car, seated in front of us, whose coat collar was turned far down upon the shoulders. I saw directly that he had a large wen on his neck. I said to Mr. Clay, That wen represents slavery; it bears the same relation to that man that slavery does to the country. That wen is a great evil; the man that bears it will say so. But he does not dare to cut it out. He bleeds to death if he does, directly. If he does *not* cut it out; it will shorten his life materially.

This is only applicable to men who think slavery is wrong. Those who think it right, of course will look upon the rattlesnake as a jewel, and call the wen an ornament. I suppose the only way to get rid of it is, for those who think it wrong, to work together, and to vote no longer with the Democracy who love it so well.

Do you who think slavery is wrong, but still vote with the Democracy, act towards it as you do towards any other thing you consider wrong? I think not; on the contrary, you find fault with those who denounce it. In your view of the case it must not be discussed at all. In your view it must not be spoken of in the free States, because slavery is *not* there; nor in the slave States, because it *is* there; you do not want it brought into politics because it stirs up agitation; you do not want to hear of it from the pulpit because it is not religion; you do not want to take it into your Tract Societies because it creates disturbance *there*. . . .

The Republicans want to see all parts of the Union in harmony with one another. Let us do our duty, but let us look to what our duty is, and do nothing except after due deliberation. Let us determine, if we can, what will satisfy the South. Will they be satisfied that we surrender the territories to them unconditionally? No. If we promise never to instigate an invasion upon slavery? No. Equally without avail is the fact that they have found nothing to detect us in doing them any wrong. What then? We must say that slavery is right; we must vote for Douglas's new Sedition laws; we must withdraw our statement that slavery is wrong. If a slave runs away, they overlook the natural causes which impelled him to the act; do not remember the oppression or the lashes he received, but charge us with instigating him to flight. If he screams when whipped, they say it is not caused by the pains he suffers, but he screams because we instigate him to outcrying. We do let them alone, to be sure, but they object to our saying anything against their system. They do not ask us to change our free State constitutions, but they will yet do that. After demanding *what* they do, and *as* they do, they cannot stop short of this. They may be justified in this, believing, as they do, that slavery is right, and a social blessing. We cannot act otherwise than we do, believing that slavery is wrong. If it is right, we may not contract its limits. If it is wrong, they cannot ask us to extend it. Upon these different views, hinges the whole controversy. Thinking it right, they are justified in asking its protection; thinking it wrong, we cannot consent to vote for it, or to let it extend itself. If our sense of duty forbids this extension, let us do that duty. This contrivance of a middle ground is such that he who occupies it is neither a dead or a living man. Their "Union" contrivances are not for us, for they reverse the scriptural order and call the righteous, not sinners to repentance. They ask men who never had an aspiration except for the Union, to swear fealty to the Union. Let us not be slandered from our duties, or intimidated from preserving our dignity and our rights by any menace; but let us have faith that Right, Eternal Right makes might, and as we understand our duty, so do it!

41

AL to John A. Gilmer
CW, 4:151–152

John A. Gilmer, the conservative Whig politician from North Carolina who opposed secession, belonged to a small group of Southerners that Lincoln labeled "white crows." The president-elect hoped to include Gilmer in his cabinet to shore up Unionist strength in the South and keep secessionist spirit from growing. Gilmer, however, understood that most Southerners insisted on the right to extend slavery into the territories, and submitted a list of questions to Lincoln which showed how much that meant to the South and to the survival of the Union. Lincoln, however, could hardly abandon the founding principle of the Republican Party, and Gilmer was dropped from consideration for any post in the administration. In his reply to Gilmer's queries, which Lincoln hoped would be shared with others in the South—despite being marked "Strictly confidential"—the president advised the North Carolinian that he had no intention of reversing the principled stand that had resulted in his election. Furthermore, drafting any new political statement, as Gilmer desired, was entirely pointless. Lincoln's views and those of the Republican Party were well known, and he even referred Gilmer to a published edition of his debates with Stephen A. Douglas. But he also offered assurances that he had no intention of seeking an end to slavery in the District of Columbia or to the interstate slave trade. He sought to allay Gilmer's anxiety over patronage: "I do not expect to inquire for the politics of the appointee, or whether he does or not own slaves." While he reiterated his unwavering stand on the matter of slavery in the territories, he tried to convince his Southern colleague that such a difference of opinion should not overshadow everything. "You think slavery is right and ought to be extended; we think it is wrong and ought to be restricted. For this, neither has any just occasion to be angry with the other." Less than a week later, South Carolina seceded from the Union, and

Lincoln wrote to another "white crow," Alexander H. Stephens, offering identical assurances and downplaying their differences over slavery. Stephens, who would soon become vice president of the Confederacy, at first balked at secession and advised Lincoln, "I am not your enemy—far from it; and however widely we may differ politically, yet I trust we both have an earnest desire to preserve and maintain the Union." For Lincoln's contacts with Gilmer and Stephens, see: David Herbert Donald, *Lincoln* (London: Jonathan Cape, 1995), 263; *CW*, 4:160–161.

Strictly confidential.

Hon. John A. Gilmer: Springfield, Ill.
Dec 15, 1860.

My dear Sir—Yours of the 10th is received. I am greatly disinclined to write a letter on the subject embraced in yours; and I would not do so, even privately as I do, were it not that I fear you might misconstrue my silence. Is it desired that I shall shift the ground upon which I have been elected? I can not do it. You need only to acquaint yourself with that ground, and press it on the attention of the South. It is all in print and easy of access. May I be pardoned if I ask whether even you have ever attempted to procure the reading of the Republican platform, or my speeches, by the Southern people? If not, what reason have I to expect that any additional production of mine would meet a better fate? It would make me appear as if I repented for the crime of having been elected, and was anxious to apologize and beg forgiveness. To so represent me, would be the principal use made of any letter I might now thrust upon the public. My old record cannot be so used; and that is precisely the reason that some new dec-laration is so much sought.

Now, my dear sir, be assured, that I am not questioning *your* candor; I am only pointing out, that, while a new letter would hurt the cause which I think a just one, you can quite as well effect every patriotic object with the old record. Carefully read pages 18, 19, 74, 75, 88, 89, & 267 of the volume of Joint Debates between Senator Douglas and myself, with the Republican Platform adopted at Chicago, and all your questions will be substantially answered. I have no thought of recommending the abolition of slavery in the District of Columbia, nor the slave trade among the slave states, even on the conditions indicated; and if I were to make such recommendation, it is quite clear Congress would not follow it.

As to employing slaves in Arsenals and Dockyards, it is a thing I never thought of in my life, to my recollection, till I saw your letter; and I may say of it, precisely as I have said of the two points above.

As to the use of patronage in the slave states, where there are few or no Republicans, I do not expect to inquire for the politics of the appointee, or whether he does or not own slaves. I intend in that matter to accommodate the people in the several localities, if they themselves will allow me to accommodate them. In one word, I never have been, am not now, and probably never shall be, in a mood of harassing the people, either North or South.

On the territorial question, I am inflexible, as you see my position in the book. On that, there is a difference between you and us; and it is the only substantial difference. You think slavery is right and ought to be extended; we think it is wrong and ought to be restricted. For this, neither has any just occasion to be angry with the other.

As to the state laws, mentioned in your sixth question, I really know very little of them. I never have read one. If any of them are in conflict with the fugitive slave clause, or any other part of the constitution, I certainly should be glad of their repeal; but I could hardly be justified, as a citizen of Illinois, or as President of the United States, to recommend the repeal of a statute of Vermont, or South Carolina.

With the assurance of my highest regards I subscribe myself Your obt. Servt.,

A. Lincoln

P.S. The documents referred to, I suppose you will readily find in Washington.

A. L.

42

First Inaugural Address
CW, 4:262–264, 268–269

Secessionists raised the palmetto flag in Charleston, South Carolina, the day after Lincoln's election on November 6, 1860. The state officially voted for secession on December 20, and headlines splashed across the nation's newspapers, "Union Dissolved!" The next month, one Southern state after another voted for secession, and by the time Lincoln gave his first inaugural address seven states had left the Union—four more would leave after the attack on Fort Sumter. Lincoln knew many Southern politicians who wished to preserve slavery and the Union, and he believed that some accommodation remained possible. In fact, Unionism persisted in the South, and all the states except South Carolina eventually sent considerable numbers of men to serve in the *Union* army. Nevertheless, in the spring of 1861, the loss of the presidential election left the overwhelming number of Southerners in dead fear that their power and the institution of slavery would fall before an aggrandizing, abolitionist North. To combat such anxieties, Lincoln distanced himself and his party from abolitionism, and assured the South that he would never "directly or indirectly" interfere with slavery where it already existed. He repudiated the actions of men like John Brown, whose 1859 attack at Harpers Ferry caused such distress, and assured the nation that he fully intended to enforce the Fugitive Slave Law. The only difference between North and South, he maintained in his first remarks as president, was over extending slavery to places where it did not previously exist.

March 4, 1861

Fellow citizens of the United States:

. . . Apprehension seems to exist among the people of the Southern States, that by the accession of a Republican Administration, their property, and their peace, and personal security, are to be endangered. There has never been any reasonable cause for such apprehension. Indeed, the most ample evidence to the contrary has all the while existed, and been open to their inspection. It is found in nearly all the published speeches of him who now addresses you. I do but quote from one of those speeches when I declare that "I have no purpose, directly or indirectly, to interfere with the institution of slavery in the States where it exists. I believe I have no lawful right to do so, and I have no inclination to do so." Those who nominated and elected me did so with full knowledge that I had made this, and many similar declarations, and had never recanted them. And more than this, they placed in the platform, for my acceptance, and as a law to themselves, and to me, the clear and emphatic resolution which I now read:

"*Resolved*, That the maintenance inviolate of the rights of the States, and especially the right of each State to order and control its own domestic institutions according to its own judgment exclusively, is essential to that balance of power on which the perfection and endurance of our political fabric depend; and we denounce the lawless invasion by armed force of the soil of any State or Territory, no matter under what pretext, as among the gravest of crimes."

I now reiterate these sentiments: and in doing so, I only press upon the public attention the most conclusive evidence of which the case is susceptible, that the property, peace and security of no section are to be in anywise endangered by the now incoming Administration. I add too, that all the protection which, consistently with the Constitution and the laws, can be given, will be cheerfully given to all the States when lawfully demanded, for whatever cause—as cheerfully to one section, as to another.

There is much controversy about the delivering up of fugitives from service or labor. The clause I now read is as plainly written in the Constitution as any other of its provisions:

"No person held to service or labor in one State, under the laws thereof, escaping into another, shall, in consequence of any law or regulation therein, be discharged from such service or labor, but shall be delivered up on claim of the party to whom such service or labor may be due."

It is scarcely questioned that this provision was intended by those who made it, for the reclaiming of what we call fugitive slaves; and the intention of the law-giver is the law. All members of Congress swear their support to the whole Constitution—to this provision as much as to any other. To the proposition, then, that slaves whose cases come within the terms of this clause, "shall be delivered up," their oaths are unanimous. Now, if they would make the effort in good temper, could they not, with nearly equal unanimity, frame and pass a law, by means of which to keep good that unanimous oath?

There is some difference of opinion whether this clause should be enforced by national or by state authority; but surely that difference is not a very material one. If the slave is to be surrendered, it can be of but little consequence to him, or to others, by which authority it is done. And should any one, in any case, be content that his oath shall go unkept, on a merely unsubstantial controversy as to *how* it shall be kept?

Again, in any law upon this subject, ought not all the safeguards of liberty known in civilized and humane jurisprudence to be introduced, so that a free man be not, in any case, surrendered as a slave? And might it not be well, at the same time, to provide by law for the enforcement of that clause in the Constitution which guarranties [*sic*] that "The citizens of each State shall be entitled to all previleges [*sic*] and immunities of citizens in the several States? . . ."

One section of our country believes slavery is *right*, and ought to be extended, while the other believes it is *wrong*, and ought not to be extended. This is the only substantial dispute. The fugitive slave clause of the Constitution, and the law for the suppression of the foreign slave trade, are each as well enforced, perhaps, as any law can ever be in a community where the moral sense of the people imperfectly supports the law itself. The great body of the people abide by the dry legal obligation in both cases, and a few break over in each. This, I think, cannot be perfectly cured; and it would be worse in both cases *after* the separation of the sections, than before. The foreign slave trade, now imperfectly suppressed, would be ultimately revived without restriction, in one section; while fugitive slaves, now only partially surrendered, would not be surrendered at all, by the other. . . .

43

AL to Orville H. Browning

CW, 4:531–532

General John Charles Frémont, known as "The Pathfinder" for his exploits in California in the 1840s, commanded the Department of the West and was headquartered in the pivotal border state of Missouri. He appeared well placed in his command since he was married to Jessie Benton, daughter of former Missouri U.S. senator Thomas Hart Benton and an influential national figure in her own right. Her husband, worried over growing rebel strength in Missouri and his own command's weaknesses, proclaimed martial law throughout the state, threatened to execute any civilians bearing arms against the United States, and emancipated all slaves of disloyal citizens. The move proved a shock to Lincoln, who worried that if Frémont's proclamation was not quickly reversed, Kentucky and other border states would join the Confederacy. Missouri, Kentucky, and Maryland all contained considerable numbers of Confederate sympathizers, and Lincoln referred to one Union volunteer unit that refused to fight because of Frémont's order as evidence of the threat it posed. Lincoln knew Orville H. Browning as a man much like himself, a conservative Illinois Republican and former Whig. No doubt he felt heartened when Browning was named to complete the U.S. Senate term of Stephen A. Douglas, who had died the previous June—hence his shock when Browning expressed support for Frémont's emancipation order. Lincoln advised Browning that the move in Missouri was entirely unconstitutional and illegal, a reckless antislavery "dictatorship." Contrary to Lincoln's statement to Browning, Frémont refused to back down, and his wife traveled to the White House to personally appeal on behalf of her husband. Vexed, the president curtly advised the general's bold wife that "General Frémont should not have dragged the Negro into it." In November, he relieved the general of his command. For the encounter between Lincoln and the Frémonts, see: David Herbert Donald, *Lincoln* (London: Jonathan Cape, 1995), 314–316.

Private & confidential.

Hon. O. H. Browning   Executive Mansion
My dear Sir   Washington *Sept 22d 1861.*

Yours of the 17th is just received; and coming from you, I confess it astonishes me. That you should object to my adhering to a law, which you had assisted in making, and presenting to me, less than a month before, is odd enough. But this is a very small part. Genl. Fremont's proclamation, as to confiscation of property, and the liberation of slaves, is *purely political*, and not within the range of *military* law, or necessity. If a commanding General finds a necessity to seize the farm of a private owner, for a pasture, an encampment, or a fortification, he has the right to do so, and to so hold it, as long as the necessity lasts; and this is within military law, because within military necessity. But to say the farm shall no longer belong to the owner, or his heirs forever; and this as well when the farm is not needed for military purposes as when it is, is purely political, without the savor of military law about it. And the same is true of slaves. If the General needs them, he can seize them, and use them; but when the need is past, it is not for him to fix their permanent future condition. That must be settled according to laws made by law-makers, and not by military proclamations. The proclamation in the point in question, is simply "dictatorship." It assumes that the general may do *anything* he pleases—confiscate the lands and free the slaves of *loyal* people, as well as of disloyal ones. And going the whole figure I have no doubt would be more popular with some thoughtless people, than that which has been done! But I cannot assume this reckless position; nor allow others to assume it on my responsibility. You speak of it as being the only means of *saving* the government. On the contrary it is itself the surrender of the government. Can it be pretended that it is any longer the government of the U.S.—any government of Constitution and laws,—wherein a General, or a President, may make permanent rules of property by proclamation?

I do not say Congress might not with propriety pass a law, on the point, just such as General Fremont proclaimed. I do not say I might not, as a member of Congress, vote for it. What I object to, is, that I as President, shall expressly or impliedly seize and exercise the permanent legislative functions of the government.

So much as to principle. Now as to policy. No doubt the thing was popular in some quarters, and would have been more so if it had been a general declaration of emancipation. The Kentucky Legislature would not budge till that proclamation was modified; and Gen. [Robert] Anderson telegraphed me that on the news of Gen. Fremont having actually issued deeds of manumission, a whole company of our Volunteers threw down their arms and disbanded. I was so assured, as to think it probable, that the very arms we had furnished Kentucky would be turned against us. I think to lose Kentucky is nearly the same as to lose the whole game. Kentucky gone, we can not hold Missouri, nor, as I think, Maryland. These all against us, and the job on our hands is too large for us. We would as well consent to separation at once, including the surrender of this capitol. On the contrary, if you will give up your restlessness for new positions, and back me manfully on the grounds upon which you and other kind friends gave me the election, and have approved in my public documents, we shall go through triumphantly.

You must not understand I took my course on the proclamation *because* of Kentucky. I took the same ground in a private letter to General Fremont before I heard from Kentucky.

You think I am inconsistent because I did not also forbid Gen. Fremont to shoot men under the proclamation. I understand that part to be within military law; but I also think, and so privately wrote Gen. Fremont, that it is impolitic in this, that our adversaries have the power, and will certainly exercise it, to shoot as many of our men as we shoot of theirs. I did not say this in the public letter, because it is a subject I prefer not to discuss in the hearing of our enemies.

There has been no thought of removing Gen. Fremont on any ground connected with his proclamation. . . . Your friend as ever A. LINCOLN

44

Message to Congress
CW, 5:144–146

Lincoln preferred that Congress adopt a compensated emancipation scheme as the best way to retain the border states and satisfy the more radical members of the Republican Party, like Charles Sumner, who lobbied the president continuously to move against slavery. Lincoln hoped to convince Delaware to be the first state to voluntarily give up slavery, with significant congressional incentives, thus becoming a model for the other border states. Lincoln gained the support of his secretary of the treasury Salmon P. Chase—who also backed colonization—and Sumner agreed not to oppose any compensation plan if a border state agreed to such a program. None did. The president even went so far as to print up proposals and distribute them to members of the Delaware legislature, but the state refused to cooperate. Lincoln followed a slow, deliberate, step-by-step process that favored action by Congress and voluntary cooperation by the states. His March message to Congress did contain a warning, which border state congressmen especially in Maryland were quick to seize upon: "If, however, resistance continues, the war must also continue; and it is impossible to foresee all the incidents, which may attend and all the ruin which may follow it."

March 6, 1862

Fellow-citizens of the Senate, and House of Representatives,

I recommend the adoption of a Joint Resolution by your honorable bodies which shall be substantially as follows:

"Resolved that the United States ought to co-operate with any state which may adopt gradual abolishment of slavery, giving to such state pecuniary aid, to be used by such state in it's discretion, to compensate for the inconveniences public and private, produced by such change of system"

If the proposition contained in the resolution does not meet the approval of Congress and the country, there is the end; but if it does command such approval, I deem it of importance that the states and people immediately interested, should be at once distinctly notified of the fact, so that they may begin to consider whether to accept or reject it. The federal government would find it's highest interest in such a measure, as one of the most efficient means of self-preservation. The leaders of the existing insurrection entertain the hope that this government will ultimately be forced to acknowledge the independence of some part of the disaffected region, and that all the slave states North of such part will then say "the Union, for which we have struggled, being already gone, we now choose to go with the Southern section." To deprive them of this hope, substantially ends the rebellion; and the initiation of emancipation completely deprives them of it, as to all the states initiating it. The point is not that *all* the states tolerating slavery would very soon, if at all, initiate emancipation; but that, while the offer is equally made to all, the more Northern shall, by such initiation, make it certain to the more Southern, that in no event, will the former ever join the latter, in their proposed confederacy. I say "initiation" because, in my judgment, gradual, and not sudden emancipation, is better for all. In the mere financial, or pecuniary view, any member of Congress, with the census-tables and Treasury-reports before him, can readily see for himself how very soon the current expenditures of this war would purchase, at fair valuation, all the slaves in any named State. Such a proposition, on the part of the general government, sets up no claim of a right, by federal authority, to interfere with slavery within state limits, referring, as it does, the absolute control of the subject, in each case, to the state and it's people, immediately interested. It is proposed as a matter of perfectly free choice with them.

In the annual message last December, I thought fit to say "The Union must be preserved; and hence all indispensable means must be employed." I said this, not hastily, but deliberately. War has been made, and continues to be, an indispensable means to this end. A practical re-acknowledgement of the national authority would render the war unnecessary, and it would at once cease. If, however, resistance continues, the war must also continue; and it is impossible to foresee all the incidents, which may attend and all the ruin which may follow it. Such as may seem indispensable, or may obviously promise great efficiency towards ending the struggle, must and will come.

The proposition now made, though an offer only, I hope it may be esteemed no offence to ask whether the pecuniary consideration tendered would not be of more value to the States and private persons concerned, than are the institution, and property in it, in the present aspect of affairs.

While it is true that the adoption of the proposed resolution would be merely initiatory, and not within itself a practical measure, it is recommended in the hope that it would soon lead to important practical results. In full view of my great responsibility to my God, and to my country, I earnestly beg the attention of Congress and the people to the subject.

Abraham Lincoln
March 6. 1862.

45

AL to James A. McDougall
CW, 5:160–161

The response to Lincoln's plan for compensated emancipation mentioned in his March 6, 1862, message to Congress proved disappointing. Although the president met with a congressional delegation from the border states in an effort to change their minds, and personally drafted two bills that would end slavery in Delaware, he could not win any substantial support. Congressman John W. Crisfield, representing Maryland slave-owning Unionists, publicly rejected the president's offer, and even protested Lincoln's attempt to "bully" him and the state into accepting his plans. California U.S. senator James A. Mc-Dougall, a War Democrat, came to Crisfield's defense on the floor of the U.S. Senate, asserting that emancipation of any kind was illegal and unconstitutional. Despite the fact that the House of Representatives had approved compensated emancipation in the District of Columbia on April 11 (the Senate had done so on April 3), Maryland slaveowners damned the move, supported by Democrats like McDougall who otherwise remained loyal to the Union. Lincoln believed that compensated emancipation was the best way to keep the border states in the Union and help shorten the war. He wrote to the California senator, using statistics provided by the superintendent of the census to show that it would be cheaper to pay for the emancipation of slaves than to continue fighting the war. McDougall was not convinced and, on March 26, delivered another speech rejecting the constitutionality of any plan that used federal funds to buy slaves. For the opposition of War Democrats to Lincoln's modest plans, see: Christopher Dell, *Lincoln and the War Democrats: The Grand Erosion of Conservative Tradition* (Cranbury, N.J.: Associated University Presses, 1975), 143.

Hon. James A. McDougal[1]   Executive Mansion
U.S. Senate   Washington, *March 14, 1862*

My dear Sir: As to the expensiveness of the plan of gradual emancipation with compensation, proposed in the late Message, please allow me one or two brief suggestions.

Less than one half-day's cost of this war would pay for all the slaves in Delaware at four hundred dollars per head:

Thus, all the slaves in Delaware,

by the Census of 1860, are. 1798
400

Cost of the slaves, ... $719,200.

One day's cost of the war . . . . [$]2,000,000.

Again, less than eighty seven days cost of this war would, at the same price, pay for all in Delaware, Maryland, District of Columbia, Kentucky, and Missouri.

Thus, slaves in Delaware 1798
"   "   Maryland 87,188
"   "   Dis. of Col. 3,181
"   "   Kentucky. 225,490
"   "   Missouri. 114,965

432,622
400

Cost of the slaves. $173,048,800
Eightyseven days' cost of
the war. . . . . [$]174,000,000.

Do you doubt that taking the initiatory steps on the part of those states and this District, would shorten the war more than eighty-seven days, and thus be an actual saving of expense?

A word as to the *time* and *manner* of incurring the expence. [*sic*] Suppose, for instance, a State devises and adopts a system by which the institution absolutely ceases therein by a named day—say January 1st. 1882. Then, let the sum to be paid to such state by the United States, be ascertained by taking from the Census of 1860, the number of slaves within the state, and multiplying that number by four hundred—the United States to pay such sum to the state in twenty equal annual instalments, [*sic*] in six per cent. bonds of the United States.

The sum thus given, as to *time* and *manner*, I think would not be half as onerous, as would be an equal sum, raised *now*, for the indefinite prossecution [*sic*] of the war; but of this you can judge as well as I.

I inclose [*sic*] a Census-table for your convenience.

Yours very truly
A. Lincoln

46

AL to Horace Greeley
CW, 5:169

& Message to Congress
CW, 5:192

Throughout the early spring of 1862, Lincoln lobbied furiously for Congress to adopt compensated emancipation in the District of Columbia, which the Senate approved on April 3 and the House on April 11. Lincoln believed that an orderly and *compensated* end to slavery in the nation's capital would prove to the border states that they could safely abandon slavery and remain in the Union. Lincoln preferred to pressure legislators through influential newspapermen like Horace Greeley, famed editor of the *New York Tribune*, but he lobbied some directly, particularly Schuyler Colfax, an Indiana congressman who maintained influential friendships with many journalists. The new drive to end slavery in the nation's capital fit well into Lincoln's long-standing principle that Congress had the authority to legislate in all matters for the District and in the territories. He repeated his desire, first enunciated in 1837, that white residents in the District should have some say in the process. The measure also contained the president's proposal to compensate loyal slaveholders for their losses (a measure that Congress passed in July) and offered colonization to the former slaves. The move, however disappointing, assuaged some radicals who had come to expect little or nothing from Lincoln on this issue. Many had been deeply disappointed by Lincoln's removal of General John C. Frémont the previous year for issuing a proclamation liberating the slaves of Missourians who aided the rebellion. For the congressional debate over emancipation in the District of Columbia, see: Allen C. Guelzo, *Lincoln's Emancipation Proclamation: The End of Slavery in America* (New York: Simon & Schuster, 2004), 81–89.

Private

Hon. Horace Greeley—   Executive Mansion,
My dear Sir: Washington, *March 24, 1862.*

Your very kind letter of the 16th. to Mr. [Schuyler] Colfax, has been shown me by him. I am grateful for the generous sentiments and purposes expressed towards the administration. Of course I am anxious to see the policy proposed in the late special message, go forward; but you have advocated it from the first, so that I need to say little to you on the subject. If I were to suggest anything it would be that as the North are already for the measure, we should urge it *persuasively*, and not *menacingly*, upon the South. I am a little uneasy about the abolishment of slavery in this District, not but I would be glad to see it abolished, but as to the time and manner of doing it. If some one or more of the border-states would move fast, I should greatly prefer it; but if this can not be in a reasonable time, I would like the bill to have the three main features—gradual—compensation—and vote of the people—I do not talk to members of congress on the subject, except when they ask me. I am not prepared to make any suggestion about confiscation. I may drop you a line hereafter.

Yours truly
A. Lincoln

April 16, 1862

Fellow citizens of the Senate, and House of Representatives.

The Act entitled "An Act for the release of certain persons held to service, or labor in the District of Columbia" has this day been approved, and signed.

I have never doubted the constitutional authority of congress to abolish slavery in this District; and I have ever desired to see the national capital freed from the institution in some satisfactory way. Hence there has never been, in my mind, any question upon the subject, except the one of expediency, arising in view of all the circumstances. If there be matters within and about this act, which might have taken a course or shape, more satisfactory to my jud[g]ment, I do not attempt to specify them. I am gratified that the two principles of compensation, and colonization, are both recognized, and practically applied in the act.

In the matter of compensation, it is provided that claims may be presented within ninety days from the passage of the act "but not thereafter"; and there is no saving for minors, femes-covert, insane, or absent persons. I presume this is an omission by mere over-sight, and I recommended that it be supplied by an amendatory or supplemental act.

April 16. 1862.
Abraham Lincoln

47

Appeal to Border State Representatives to Favor Compensated Emancipation
CW, 5:317–319

Lincoln failed to convince the state of Delaware, with only eighteen hundred slaves, to adopt his compensated emancipation scheme. Intent on pushing his plan, which included federal funds for colonization as in the case of the District of Columbia, Lincoln invited the representatives and senators from the border states to the White House to hear the following address. He expressed his disappointment that his plan had been rejected in the spring, admonishing the group that if it had been accepted, the war would "now be substantially ended." Lincoln believed that if his offer had been accepted, the South would have realized that the border states would not join them in the rebellion and that "they can not, much longer maintain the contest." In this address, Lincoln issued his sternest warning to date of the consequences of failing to agree to the compensation plan: "The incidents of the war can not be avoided. If the war continue long, as it must, if the object be not sooner attained, the institution in your states will be extinguished by mere friction and abrasion—by the mere incidents of the war. It will be gone, and you will have nothing valuable in lieu of it. Much of it's value is gone already. How much better for you, and for your people, to take the step which, at once, shortens the war, and secures substantial compensation for that which is sure to be wholly lost in any other event." He also referred to the controversial case of General David Hunter, commander of the Department of the South, headquartered on the Sea Islands off the South Carolina coast. On April 13, 1862, the general declared that all slaves under his jurisdiction would be "confiscated and declared free." Then on May 8 he declared that all slaves in Georgia, Florida, and South Carolina "are therefore declared forever free." He also began raising a regiment of black troops (later becoming the First South Carolina Volunteers). The emancipation order, which sparked outrage among Democrats and in the border states, was repudiated by the president, as he had done in Missouri, and a congressional inquiry began over Hunter's efforts to raise black troops. Clearly, Lincoln used the case of Hunter as a warning of what could be expected if resistance to compensated or gradual emancipation continued. Nevertheless, only eight of the congressmen approved Lincoln's plans. The overwhelming number rejected them, declaring that the country could not afford the cost, that emancipation would only harden rebel resistance and increase support for secession among the border states. Furthermore they declared that any attempt to emancipate the slaves in the rebel states would be completely unconstitutional. For the case of General Hunter, see: Dudley Taylor Cornish, *The Sable Arm: Negro Troops in the Union Army, 1861–1865* (New York: W. W. Norton, 1966), 35.

July 12, 1862

Gentlemen. After the adjournment of Congress, now very near, I shall have no opportunity of seeing you for several months. Believing that you of the border-states hold more power for good than any other equal number of members, I feel it a duty which I can not justifiably waive, to make this appeal to you. I intend no reproach or complaint when I assure you that in my opinion, if you all had voted for the resolution in the gradual emancipation message of last March, the war would now be substantially ended. And the plan therein proposed is yet one of the most potent, and swift means of ending it. Let the states which are in rebellion see, definitely and certainly, that, in no event, will the states you represent ever join their proposed Confederacy, and they can not, much longer maintain the contest. But you can not divest them of their hope to ultimately have you with them so long as you show a determination to perpetuate the institution within your own states. Beat them at elections, as you have overwhelmingly done, and, nothing daunted, they still claim you as their own. You and I know what the lever of their power is. Break that lever before their faces, and they can shake you no more forever.

Most of you have treated me with kindness and consideration; and I trust you will not now think I improperly touch what is exclusively your own, when, for the sake of the whole country I ask "Can you, for your states, do better than to take the course I urge? ["] Discarding *punctillio* and maxims adapted to more manageable times, and looking only to the unprecedentedly stern facts of our case, can you do better in any possible event? You prefer that the constitutional relation of the states to the nation shall be practically restored, without disturbance of the institution; and if this were done, my whole duty, in this respect, under the constitution, and my oath of office, would be performed. But it is not done, and we are trying to accomplish it by war. The incidents of the war can not be avoided. If the war continue long, as it must, if the object be not sooner attained, the institution in your states will be extinguished by mere friction and abrasion—by the mere incidents of the war. It will be gone, and you will have nothing valuable in lieu of it. Much of it's value is gone already. How much better for you, and for your people, to take the step which, at once, shortens the war, and secures substantial compensation for that which is sure to be wholly lost in any other event. How much better to thus save the money which else we sink forever in the war. How much better to do it while we can, lest the war ere long render us pecuniarily unable to do it. How much better for you, as seller, and the nation as buyer, to sell out, and buy out, that without which the war could never have been, than to sink both the thing to be sold, and the price of it, in cutting one another's throats.

I do not speak of emancipation *at once*, but of a *decision* at once to emancipate *gradually*. Room in South America for colonization, can be obtained cheaply, and in abundance; and when numbers shall be large enough to be company and encouragement for one another, the freed people will not be so reluctant to go.

I am pressed with a difficulty not yet mentioned— one which threatens division among those who, united are none too strong. An instance of it is known to you. Gen. [David] Hunter is an honest man. He was, and I hope, still is, my friend. I valued him none the less for his agreeing with me in the general wish that all men everywhere, could be free. He proclaimed all men free within certain states, and I repudiated the proclamation. He expected more good, and less harm from the measure, than I could believe would follow. Yet in repudiating it, I gave dissatisfaction, if not offence, to many whose support the country can not afford to lose. And this is not the end of it. The pressure, in this direction, is still upon me, and is increasing. By conceding what I now ask, you can relieve me, and much more, can relieve the country, in this important point. Upon these considerations I have again begged your attention to the message of March last. Before leaving the Capital, consider and discuss it among yourselves. You are patriots and statesmen; and, as such, I pray you, consider this proposition; and, at the least, commend it to the consideration of your states and people. As you would perpetuate popular government for the best people in the world, I beseech you that you do in no wise omit this. Our common country is in great peril, demanding the loftiest views, and boldest action to bring it speedy relief. Once relieved, it's form of government is saved to the world; it's beloved history, and cherished memories, are vindicated; and it's happy future fully assured, and rendered inconceivably grand. To you, more than to any others, the previlege [*sic*] is given, to assure that happiness, and swell that grandeur, and to link your own names therewith forever.

48

Address on Colonization to a Deputation of Negroes
CW, 5:370–375

Following up on President Lincoln's request to provide funding for the abolition of slavery in the District of Columbia, Congress appropriated about six million dollars to colonize the newly emancipated slaves in Central America. Although Lincoln no longer believed that the entire African American population could be removed from the United States, he remained committed to racial segregation and colonization as a way to increase white support for emancipation. By continuing to advocate colonization, Lincoln sought to discourage border state Unionists from joining the rebellion, especially as he considered issuing the Preliminary Emancipation Proclamation. His interview with prominent members of the District's black community on August 14 aimed at securing black support for resettlement in the Chiriqui region of Central America. Lincoln believed coal deposits there (later proved worthless) would provide a sound economic basis for the venture. Edward M. Thomas, Reverend John F. Cook, Cornelius C. Clark, John T. Costin, and Benjamin McCoy, Freemasons, abolitionists, community organizers, A.M.E. Church leaders, and a Presbyterian minister, listened respectfully to the president explain that while he understood that blacks suffered "the greatest wrong inflicted on any people," they still could not live in freedom with whites. Not only did he deny the black quest for full citizenship, but he went on to label the African American presence in the United States as the root cause of the Civil War: without "the institution of Slavery and the colored race as a basis, the war could not have an existence." Lincoln's remarks, widely reprinted in the Northern press, enraged African Americans, who saw in them a scheme to deny their quest for equal rights. Many of the District's black citizens even denounced the committee that had met with Lincoln. Frances Ellen Watkins Harper, the famed black poet, spoke for most free blacks when she repudiated Lincoln's revival of the colonizationist delusion in the midst of civil war. "The President's dabbling with colonization," Harper lamented in the September 27 issue of the *Christian Recorder*, "just now suggests to my mind the idea of a man almost dying with a loathsome cancer, and busying himself about having his hair trimmed according to the latest fashion." Rather than expatriate them, others advised the president to send African Americans to the battlefield. Even after the Emancipation Proclamation, Northern blacks believed that Lincoln remained a colonizationist and would do nothing to advance their claims to full citizenship.

August 14, 1862

This afternoon the President of the United States gave audience to a Committee of colored men at the White House. They were introduced by the Rev. J. Mitchell, Commissioner of Emigration. E. M. Thomas, the Chairman, remarked that they were there by invitation to hear what the Executive had to say to them. Having all been seated, the President, after a few preliminary observations, informed them that a sum of money had been appropriated by Congress, and placed at his disposition for the purpose of aiding the colonization in some country of the people, or a portion of them, of African descent, thereby making it his duty, as it had for a long time been his inclination, to favor that cause; and why, he asked, should the people of your race be colonized, and where? Why should they leave this country? This is, perhaps, the first question for proper consideration. You and we are different races. We have between us a broader difference than exists between almost any other two races. Whether it is right or wrong I need not discuss, but this physical difference is a great disadvantage to us both, as I think your race suffer very greatly, many of them by living among us, while ours suffer from your presence. In a word we suffer on each side. If this is admitted, it affords a reason at least why we should be separated. You here are freemen I suppose.

A VOICE:

Yes, sir.

The President—Perhaps you have long been free, or all your lives. Your race are suffering, in my judgment, the greatest wrong inflicted on any people. But even when you cease to be slaves, you are yet far removed from being placed on an equality with the white race. You are cut off from many of the advantages which the other race enjoy. The aspiration of men is to enjoy equality with the best when free, but on this broad continent, not a single man of your race is made the equal of a single man of ours. Go where you are treated the best, and the ban is still upon you.

I do not propose to discuss this, but to present it as a fact with which we have to deal. I cannot alter it if I would. It is a fact, about which we all think and feel alike, I and you. We look to our condition, owing to the existence of the two races on this continent. I need not recount to you the effects upon white men, growing out of the institution of Slavery. I believe in its general evil effects on the white race. See our present condition—the country engaged in war!—our white men cutting one another's throats, none knowing how far it will extend; and then consider what we know to be the truth. But for your race among us there could not be war, although many men engaged on either side do not care for you one way or the other. Nevertheless, I repeat, without the institution of Slavery and the colored race as a basis, the war could not have an existence.

It is better for us both, therefore, to be separated. I know that there are free men among you, who even if they could better their condition are not as much inclined to go out of the country as those, who being slaves could obtain their freedom on this condition. I suppose one of the principal difficulties in the way of colonization is that the free colored man cannot see that his comfort would be advanced by it. You may believe you can live in Washington or elsewhere in the United States the remainder of your life [as easily], perhaps more so than you can in any foreign country, and hence you may come to the conclusion that you have nothing to do with the idea of going to a foreign country. This is (I speak in no unkind sense) an extremely selfish view of the case.

But you ought to do something to help those who are not so fortunate as yourselves. There is an unwillingness on the part of our people, harsh as it may be, for you free colored people to remain with us. Now, if you could give a start to white people, you would open a wide door for many to be made free. If we deal with those who are not free at the beginning, and whose intellects are clouded by Slavery, we have very poor materials to start with. If intelligent colored men, such as are before me, would move in this matter, much might be accomplished. It is exceedingly important that we have men at the beginning capable of thinking as white men, and not those who have been systematically oppressed.

There is much to encourage you. For the sake of your race you should sacrifice something of your present comfort for the purpose of being as grand in that respect as the white people. It is a cheering thought throughout life that something can be done to ameliorate the condition of those who have been subject to the hard usage of the world. It is difficult to make a man miserable while he feels he is worthy of himself, and claims kindred to the great God who made him. In the American Revolutionary war sacrifices were made by men engaged in it; but they were cheered by the future. Gen. Washington himself endured greater physical hardships than if he had remained a British subject. Yet he was a happy man, because he was engaged in benefiting his race—something for the children of his neighbors, having none of his own.

The colony of Liberia has been in existence a long time. In a certain sense it is a success. The old President of Liberia, Roberts, has just been with me—the first time I ever saw him. He says they have within the bounds of that colony between 300,000 and 400,000 people, or more than in some of our old States, such as Rhode Island or Delaware, or in some of our newer States, and less than in some of our larger ones. They are not all American colonists, or their descendants. Something less than 12,000 have been sent thither from this country. Many of the original settlers have died, yet, like people elsewhere, their offspring outnumber those deceased.

The question is if the colored people are persuaded to go anywhere, why not there? One reason for an unwillingness to do so is that some of you would rather remain within reach of the country of your nativity. I do not know how much attachment you may have toward our race. It does not strike me that you have the greatest reason to love them. But still you are attached to them at all events.

The place I am thinking about having for a colony is in Central America. It is nearer to us than Liberia—not much more than one-fourth as far as Liberia, and within seven days' run by steamers. Unlike Liberia it is on a great line of travel—it is a highway. The country is a very excellent one for any people, and with great natural resources and advantages, and especially because of the similarity of climate with your native land—thus being suited to your physical condition.

The particular place I have in view is to be a great highway from the Atlantic or Caribbean Sea to the Pacific Ocean, and this particular place has all the advantages for a colony. On both sides there are harbors among the finest in the world. Again, there is evidence of very rich coal mines. A certain amount of coal is valuable in any country, and there may be more than enough for the wants of the country. Why I attach so much importance to coal is, it will afford an opportunity to the inhabitants for immediate employment till they get ready to settle permanently in their homes.

If you take colonists where there is no good landing, there is a bad show; and so where there is nothing to cultivate, and of which to make a farm. But if something is started so that you can get your daily bread as soon as you reach there, it is a great advantage. Coal land is the best thing I know of with which to commence an enterprise.

To return, you have been talked to upon this subject, and told that a speculation is intended by gentlemen, who have an interest in the country, including the coal mines. We have been mistaken all our lives if we do not know whites as well as blacks look to their self-interest. Unless among those deficient of intellect everybody you trade with makes something. You meet with these things here as elsewhere.

If such persons have what will be an advantage to them, the question is whether it cannot be made of advantage to you. You are intelligent, and know that success does not as much depend on external help as on self-reliance. Much, therefore, depends upon yourselves. As to the coal mines, I think I see the means available for your self-reliance.

I shall, if I get a sufficient number of you engaged, have provisions made that you shall not be wronged. If you will engage in the enterprise I will spend some of the money intrusted [sic] to me. I am not sure you will succeed. The Government may lose the money, but we cannot succeed unless we try; but we think, with care, we can succeed.

The political affairs in Central America are not in quite as satisfactory condition as I wish. There are contending factions in that quarter; but it is true all the factions are agreed alike on the subject of colonization, and want it, and are more generous than we are here. To your colored race they have no objection. Besides, I would endeavor to have you made equals, and have the best assurance that you should be the equals of the best.

The practical thing I want to ascertain is whether I can get a number of able-bodied men, with their wives and children, who are willing to go, when I present evidence of encouragement and protection. Could I get a hundred tolerably intelligent men, with their wives and children, to "cut their own fodder," so to speak? Can I have fifty? If I could find twenty-five able-bodied men, with a mixture of women and children, good things in the family relation, I think I could make a successful commencement.

I want you to let me know whether this can be done or not. This is the practical part of my wish to see you. These are subjects of very great importance, worthy of a month's study, [instead] of a speech delivered in an hour. I ask you then to consider seriously not pertaining to yourselves merely, nor for your race, and ours, for the present time, but as one of the things, if successfully managed, for the good of mankind—not confined to the present generation, but as

> "From age to age descends the lay,
> To millions yet to be,
> Till far its echoes roll away,
> Into eternity."

The above is merely given as the substance of the President's remarks.

The Chairman of the delegation briefly replied that "they would hold a consultation and in a short time give an answer." The President said: "Take your full time—no hurry at all."

The delegation then withdrew.

49

AL to Horace Greeley
CW, 5:388–389

The following open letter printed in Greeley's *New York Tribune* on August 25, 1862, is the best known and most succinct summary of Lincoln's approach toward slavery and the Civil War. Impatient with the course of the war and the administration's apparent reluctance to do anything about the institution of slavery, Greeley challenged the president to act. On August 20 under the title "The Prayer of Twenty Millions," he published a long list of grievances accusing Lincoln of failing to enforce the laws that Congress had passed. He drew special attention to the Second Confiscation Act, which authorized the president to institute an aggressive policy of emancipation and recruit African Americans into the army—which the administration adamantly refused to consider. Greeley charged that the president labored under the influence of fossilized politicians from the border states who compelled him to be timid when the national crisis demanded boldness. He denounced Lincoln for failing to instruct his generals to accept runaway slaves into their lines; instead Union troops often murdered them. The time had long since passed, Greeley explained, for the president to follow the congressional lead and attack the South where it would most hurt: the institution of slavery. In his temperate and well-considered reply to the fiery editor, Lincoln made clear that his priority was simple and precise: preservation of the Union. His personal feelings about the institution of slavery and African Americans, he explained, occupied no part of his thinking. While privately he considered steps toward enacting emancipation as a war measure, publicly he proclaimed his single desire to do anything to end the war and restore the Union—and if the Union could be restored by preserving slavery in the South, he would gladly do it. His use of the Democratic Party's popular rallying cry of "the Union as it was" represented a transparent attempt to disarm his conservative political rivals, which simultaneously convinced black leaders that Lincoln could not be trusted.

Hon. Horace Greely: [*sic*]   Executive Mansion,
Dear Sir   Washington, *August 22, 1862.*

I have just read yours of the 19th. addressed to myself through the New-York Tribune. If there be in it any statements, or assumptions of fact, which I may know to be erroneous, I do not, now and here, controvert them. If there be in it any inferences which I may believe to be falsely drawn, I do not now and here, argue against them. If there be perceptable [*sic*] in it an impatient and dictatorial tone, I waive it in deference to an old friend, whose heart I have always supposed to be right.

As to the policy I "seem to be pursuing" as you say, I have not meant to leave any one in doubt.

I would save the Union. I would save it the shortest way under the Constitution. The sooner the national authority can be restored; the nearer the Union will be "the Union as it was." If there be those who would not save the Union, unless they could at the same time *save* slavery, I do not agree with them. If there be those who would not save the Union unless they could at the same time *destroy* slavery, I do not agree with them. My paramount object in this struggle *is* to save the Union, and is *not* either to save or to destroy slavery. If I could save the Union without freeing *any* slave I would do it, and if I could save it by freeing *all* the slaves I would do it; and if I could save it by freeing some and leaving others alone I would also do that. What I do about slavery, and the colored race, I do because I believe it helps to save the Union; and what I forbear, I forbear because I do *not* believe it would help to save the Union. I shall do *less* whenever I shall believe what I am doing hurts the cause, and I shall do *more* whenever I shall believe doing more will help the cause. I shall try to correct errors when shown to be errors; and I shall adopt new views so fast as they shall appear to be true views.

I have here stated my purpose according to my view of *official* duty; and I intend no modification of my oft-expressed *personal* wish that all men every where could be free. Yours,

A. Lincoln

50

Reply to Emancipation Memorial Presented by Chicago Christians of All Denominations
CW, 5:419–421, 423–425

William W. Patton, a Congregational minister, fierce abolitionist, and later president of Howard University, and John Dempster, a Methodist minister and educator, presented Lincoln with antislavery memorials from an interdenominational convention of Chicago Christians and one in German signed by Chicagoans of German descent. In his reply to the memorials, which appeared in the ministers' report published in the *Chicago Tribune* and in Washington, D.C.'s *National Intelligencer*, Lincoln joked about all the recommendations he received concerning slavery. Although privately he had decided to issue a decree and would actually issue the Preliminary Emancipation Proclamation in a little more than a week, Lincoln gave no hint of his impending move. In these public remarks, he questioned the utility of such a declaration: "Would *my word* free the slaves, when I cannot even enforce the Constitution in the rebel States?" The administration, unwilling to appear desperate, waited only upon a major military victory to adopt emancipation as policy. Yet, as Lincoln confessed, the federal government was entirely unprepared for the number of slaves that would begin seeking protection in Union lines. Employing them as soldiers, an idea hotly debated over the previous year, remained impossible since Lincoln did not believe blacks capable of such a role: "I fear that in a few weeks the[ir] arms would be in the hands of the rebels." Nevertheless, Lincoln closed his remarks with a hint that given the right circumstances, the ministers' wish might be realized.

"The subject presented in the memorial is one upon which I have thought much for weeks past, and I may even say for months. I am approached with the most opposite opinions and advice, and that by religious men, who are equally certain that they represent the Divine will. I am sure that either the one or the other class is mistaken in that belief, and perhaps in some respects both. I hope it will not be irreverent for me to say that if it is probable that God would reveal his will to others, on a point so connected with my duty, it might be supposed he would reveal it directly to me; for, unless I am more deceived in myself than I often am, it is my earnest desire to know the will of Providence in this matter. *And if I can learn what it is I will do it!* These are not, however, the days of miracles, and I suppose it will be granted that I am not to expect a direct revelation. I must study the plain physical facts of the case, ascertain what is possible and learn what appears to be wise and right. The subject is difficult, and good men do not agree. For instance, the other day four gentlemen of standing and intelligence (naming one or two of the number) from New York called, as a delegation, on business connected with the war; but, before leaving, two of them earnestly beset me to proclaim general emancipation, upon which the other two at once attacked them! You know, also, that the last session of Congress had a decided majority of anti-slavery men, yet they could not unite on this policy. And the same is true of the religious people. Why, the rebel soldiers are praying with a great deal more earnestness, I fear, than our own troops, and expecting God to favor their side; for one of our soldiers, who had been taken prisoner, told Senator Wilson, a few days since, that he met with nothing so discouraging as the evident sincerity of those he was among in their prayers. But we will talk over the merits of the case.

"What *good* would a proclamation of emancipation from me do, especially as we are now situated? I do not want to issue a document that the whole world will see must necessarily be inoperative, like the Pope's bull against the comet! Would *my word* free the slaves, when I cannot even enforce the Constitution in the rebel States? Is there a single court, or magistrate, or individual that would be influenced by it there? And what reason is there to think it would have any greater effect upon the slaves than the late law of Congress, which I approved, and which offers protection and freedom to the slaves of rebel masters who come within our lines? Yet I cannot learn that that law has caused a single slave to come over to us. And suppose they could be induced by a proclamation of freedom from me to throw themselves upon us, *what should we do with them*? How can we feed and care for such a multitude? Gen. Butler wrote me a few days since that he was issuing more rations to the slaves who have rushed to him than to all the white troops under his command. They *eat*, and that is all, though it is true Gen.[Benjamin F.] Butler is feeding the whites also by the thousand; for it nearly amounts to a famine there. If, now, the pressure of the war should call off our forces from New Orleans to defend some other point, what is to prevent the masters from reducing the blacks to slavery again; for I am told that whenever the rebels take any black prisoners, free or slave, they immediately auction them off! They did so with those they took from a boat that was aground in the Tennessee river a few days ago. And then *I am very ungenerously attacked for it*! For instance, when, after the late battles at and near Bull Run, an expedition went out from Washington under a flag of truce to bury the dead and bring in the wounded, and the rebels seized the blacks who went along to help and sent them into slavery, Horace Greeley said in his paper that the Government would probably do nothing about it. What *could* I do? [Here your delegation suggested that this was a gross outrage on a flag of truce, which covers and protects all over which it waves, and that whatever he *could* do if *white* men had been similarly detained he could do in this case.]

"Now, then, tell me, if you please, what possible result of good would follow the issuing of such a proclamation as you desire? Understand, I raise no objections against it on legal or constitutional grounds; for, as commander-in-chief of the army and navy, in time of war, I suppose I have a right to take any measure which may best subdue the enemy. Nor do I urge objections of a moral nature, in view of possible consequences of insurrection and massacre at the South. I view the matter as a practical war measure, to be decided upon according to the advantages or disadvantages it may offer to the suppression of the rebellion. . . ."

"I admit that slavery is the root of the rebellion, or at least its *sine qua non*. The ambition of politicians may have instigated them to act, but they would have been impotent without slavery as their instrument. I will also concede that emancipation would help us in Europe, and convince them that we are incited by something more than ambition. I grant further that it would help *somewhat* at the North, though not so much, I fear, as you and those you represent imagine. Still, some additional strength would be added in that way to the war. And then un-questionably it would weaken the rebels by drawing off their laborers, which is of great importance. But I am not so sure we could do much with the blacks. If we were to arm them, I fear that in a few weeks the arms would be in the hands of the rebels; and indeed thus far we have not had arms enough to equip our white troops. I will mention another thing, though it meet only your scorn and contempt: There are fifty thousand bayonets in the Union armies from the Border Slave States. It would be a serious matter if, in consequence of a proclamation such as you desire, they should go over to the rebels. I do not think they all would—not so many indeed as a year ago, or as six months ago—not so many to-day as yesterday. Every day increases their Union feeling. They are also getting their pride enlisted, and want to beat the rebels. Let me say one thing more: I think you should admit that we already have an important principle to rally and unite the people in the fact that constitutional government is at stake. This is a fundamental idea, going down about as deep as any thing. . . ."

[In bringing our interview to a close, after an hour of earnest and frank discussion, of which the foregoing is a specimen, Mr. Lincoln remarked:] "Do not misunderstand me, because I have mentioned these objections. They indicate the difficulties that have thus far prevented my action in some such way as you desire. I have not decided against a proclamation of liberty to the slaves, but hold the matter under advisement. And I can assure you that the subject is on my mind, by day and night, more than any other. Whatever shall appear to be God's will I will do. I trust that, in the freedom with which I have canvassed your views, I have not in any respect injured your feelings."

51

Preliminary Emancipation Proclamation
CW, 5:433–436

On the day that Lincoln received the Chicago ministers' emancipation memorials, Union soldiers discovered General Robert E. Lee's plans for his campaign in Maryland—part of his drive north into Pennsylvania—wrapped around some cigars accidentally dropped by a rebel courier. In one of the bloodiest battles in American history, the Union Army under General George B. McClellan intercepted Lee, forcing him to fight at Antietam. The results proved enough of a "victory" for Lincoln to issue the proclamation from a position of strength and help avert European recognition of the Confederacy. How long Lincoln considered issuing a proclamation regarding slavery is uncertain, but he first announced his decision on July 13, 1862, to Secretary of the Navy Gideon Welles. Lincoln issued the preliminary emancipation statement with the situation of the border states still central to his strategy. He allowed loyal slaveowners to keep their "property" and offered colonization as an inducement for slaveowners to give up their property without fear of creating a large free black population. For states in rebellion, Lincoln decreed that if they did not return to the Union, all their slaves would be "thenceforth, and forever free" as of January 1, 1863. The proclamation reaffirmed Congress's confiscation acts and pledged to compensate all loyal slaveowners for the loss of their property, "including the loss of slaves." Lincoln's initial proclamation completely avoided any mention of the status of newly freed slaves and said nothing about possible recruitment for the army, although blacks had been serving successfully in the navy since the start of the war. For Lincoln's move toward emancipation, see: Allen C. Guelzo, *Lincoln's Emancipation Proclamation: The End of Slavery in America* (New York: Simon & Schuster, 2004).

September 22, 1862

By the President of the United States of America A Proclamation.

I, Abraham Lincoln, President of the United States of America, and Commander-in-chief of the Army and Navy thereof, do hereby proclaim and declare that hereafter, as heretofore, the war will be prosecuted for the object of practically restoring the constitutional relation between the United States, and each of the states, and the people thereof, in which states that relation is, or may be suspended, or disturbed.

That it is my purpose, upon the next meeting of Congress to again recommend the adoption of a practical measure tendering pecuniary aid to the free acceptance or rejection of all slave-states, so called, the people whereof may not then be in rebellion against the United States, and which states, may then have voluntarily adopted, or thereafter may voluntarily adopt, immediate, or gradual abolishment of slavery within their respective limits; and that the effort to colonize persons of African descent, with their consent, upon this continent, or elsewhere, with the previously obtained consent of the Governments existing there, will be continued.

That on the first day of January in the year of our Lord, one thousand eight hundred and sixty-three, all persons held as slaves within any state, or designated part of a state, the people whereof shall then be in rebellion against the United States shall be then, thenceforward, and forever free; and the executive government of the United States, including the military and naval authority thereof, will recognize and maintain the freedom of such persons, and will do no act or acts to repress such persons, or any of them, in any efforts they may make for their actual freedom.

That the executive will, on the first day of January aforesaid, by proclamation, designate the States, and parts of states, if any, in which the people thereof respectively, shall then be in rebellion against the United States; and the fact that any state, or the people thereof shall, on that day be, in good faith represented in the Congress of the United States, by members chosen thereto, at elections wherein a majority of the qualified voters of such state shall have participated, shall, in the absence of strong countervailing testimony, be deemed conclusive evidence that such state and the people thereof, are not then in rebellion against the United States.

That attention is hereby called to an act of Congress entitled "An act to make an additional Article of War" approved March 13, 1862, and which act is in the words and figure following: *Be it enacted by the Senate and House of Representatives of the United States of America in Congress assembled*, That hereafter the following shall be promulgated as an additional article of war for the government of the army of the United States, and shall be obeyed and observed as such:

Article—. All officers or persons in the military or naval service of the United States are prohibited from employing any of the forces under their respective commands for the purpose of returning fugitives from service or labor, who may have escaped from any persons to whom such service or labor is claimed to be due, and any officer who shall be found guilty by a court-martial of violating this article shall be dismissed from the service.

Sec. 2. *And be it further enacted*, That this act shall take effect from and after its passage.

Also to the ninth and tenth sections of an act entitled "An Act to suppress Insurrection, to punish Treason and Rebellion, to seize and confiscate property of rebels, and for other purposes," approved July 17, 1862, and which sections are in the words and figures following:

Sec. 9. *And be it further enacted,* That all slaves of persons who shall hereafter be engaged in rebellion against the government of the United States, or who shall in any way give aid or comfort thereto, escaping from such persons and taking refuge within the lines of the army; and all slaves captured from such persons or deserted by them and coming under the control of the government of the United States; and all slaves of such persons found on (or) being within any place occupied by rebel forces and afterwards occupied by the forces of the United States, shall be deemed captives of war, and shall be forever free of their servitude and not again held as slaves.

Sec. 10. *And be it further enacted,* That no slave escaping into any State, Territory, or the District of Columbia, from any other State, shall be delivered up, or in any way impeded or hindered of his liberty, except for crime, or some offence against the laws, unless the person claiming said fugitive shall first make oath that the person to whom the labor or service of such fugitive is alleged to be due is his lawful owner, and has not borne arms against the United States in the present rebellion, nor in any way given aid and comfort thereto; and no person engaged in the military or naval service of the United States shall, under any pretence whatever, assume to decide on the validity of the claim of any person to the service or labor of any other person, or surrender up any such person to the claimant, on pain of being dismissed from the service.

And I do hereby enjoin upon and order all persons engaged in the military and naval service of the United States to observe, obey, and enforce, within their respective spheres of service, the act, and sections above recited.

And the executive will in due time recommend that all citizens of the United States who shall have remained loyal thereto throughout the rebellion, shall (upon the restoration of the constitutional relation between the United States, and their respective states, and people, if that relation shall have been suspended or disturbed) be compensated for all losses by acts of the United States, including the loss of slaves. . . .

By the President: Abraham Lincoln
William H. Seward, Secretary of State.

52

Annual Message to Congress
CW, 5:518, 520–521, 527, 529–532, 534–537

In his address to Congress on the eve of the final Emancipation Proclamation, Lincoln continued to favor colonization of newly emancipated blacks. He characterized his support as motivated by calls from "many free Americans of African descent." A minority of African Americans had been interested in colonization and in the Haytian Emigration Bureau, headed by the former John Brown supporter James Redpath. The bureau had sent some two thousand blacks to Haiti earlier in the year, but by the fall—long before Lincoln's address—black interest in removal to Haiti had effectively ended. Lincoln recognized black reluctance to resettle in Haiti and Liberia, but seemed completely unaware of the depth of black opposition to colonization. His continued expression of support for the hated scheme infuriated Northern blacks, who saw it as yet one more attempt by whites to deny black citizenship. But Lincoln also began to back away from the scheme, even chastising those whose hatred for African Americans knew no bounds. He assured working-class whites that free blacks would not deny them work: "Is it true, then, that colored people can displace any more white labor, by being free, than by remaining slaves? If they stay in their old places, they jostle no white laborers; if they leave their old places, they leave them open to white laborers." Moreover, Lincoln hinted that the nation would need the labor of blacks, perhaps reflecting his newfound confidence—although he would not publicly say so until the final Emancipation Proclamation—that blacks could successfully serve as soldiers. With border states again in mind, Lincoln offered compensation to those states that voluntarily abandoned slavery and to loyal slaveowners who lost their property "by the chances of the war." Attempting to comfort those who feared the impact of a large free black population, Lincoln suggested a gradual emancipation program, but one that would not be realized until *1900*.

Lincoln expressed no hesitation in having African Americans bear the cost of freedom through a prolonged apprenticeship, but he also recognized the opportunity embedded in the tragedy of war. "In *giving* freedom to the *slave*, we assure *freedom* to the *free*—honorable alike in what we give, and what we preserve. We shall nobly save, or meanly lose, the last best, hope of earth."

December 1, 1862

Fellow-citizens of the Senate and House of Representatives:

. . . Applications have been made to me by many free Americans of African descent to favor their emigration, with a view to such colonization as was contemplated in recent acts of Congress. Other parties, at home and abroad—some from interested motives, others upon patriotic considerations, and still others influenced by philanthropic sentiments—have suggested similar measures; while, on the other hand, several of the Spanish-American republics have protested against the sending of such colonies to their respective territories. Under these circumstances, I have declined to move any such colony to any state, without first obtaining the consent of its government, with an agreement on its part to receive and protect such emigrants in all the rights of freemen; and I have, at the same time, offered to the several states situated within the tropics, or having colonies there, to negotiate with them, subject to the advice and consent of the Senate, to favor the voluntary emigration of persons of that class to their respective territories, upon conditions which shall be equal, just, and humane. Liberia and Hayti are, as yet, the only countries to which colonists of African descent from here, could go with certainty of being received and adopted as citizens; and I regret to say such persons, contemplating colonization, do not seem so willing to migrate to those countries, as to some others, nor so willing as I think their interest demands. I believe, however, opinion among them, in this respect, is improving; and that, ere long, there will be an augmented, and considerable migration to both these countries, from the United States. . . .

In the inaugural address I briefly pointed out the total inadequacy of disunion, as a remedy for the differences between the people of the two sections. I did so in language which I cannot improve, and which, therefore I beg to repeat:

. . . "One section of our country believes slavery is *right*, and ought to be extended, while the other believes it is *wrong*, and ought not to be extended. This is the only substantial dispute. The fugitive slave clause of the Constitution, and the law for the suppression of the foreign slave trade, are each as well enforced, perhaps, as any law can ever be in a community where the moral sense of the people imperfectly supports the law itself. The great body of the people abide by the dry legal obligation in both cases, and a few break over in each. This, I think, cannot be perfectly cured; and it would be worse in both cases *after* the separation of the sections, than before. The foreign slave trade, now imperfectly suppressed, would be ultimately revived without restriction in one section; while fugitive slaves, now only partially surrendered, would not be surrendered at all by the other. . . .["]

In this view, I recommend the adoption of the following resolution and articles amendatory to the Constitution of the United States:

"*Resolved by the Senate and House of Representatives of the United States of America in Congress assembled*, (two thirds of both houses concurring,) That the following articles be proposed to the legislatures (or conventions) of the several States as amendments to the Constitution of the United States, all or any of which articles when ratified by three-fourths of the said legislatures (or conventions) to be valid as part or parts of the said Constitution, viz:

"ARTICLE —.

"Every State, wherein slavery now exists, which shall abolish the same therein, at any time, or times, before the first day of January, in the year of our Lord one thousand and nine hundred, shall receive compensation from the United States as follows, to wit:

"The President of the United States shall deliver to every such State, bonds of the United States, bearing interest at the rate of ——— per cent, per annum, to an amount equal to the aggregate sum of for each slave shown to have been therein, by the eig[h]th census of the United States, said bonds to be delivered to such State by instalments, [sic] or in one parcel, at the completion of the abolishment, accordingly as the same shall have been gradual, or at one time, within such State; and interest shall begin to run upon any such bond, only from the proper time of its delivery as aforesaid. Any State having received bonds as aforesaid, and afterwards reintroducing or tolerating slavery therein, shall refund to the United States the bonds so received, or the value thereof, and all interest paid thereon.

"ARTICLE —.

"All slaves who shall have enjoyed actual freedom by the chances of the war, at any time before the end of the rebellion, shall be forever free; but all owners of such, who shall not have been disloyal, shall be compensated for them, at the same rates as is provided for States adopting abolishment of slavery, but in such way, that no slave shall be twice accounted for.

"ARTICLE —.

"Congress may appropriate money, and otherwise provide, for colonizing free colored persons, with their own consent, at any place or places without the United States."

I beg indulgence to discuss these proposed articles at some length. Without slavery the rebellion could never have existed; without slavery it could not continue.

Among the friends of the Union there is great diversity, of sentiment, and of policy, in regard to slavery, and the African race amongst us. Some would perpetuate slavery; some would abolish it suddenly, and without compensation; some would abolish it gradually, and with compensation; some would remove the freed people from us, and some would retain them with us; and there are yet other minor diversities. Because of these diversities, we waste much strength in struggles among ourselves. By mutual concession we should harmonize, and act together. This would be compromise; but it would be compromise among the friends, and not with the enemies of the Union. These articles are intended to embody a plan of such mutual concessions. If the plan shall be adopted, it is assumed that emancipation will follow, at least, in several of the States.

As to the first article, the main points are: first, the emancipation; secondly, the length of time for consummating it—thirty-seven years; and thirdly, the compensation.

The emancipation will be unsatisfactory to the advocates of perpetual slavery; but the length of time should greatly mitigate their dissatisfaction. The time spares both races from the evils of sudden derangement—in fact, from the necessity of any derangement—while most of those whose habitual course of thought will be disturbed by the measure will have passed away before its consummation. They will never see it. Another class will hail the prospect of emancipation, but will deprecate the length of time. They will feel that it gives too little to the now living slaves. But it really gives them much. It saves them from the vagrant destitution which must largely attend immediate emancipation in localities where their numbers are very great; and it gives the inspiring assurance that their posterity shall be free forever. The plan leaves to each State, choosing to act under it, to abolish slavery now, or at the end of the century, or at any intermediate time, or by degrees, extending over the whole or any part of the period; and it obliges no two states to proceed alike. It also provides for compensation, and generally the mode of making it. This, it would seem, must further mitigate the dissatisfaction of those who favor perpetual slavery, and especially of those who are to receive the compensation. Doubtless some of those who are to pay, and not to receive will object. Yet the measure is both just and economical. In a certain sense the liberation of property acquired by descent, or by purchased, slaves is the destruction of property— the same as any other property. It is no less true for having been often said, that the people of the south are not more responsible for the original introduction of this property, than are the people of the north; and when it is remembered how unhesitatingly we all use cotton and sugar, and share the profits of dealing in them, it may not be quite safe to say, that the south has been more responsible than the north for its continuance. If then, for a common object, this property is to be sacrificed is it not just that it be done at a common charge? . . .

As to the second article, I think it would be impracticable to return to bondage the class of persons therein contemplated. Some of them, doubtless, in the property sense, belong to loyal owners; and hence, provision is made in this article for compensating such.

The third article relates to the future of the freed people. It does not oblige, but merely authorizes, Congress to aid in colonizing such as may consent. This ought not to be regarded as objectionable, on the one hand, or on the other, in so much as it comes to nothing, unless by the mutual consent of the people to be deported, and the American voters, through their representatives in Congress.

I cannot make it better known than it already is, that I strongly favor colonization. And yet I wish to say there is an objection urged against free colored persons remaining in the country, which is largely imaginary, if not sometimes malicious.

It is insisted that their presence would injure, and displace white labor and white laborers. If there ever could be a proper time for mere catch arguments, that time surely is not now. In times like the present, men should utter nothing for which they would not willingly be responsible through time and in eternity. Is it true, then, that colored people can displace any more white labor, by being free, than by remaining slaves? If they stay in their old places, they jostle no white laborers; if they leave their old places, they leave them open to white laborers. Logically, there is neither more nor less of it. Emancipation, even without deportation, would probably enhance the wages of white labor, and, very surely, would not reduce them. Thus, the customary amount of labor would still have to be performed; the freed people would surely not do more than their old proportion of it, and very probably, for a time, would do less, leaving an increased part to white laborers, bringing their labor into greater demand, and, consequently, enhancing the wages of it. With deportation, even to a limited extent, enhanced wages to white labor is mathematically certain. Labor is like any other commodity in the market—increase the demand for it, and you increase the price of it. Reduce the supply of black labor, by colonizing the black laborer out of the country, and, by precisely so much, you increase the demand for, and wages of, white labor.

But it is dreaded that the freed people will swarm forth, and cover the whole land? Are they not already in the land? Will liberation make them any more numerous? Equally distributed among the whites of the whole country, and there would be but one colored to seven whites. Could the one, in any way, greatly disturb the seven? There are many communities now, having more than one free colored person, to seven whites; and this, without any apparent consciousness of evil from it. The District of Columbia, and the States of Maryland and Delaware, are all in this condition. The District has more than one free colored to six whites; and yet, in its frequent petitions to Congress, I believe it has never presented the presence of free colored persons as one of its grievances. But why should emancipation south, send the free people north? People, of any color, seldom run, unless there be something to run from. *Heretofore* colored people, to some extent, have fled north from bondage; and *now*, perhaps, from both bondage and destitution. But if gradual emancipation and deportation be adopted, they will have neither to flee from. Their old masters will give them wages at least until new laborers can be procured; and the freed men, in turn, will gladly give their labor for the wages, till new homes can be found for them, in congenial climes, and with people of their own blood and race. This proposition can be trusted on the mutual interests involved. And, in any event, cannot the north decide for itself, whether to receive them?

Again, as practice proves more than theory, in any case, has there been any irruption of colored people northward, because of the abolishment of slavery in this District last spring?

What I have said of the proportion of free colored persons to the whites, in the District, is from the census of 1860, having no reference to persons called contrabands, nor to those made free by the act of Congress abolishing slavery here.

The plan consisting of these articles is recommended, not but that a restoration of the national authority would be accepted without its adoption.

Nor will the war, nor proceedings under the proclamation of September 22, 1862, be stayed because of the *recommendation* of this plan. Its timely *adoption*, I doubt not, would bring restoration and thereby stay both.

And, notwithstanding this plan, the recommendation that Congress provide by law for compensating any State which may adopt emancipation, before this plan shall have been acted upon, is hereby earnestly renewed. Such would be only an advance part of the plan, and the same arguments apply to both.

This plan is recommended as a means, not in exclusion of, but additional to, all others for restoring and preserving the national authority throughout the Union. The subject is presented exclusively in its economical aspect. The plan would, I am confident, secure peace more speedily, and maintain it more permanently, than can be done by force alone; while all it would cost, considering amounts, and manner of payment, and times of payment, would be easier paid than will be the additional cost of the war, if we rely solely upon force. It is much—very much—that it would cost no blood at all.

The plan is proposed as permanent constitutional law. It cannot become such without the concurrence of, first, two-thirds of Congress, and, afterwards, three-fourths of the States. The requisite three-fourths of the States will necessarily include seven of the Slave states. Their concurrence, if obtained, will give assurance of their severally adopting emancipation, at no very distant day, upon the new constitutional terms. This assurance would end the struggle now, and save the Union forever. . . .

Fellow-citizens, *we* cannot escape history. We of this Congress and this administration, will be remembered in spite of ourselves. No personal significance, or insignificance, can spare one or another of us. The fiery trial through which we pass, will light us down, in honor or dishonor, to the latest generation. We say we are for the Union. The world will not forget that we say this. We know how to save the Union. The world knows we do know how to save it. We—even *we here*—hold the power, and bear the responsibility. In *giving* freedom to the *slave*, we assure *freedom* to the *free*—honorable alike in what we give, and what we preserve. We shall nobly save, or meanly lose, the last best, hope of earth. Other means may succeed; this could not fail. The way is plain, peaceful, generous, just—a way which, if followed, the world will forever applaud, and God must forever bless.

December 1, 1862.
Abraham Lincoln

53

Emancipation Proclamation
CW, 6:28–30

Lincoln issued the final Emancipation Proclamation on the first of the new year as promised in his Preliminary Proclamation of September 22, 1862. Keenly aware of the constitutional limits of his office, the president justified the new policy on the basis of military necessity and the war powers invested in the presidency. With the precision of a constitutional legal brief, Lincoln's document carefully crafted its impact upon slavery in those areas that had seceded and excluded states that had remained in the Union but still maintained slavery. Lincoln remained true to his famed response to Horace Greeley that he would abolish slavery only as a necessary means to restore the Union. With battle casualties rising and the prospects of victory diminishing, he believed the time had finally arrived to attack the central cause of the war. In a dramatic change from the Preliminary Proclamation, Lincoln authorized the recruitment of African Americans for the army. By the late summer of 1862, he had been persuaded by the writings of George Livermore, a Boston merchant, that the Founding Fathers had supported use of black troops in the American Revolution and that they had performed with distinction. Nevertheless, to Lincoln and the War Department black recruitment remained a volatile experiment. In response to the Emancipation Proclamation, rallies from Boston to San Francisco celebrated the move, heralding the beginning of the end of slavery. While all thanked Lincoln for keeping his word, most Northern blacks gave credit to God for the dramatic change in war policy, rather than to the president, who had heretofore professed a greater interest in colonization than in freedom.

Abraham Lincoln Writing the Emancipation Proclamation, *oil painting by David Gilmour Blythe, 21 ¾ × 27 ½ inches, 1863, also appeared in revised form as a lithograph. The many influences compelling Lincoln to issue the Emancipation Proclamation are displayed, from antislavery petitions to the conduct of the war. But most prominent among the many factors are the Bible and the U.S. Constitution, which rest on the president's lap. Photograph ©️ 2007 Carnegie Museum of Art, Pittsburgh.*

January 1, 1863

By the President of the United States of America:

A Proclamation.

Whereas, on the twentysecond day of September, in the year of our Lord one thousand eight hundred and sixty two, a proclamation was issued by the President of the United States, containing, among other things, the following, to wit:

"That on the first day of January, in the year of our Lord one thousand eight hundred and sixty-three, all persons held as slaves within any State or designated part

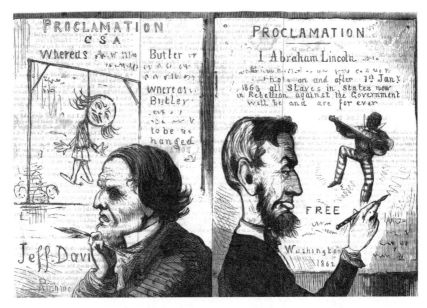

Butler Hanged—the Negro Freed—on paper—1863, *from Frank Leslie's Budget of Fun, February 1, 1863. This cartoon expressed the English-born, New York publishing magnate Frank Leslie's stand against the political leadership of both sides in the war. A vindictive Jefferson Davis is shown dreaming of hanging Union General Benjamin F. Butler, and Lincoln is characterized as a tool of the abolitionists. Leslie's highly illustrated journals, especially his Weekly, regularly published hideous stereotypes of African Americans. Courtesy, American Antiquarian Society.*

of a State, the people whereof shall then be in rebellion against the United States, shall be then, thenceforward, and forever free; and the Executive Government of the United States, including the military and naval authority thereof, will recognize and maintain the freedom of such persons, and will do no act or acts to repress such persons, or any of them, in any efforts they may make for their actual freedom.

"That the Executive will, on the first day of January aforesaid, by proclamation, designate the States and parts of States, if any, in which the people thereof, respectively, shall then be in rebellion against the United States; and the fact that any State, or the people thereof, shall on that day be, in good faith, represented in the Congress of the

United States by members chosen thereto at elections wherein a majority of the qualified voters of such State shall have participated, shall, in the absence of strong countervailing testimony, be deemed conclusive evidence that such State, and the people thereof, are not then in rebellion against the United States."

Now, therefore I, Abraham Lincoln, President of the United States, by virtue of the power in me vested as Commander-in-Chief, of the Army and Navy of the United States in time of actual armed rebellion against authority and government of the United States, and as a fit and necessary war measure for suppressing said re-bellion, do, on this first day of January, in the year of our Lord one thousand eight hundred and sixty three, and in accordance with my purpose so to do publicly proclaimed for the full period of one hundred days, from the day first above mentioned, order and designate as the States and parts of States wherein the people thereof respectively, are this day in rebellion against the United States, the fol-lowing, to wit:

Arkansas, Texas, Louisiana, (except the Parishes of St. Bernard, Plaquemines, Jefferson, St. Johns, St. Charles, St. James[,] Ascension, Assumption, Terrebonne, La-fourche, St. Mary, St. Martin, and Orleans, including the City of New-Orleans) Mississippi, Alabama, Florida, Georgia, South-Carolina, North-Carolina, and Virginia, (except the fortyeight counties designated as West Virginia, and also the counties of Berkley, Accomac, Northampton, Elizabeth-City, York, Princess Ann, and Norfolk, including the cities of Norfolk & Portsmouth [)]; and which excepted parts are, for the present, left precisely as if this proclamation were not issued.

And by virtue of the power, and for the purpose aforesaid, I do order and declare that all persons held as slaves within said designated States, and parts of States, are, and henceforward shall be free; and that the Ex-ecutive government of the United States, including the military and naval authorities thereof, will recognize and maintain the freedom of said persons.

And I hereby enjoin upon the people so declared to be free to abstain from all violence, unless in necessary self-defence; and I recommend to them that, in all cases when allowed, they labor faithfully for reasonable wages.

And I further declare and make known, that such persons of suitable condition, will be received into the armed service of the United States to garrison forts, positions, stations, and other places, and to man vessels of all sorts in said service.

And upon this act, sincerely believed to be an act of justice, warranted by the Constitution, upon military necessity, I invoke the considerate judgment of mankind, and the gracious favor of Almighty God.

In witness whereof, I have hereunto set my hand and caused the seal of the United States to be affixed.

Done at the City of Washington, this first day of January, in the year of our Lord one thousand eight hundred and sixty three, and of the Independence of the United States of America the eighty-seventh.

By the President: Abraham Lincoln
William H. Seward, Secretary of State.

54

AL to Andrew Johnson
CW, 7:149–150

After issuing the Emancipation Proclamation, Lincoln put aside his colonization plans, understanding that he needed African Americans in the army. With casualty lists growing each day and Northern support for the costly war effort flagging, Lincoln concluded that by placing liberated slaves in the army, he not only would increase military manpower but would deny the South an invaluable resource it needed to conduct the war. Until late in the summer of 1862, however, he had rejected the idea of black recruitment, believing that Northern whites would not accept the move and that African Americans were largely incapable of becoming effective soldiers. He even rejected the pleas of his first secretary of war, Simon Cameron, to recruit blacks and ignored many other voices that called for black troops. But the heroism of black soldiers along the Kansas-Missouri border, in Louisiana, and along the coasts of South Carolina and north Florida proved to many Union field commanders that blacks could fight, and even public opinion, among Northerners, began to change. Sometime in August 1862, Charles Sumner gave Lincoln a copy of George Livermore's *An Historical Research Respecting the Opinions of the Founders of the Republic on Negroes as Slaves, as Citizens, and as Soldiers* (1862). Livermore, a Boston merchant and bibliophile, launched into an exploration of the black role in the Revolutionary War soon after the start of the war and after reading the black abolitionist William C. Nell's *Colored Patriots of the American Revolution* (1855). Lincoln felt so indebted to Livermore that he gave him the pen that he had used to sign the Emancipation Proclamation. When he heard a rumor that Andrew Johnson had considered raising a unit of black troops, Lincoln fired off a letter to the Tennessean. Johnson, the only Southern senator not to resign and join the rebellion, enjoyed a reputation as a great enemy of the planter class and of slavery. The image of a prominent Southerner behind the black recruitment effort overwhelmed Lincoln: "The bare sight of fifty thousand armed, and drilled black soldiers on the banks of the Mississippi, would end the rebellion at once." Johnson, however, did not respond to Lincoln's inquiry.

Private

Hon. Andrew Johnson   Executive Mansion,
My dear Sir: Washington, *March 26, 1863.*

I am told you have at least *thought* of raising a negro military force. In my opinion the country now needs no specific thing so much as some man of your ability, and position, to go to this work. When I speak of your position, I mean that of an eminent citizen of a slave-state, and himself a slave-holder. The colored population is the great *available* and yet *unavailed* of, force for restoring the Union. The bare sight of fifty thousand armed, and drilled black soldiers on the banks of the Mississippi, would end the rebellion at once. And who doubts that we can present that sight, if we but take hold in earnest? If you *have* been thinking of it please do not dismiss the thought.

Yours truly
A. Lincoln

55

Resolution on Slavery
CW, 6:176

The Lincoln administration faced critical challenges from abroad, above all keeping Great Britain and other European powers from recognizing the independence of the Confederacy. Britain already provided ships and munitions to the South and safe neutral harbors for rebel vessels. Lincoln correctly feared that diplomatic recognition would open the floodgates, leading to a permanent division of the Union. Relations between the United States and Great Britain had nearly ruptured in November 1861, over the *Trent* Affair, when a U.S. warship stopped a British vessel in international waters to seize Confederate emissaries. British public opinion divided over recognition of the Confederacy, with many elites and working classes supporting the South because of the *Trent* Affair. Yet equal numbers supported the North and emancipation. Through his friendship with Charles Sumner, the antislavery senator from Massachusetts, Lincoln attempted to influence British policy. He asked Sumner to pass on this draft resolution to John Bright, a Quaker industrialist, reform parliamentarian from Birmingham, and England's greatest supporter of the United States. Bright's enormous popularity could help strengthen the Union cause if, as Lincoln hoped, Bright could arrange for public meetings to adopt the resolution. Lincoln's handiwork emphasized the fundamental issue at stake in the war—something he could not have done before issuing the Emancipation Proclamation. For conflicted British opinion on the American Civil War, see: R.J.M. Blackett, *Divided Hearts: Britain and the American Civil War* (Baton Rouge: Louisiana State University Press, 2001).

Whereas, while heretofore, States, and Nations, have tolerated slavery, recently, for the first [time] in the world, an attempt has been made to construct a new Nation, upon the basis of, and with the primary, and fundamental object to maintain, enlarge, and perpetuate human slavery, therefore,

Resolved, That no such embryo State should ever be recognized by, or admitted into, the family of christian and civilized nations; and that all ch[r]istian and civilized men everywhere should, by all lawful means, resist to the utmost, such recognition or admission.

56

AL to John M. Schofield
CW, 6:291

Missouri, a critical border state, suffered deep divisions during the Civil War. Many of its citizens openly served the Confederate cause. The state also became a testing ground for the administration's emancipation policy as the president sought simultaneously to prevent Missourians from joining the rebellion and to respect constitutional order. In 1863, a state convention attempted to end slavery, but divided into "Charcoals," radical abolitionists favoring immediate emancipation, and "Claybanks," conservative Republicans who favored a gradual process lasting as long as ten years. In July, the "Claybanks" succeeded in adopting a measure that would end slavery on July 4, 1870. Lincoln relied on Major General John Schofield to recruit local volunteers into federal service and "keep the peace" in a state that could influence further emancipation in the South and West. Unsure of how to proceed, the general appealed to Lincoln. The president agreed that loyal slaveowners should receive federal protection, provided that the gradual emancipation they adopted be "comparatively short" and that no slaves be sold "during that period, into more lasting slavery." He cautioned Schofield to exercise patience and not use the military at his disposal, as General Frémont had done early in the war, to hastily terminate slaveholders' rights. As elsewhere, Lincoln continued to move slowly toward emancipation, hoping to cement Unionist sentiment in the border states. On January 11, 1865, a constitutional convention met in St. Louis, reversed course, and immediately abolished slavery. Donald B. Connelly, *John M. Schofield and the Politics of Generalship* (Chapel Hill: University of North Carolina Press, 2006), 70–71.

Gen. John M. Schofield   Executive Mansion,
My dear Sir: Washington, *June 22, 1863.*

Your despatch, [*sic*] asking in substance, whether, in case Missouri shall adopt gradual emancipation, the general government will protect slave owners in that species of property during the short time it shall be permitted by the State to exist within it, has been received. Desirous as I am, that emancipation shall be adopted by Missouri, and believing as I do, that *gradual* can be made better than *immediate* for both black and white, except when military necessity changes the case, my impulse is to say that such protection would be given. I can not know exactly what shape an act of emancipation may take. If the period from the initiation to the final end, should be comparatively short, and the act should prevent persons being sold, during that period, into more lasting slavery, the whole would be easier. I do not wish to pledge the general government to the affirmative support of even temporary slavery, beyond what can be fairly claimed under the constitution. I suppose, however, this is not desired; but that it is desired for the Military force of the United States, while in Missouri, to not be used in subverting the temporarily reserved legal rights in slaves during the progress of emancipation. This I would desire also. I have very earnestly urged the slave-states to adopt emancipation; and it ought to be, and is an object with me not to overthrow, or thwart what any of them may in good faith do, to that end.

You are therefore authorized to act in the spirit of this letter, in conjunction with what may appear to be the military necessities of your Department.

Although this letter will become public at some time, it is not intended to be made so now.

Yours truly
A. Lincoln

57

Order of Retaliation
CW, 6:357

In December 1862, Confederate president Jefferson Davis ordered that "all negro slaves captured in arms be at once delivered over to the executive authorities of the respective States to which they belong to be dealt with according to the laws of said States." Officially, the Confederate government considered all African Americans caught in Union blue to be criminals—not prisoners of war—and "in insurrection against the state." Eight months later, in the wake of the battle at Fort Wagner (outside of Charleston, South Carolina), state authorities charged captured soldiers from the famed Fifty-fourth Massachusetts Regiment with fomenting rebellion. While awaiting their trials, which proved inconclusive and were not repeated, the black soldiers of the Fifty-fourth Massachusetts endured harsh conditions and abuse in a Confederate prison. As news spread about the egregious Confederate policy and the maltreatment of captured African American soldiers, Lincoln came under enormous pressure to respond. His Order of Retaliation (General Order No. 252) put the Confederacy on notice that the United States would insist on proper treatment for all its soldiers, regardless of "class, color, or condition." Yet its threat to execute one rebel soldier for every Union soldier killed in violation of "the laws of war" proved toothless and was never enforced. Confederate leaders quickly abandoned attempts to try black soldiers as insurrectionists and allowed individual units to resolve the issue on the battlefield, where summary executions became common. Confederate atrocities reached new depths at the April 12, 1864, Battle of Fort Pillow, but Lincoln concluded that retaliation would only spark an unending cycle of retribution, and failed to support his black troops. Howard C. Westwood, "Captive Black Union Soldiers in Charleston—What to Do?" *Civil War History* 28 (March 1982): 28–44.

UNITED STATES SOLDIERS AT CAMP "WILLIAM PENN" PHILADELPHIA, PA.

"Rally Round the Flag, boys! Rally once again,
Shouting the battle cry of FREEDOM!"

United States Soldiers at Camp "William Penn" Philadelphia, Pa. *Chromolithograph with hand-coloring, 1863, published by the Supervisory Committee for Recruiting Colored Regiments. This recruitment print accurately reflects the photograph it is based upon. The state's first black regiment was the Third USCT. Eventually, Pennsylvania raised ten more black units. Courtesy of The Library Company of Philadelphia.*

Executive Mansion, Washington D.C[.] July 30. 1863

It is the duty of every government to give protection to its citizens, of whatever class, color, or condition, and especially to those who are duly organized as soldiers in the public service. The law of nations and the usages and customs of war as carried on by civilized powers, permit no distinction as to color in the treatment of prisoners of war as public enemies. To sell or enslave any captured person, on account of his color, and for no offence against the laws of war, is a relapse into barbarism and a crime against the civilization of the age.

The government of the United States will give the same protection to all its soldiers, and if the enemy shall sell or enslave anyone because of his color, the offense shall be punished by retaliation upon the enemy's prisoners in our possession.

It is therefore ordered that for every soldier of the United States killed in violation of the laws of war, a rebel soldier shall be executed; and for every one enslaved by the enemy or sold into slavery, a rebel soldier shall be placed at hard labor on the public works and continued at such labor until the other shall be released and receive the treatment due to a prisoner of war[.]

Abraham Lincoln

58

AL to Nathaniel P. Banks

CW, 6:364–365

Nathaniel Prentice Banks, a politically appointed general and career politician from Massachusetts, commanded the military department that included Louisiana and played a key role in developing Reconstruction plans for the state. Captured by the Union early in 1862, Louisiana offered a critical look into the administration's early Reconstruction policies and a glimpse into the fate of African Americans of the South had Lincoln survived his second term. The state possessed a large African American population; New Orleans alone was home to twenty-five thousand blacks, including a wealthy and well-educated black community of eleven thousand. This group also provided some of the first black troops permitted to join the Union army; under Banks these men fought heroically at Port Hudson and at Milliken's Bend. When Lincoln learned from George S. Boutwell, who had been governor of Massachusetts in the 1850s and began serving in Congress the previous March, that Louisiana Unionists had begun drafting a new constitution, he offered Banks his views. Lincoln insisted that emancipation be permanent and that the document address slavery in those areas still under rebel control. What happened in Louisiana mattered to the president, and he kept in close contact with the military governor of the state, George Foster Shepley, and even knew the head of the committee charged with drafting the new constitution, Thomas J. Durant. The president's primary concerns, however, did not go much beyond restoring Louisiana to the Union and providing "some practical system" that would allow the races to coexist in the postwar world. Reeducation of whites did not occur to him, only the education of young African Americans. While he said nothing else of consequence to Banks, Lincoln did address a letter to Louisiana governor Michael Hahn on March 13, 1864, suggesting that the state might consider en-franchising "very intelligent . . . colored people" and those who had served "gallantly in our ranks. They would probably help, in some trying time to come, to keep the jewel of liberty within the family of freedom." Lincoln refused to insist on even these minimal concessions to the rights of African Americans: "But this is only a suggestion, not to the public, but to you alone." The state struggled over developing a constitution, with Hahn and Banks—not Lincoln—pressing for granting limited black suffrage. On Louisiana and Governor Hahn, see: Eric Foner, *Reconstruction: America's Unfinished Revolution, 1863–1877* (New York: Harper & Row, 1988), 35–50 and *CW*, 7:243.

Executive Mansion, Washington,
My dear General Banks   *August 5, 1863.*

. . . Governor Boutwell read me to-day that part of your letter to him, which relates to Louisiana affairs. While I very well know what I would be glad for Louisiana to do, it is quite a different thing for me to assume direction of the matter. I would be glad for her to make a new Constitution recognizing the emancipation proclamation, and adopting emancipation in those parts of the state to which the proclamation does not apply. And while she is at it, I think it would not be objectionable for her to adopt some practical system by which the two races could gradually live themselves out of their old relation to each other, and both come out better prepared for the new. Education for young blacks should be included in the plan. After all, the power, or element, of "contract" may be sufficient for this probationary period; and, by it's simplicity, and flexibility, may be the better.

As an anti-slavery man I have a motive to desire emancipation, which pro-slavery men do not have; but even they have strong enough reason to thus place themselves again under the shield of the Union; and to thus perpetually hedge against the recurrence of the scenes through which we are now passing.

Gov. Shepley has informed me that Mr. Durant is now taking a registry, with a view to the election of a Constitutional convention in Louisiana. This, to me, appears proper. If such convention were to ask my views, I could present little else than what I now say to you. I think the thing should be pushed forward, so that if possible, it's mature work may reach here by the meeting of Congress.

For my own part I think I shall not, in any event, retract the emancipation proclamation; nor, as executive, ever return to slavery any person who is free by the terms of that proclamation, or by any of the acts of Congress. . . .

59

AL to Gen. Ulysses S. Grant
CW, 6:374–375

In the summer of 1863 General Ulysses S. Grant commanded all Union forces in the District of Western Tennessee and Northern Mississippi. After a prolonged and costly siege, Vicksburg had fallen to Grant, and his army had gained control of the Mississippi River, splitting the Confederacy in two. Displaying his deep involvement in planning military strategy and the next move for his favorite general, Lincoln expressed his concern over the French in Mexico and continued blockade running out of Mobile, Alabama. He also sought to gauge Grant's opinion on the use of black troops. While the general shared the president's prejudiced views on African Americans, he needed no further convincing over their fighting ability. During the siege of Vicksburg, Grant learned of the untested unit of black soldiers that had repulsed a vicious Confederate attack at Milliken's Bend on June 7 and of the heroism of the men of the Corps d' Afrique that had served so gallantly, if unsuccessfully, at Port Hudson on July 9. In his reply to Lincoln on August 23, Grant—whose army was exhausted—told the president that "I have given the subject of arming the negro my hearty support. This, with the emancipation . . . is the heaviest blow yet given the Confederacy." Lincoln, who only the year before thought blacks incapable of serving as soldiers, now saw them as indispensable to victory. "It works doubly, weakening the enemy and strengthening us." The newly appointed Adjutant General Lorenzo Thomas, head of recruitment for the United States Colored Troops (USCT), arrived in Grant's district in the spring to assess the willingness of Union officers to accept black soldiers and to help raise men for the USCT. Recruitment in the Mississippi Valley, however, proved difficult at first as Confederates removed as many of their slaves as possible to Texas and Georgia. For a discussion of Lincoln's and Grant's views on the recruitment of black troops in the Mississippi Valley, see: James

M. McPherson, *Tried by War: Abraham Lincoln as Commander-in-Chief* (New York: The Penguin Press, 2008), 201–202.

Executive Mansion,   Washington,
My dear General Grant: *August 9, 1863.*

I see by a despatch of yours that you incline quite strongly towards an expedition against Mobile. This would appear tempting to me also, were it not that in view of recent events in Mexico, I am greatly impressed with the importance of re-establishing the national authority in Western Texas as soon as possible. I am not making an order, however. That I leave, for the present at least, to the General-in-Chief.

A word upon another subject. Gen. Thomas has gone again to the Mississippi Valley, with the view of raising colored troops. I have no reason to doubt that you are doing what you reasonably can upon the same subject. I believe it is a resource which, if vigorously applied now, will soon close the contest. It works doubly, weakening the enemy and strengthening us. We were not fully ripe for it until the river was opened. Now, I think at least a hundred thousand can, and ought to be rapidly organized along it's shores, relieving all the white troops to serve elsewhere.

Mr. [Charles A.] Dana understands you as believing that the emancipation proclamation has helped some in your military operations. I am very glad if this is so. Did you receive a short letter from me, dated the 13th. of July?

Yours very truly
A. Lincoln.

60

AL to James C. Conkling
CW, 6:407–410

James C. Conkling, a Republican friend and confidant of Lincoln, had served as mayor of Springfield, Illinois, and later as a state legislator. In this letter, Lincoln responded to Conkling's invitation to speak at a rally in Springfield on September 3. Lincoln regretfully declined but sent this letter to be read by Conkling at the event. "Read it slowly," he advised, so that there would be no misunderstanding. He knew that many of the "Union men" attending the rally questioned the constitutionality and purpose of the Emancipation Proclamation. He addressed the objections of conservatives with uncharacteristic impatience and defended his actions as consistent with his responsibilities as president and as commander in chief. He acknowledged that "you are dissatisfied with me about the negro," but dismissed such objections by stating his preference for freedom over slavery. Although Lincoln had displayed little regard for the black soldiers in the Union army, accepting the humiliating discrimination inflicted on them as necessary to keep whites in the fight, he could not tolerate the even more callous disregard of his opponents. "You say you will not fight to free negroes. Some of them seem willing to fight for you," he chastised. By the time of this letter, thousands of black troops had proven themselves in Louisiana, South Carolina, and Florida, putting an end to white doubts in the North over black suitability for combat. Lincoln said nothing about black citizenship claims or black patriotism. Instead, he appealed to the self-interest of those who protested black recruitment and freedom for the slaves: "I thought that whatever negroes can be got to do as soldiers, leaves just so much less for white soldiers to do, in saving the Union. Does it appear otherwise to you?" The letter was later read to a mass meeting in New York, a city that had the previous month experienced one of the worst race riots in American history. The *New York Times* exclaimed that

Miscegenation or the Millennium of Abolitionism, *lithograph by Bromley & Co., New York, 1864. This image, representative of the racist assault on black rights, casts Lincoln as an advocate of racial mixing. Senator Charles Sumner is shown introducing Miss Dinah Arabella Armintha Squash to the president. Lincoln replies that he is "proud to number among my intimate friends any member of the Squash family, especially the little Squashes." Library of Congress, Prints and Photographs Division, LC-USZ62-8840.*

The Miscegenation Ball, *lithograph by Bromley & Co., New York, 1864. This racist satire again links Abraham Lincoln to racial mixing, seeking to increase support for his Democratic presidential rival, George B. McClellan. In text below the image, the publisher claims that the event depicted occurred on September 23, 1864, involving members of the "Central Lincoln Club" and other Black Republicans. Library of Congress, Prints and Photographs Division, LC-USZ62-14828.*

WHAT MISCEGENATION IS!

—AND—

WHAT WE ARE TO EXPECT

Now that Mr. Lincoln is Re-elected.

By L. SEAMAN, LL. D.

WALLER & WILLETTS, Publishers,

NEW YORK.

L. Seaman, What Miscegenation Is! *Cover of a pamphlet designed to incite popular fears over the reelection of Abraham Lincoln (1865?). Library of Congress.*

the president's letter proved the country was lucky to be led by "a ruler who is so peculiarly adapted to the needs of the time as clear-headed, dispassionate, discreet, steadfast, honest Abraham Lincoln." For Lincoln's letter to Conkling, see: David Herbert Donald, *Lincoln* (London: Jonathan Cape, 1995), 456–457.

Hon. James C. Conkling   Executive Mansion,
My Dear Sir.   Washington, *August 26, 1863.*

. . . But, to be plain, you are dissatisfied with me about the negro. Quite likely there is a difference of opinion between you and myself upon that subject. I certainly wish that all men could be free, while I suppose you do not. Yet I have neither adopted, nor proposed any measure, which is not consistent with even your view, provided you are for the Union. I suggested compensated emancipation; to which you replied you wished not to be taxed to buy negroes. But I had not asked you to be taxed to buy negroes, except in such way, as to save you from greater taxation to save the Union exclusively by other means.

You dislike the emancipation proclamation; and, perhaps, would have it retracted. You say it is unconstitutional— I think differently. I think the constitution invests its commander-in-chief, with the law of war, in time of war. The most that can be said, if so much, is, that slaves are property. Is there—has there ever been—any question that by the law of war, property, both of enemies and friends, may be taken when needed? And is it not needed whenever taking it, helps us, or hurts the enemy? Armies, the world over, destroy enemies' property when they can not use it; and even destroy their own to keep it from the enemy. Civilized belligerents do all in their power to help themselves, or hurt the enemy, except a few things regarded as barbarous or cruel. Among the exceptions are the massacre of vanquished foes, and non-combatants, male and female.

But the proclamation, as law, either is valid, or is not valid. If it is not valid, it needs no retraction. If it is valid, it can not be retracted, any more than the dead can be brought to life. Some of you profess to think its retraction would operate favorably for the Union. Why better after the retraction, than before the issue? There was more than a year and a half of trial to suppress the rebellion before the proclamation issued, the last one hundred days of which passed under an explicit notice that it was coming, unless averted by those in revolt, returning to their allegiance. The war has certainly progressed as favorably for us, since the issue of the proclamation as before. I know as fully as one can know the opinions of others, that some of the commanders of our armies in the field who have given us our most important successes, believe the emancipation policy, and the use of colored troops, constitute the heaviest blow yet dealt to the rebellion; and that, at least one of those important successes, could not have been achieved when it was, but for the aid of black soldiers. Among the commanders holding these views are some who have never had any affinity with what is called abolitionism, or with republican party politics; but who hold them purely as military opinions. I submit these opinions as being entitled to some weight against the objections, often urged, that emancipation, and arming the blacks, are unwise as military measures, and were not adopted, as such, in good faith.

You say you will not fight to free negroes. Some of them seem willing to fight for you; but, no matter. Fight you, then, exclusively to save the Union. I issued the proclamation on purpose to aid you in saving the Union. Whenever you shall have conquered all resistance to the Union, if I shall urge you to continue fighting, it will be an apt time, then, for you to declare you will not fight to free negroes.

I thought that in your struggle for the Union, to whatever extent the negroes should cease helping the enemy, to that extent it weakened the enemy in his resistance to you. Do you think differently? I thought that whatever negroes can be got to do as soldiers, leaves just so much less for white soldiers to do, in saving the Union. Does it appear otherwise to you? But negroes, like other people, act upon motives. Why should they do any thing for us, if we will do nothing for them? If they stake their lives for us, they must be prompted by the strongest motive—even the promise of freedom. And the promise being made, must be kept. . . .

Peace does not appear so distant as it did. I hope it will come soon, and come to stay; and so come as to be worth the keeping in all future time. It will then have been proved that, among free men, there can be no successful appeal from the ballot to the bullet; and that they who take such appeal are sure to lose their case, and pay the cost. And then, there will be some black men who can remember that, with silent tongue, and clenched teeth, and steady eye, and well-poised bayonet, they have helped mankind on to this great consummation; while, I fear, there will be some white ones, unable to forget that, with malignant heart, and deceitful speech, they have strove to hinder it.

Still let us not be over-sanguine of a speedy final triumph. Let us be quite sober. Let us diligently apply the means, never doubting that a just God, in his own good time, will give us the rightful result.

Yours very truly
A. Lincoln.

61

Fragment

CW, 6:410–411

While the dating of this unpublished fragment remains uncertain, it accurately reflects Lincoln's views about the war and slavery after he issued the Emancipation Proclamation. Critics often asked the president what he would do if the South stopped fighting and desired to return to the Union. Let them try me, he once retorted. In this piece, Lincoln hinted that he could not continue the war if the other side wanted peace. The question meant little in practical terms, and Lincoln used it as a rhetorical opportunity to affirm his administration's unwavering commitment to the Union. He also made clear here and elsewhere that if peace came, he would not return anyone to slavery, especially those who had been enrolled into the army. However, he also admitted that if a court properly ordered such an action, he would be obligated to obey it. Given the right circumstances, as in a border state like Kentucky, Lincoln confessed that he might not be able to live up to his pledge that he would never return to slavery someone freed by acts of Congress or the Emancipation Proclamation.

[August 26, 1863?]

Suppose those now in rebellion should say: "We cease fighting: re-establish the national authority amongst us—customs, courts, mails, land-offices,—all as before the rebellion—we claiming to send members to both branches of Congress, as of yore, and to hold our slaves according to our State laws, notwithstanding anything or all things which has occurred during the rebellion." I probably should answer: "It will be difficult to justify in reason, or to maintain in fact, a war on one side, which shall have ceased on the other. You began the war, and you can end it. If questions remain, let them be solved by peaceful means—by courts, and votes. This war is an appeal, by you, from the ballot to the sword; and a great object with me has been to teach the futility of such appeal—to teach that what is decided by the ballot, can not be reversed by the sword—to teach that there can be no successful appeal from a fair election, but to the next election. Whether persons sent to congress, will be admitted to seats is, by the constitution, left to each House to decide, the President having nothing to do with it. Yet the question can not be one of indifference to me. I shall dread, and I think we all should dread, to see the 'the disturbing element' so brought back into the government, as to make probable a renewal of the terrible scenes through which we are now passing. During my continuance here, the government will return no person to slavery who is free according to the proclamation, or to any of the acts of congress, unless such return shall be held to be a legal duty, by the proper court of final resort, in which case I will promptly act as may then appear to be my personal duty.["]

Congress has left to me very large powers to remit forfeitures and personal penalties; and I should exercise these to the greatest extent which might seem consistent with the future public safety. I have thus told you, once more, so far as it is for me to say, what you are fighting for. The prospects of the Union have greatly improved recently; still, let us not be over-sanguine of a speedy final triumph. Let us diligently apply the means, never doubting that a just God, in his own good time, will give us the rightful result.

62

Annual Message to Congress
CW, 7:49–51

"The policy of emancipation, and of employing black soldiers, gave to the future a new aspect, about which hope, and fear, and doubt contended in uncertain conflict." In his 1863 annual message to the Congress, Lincoln underscored his reluctance to adopt emancipation as a war aim and to recruit African Americans as soldiers. Both had been unwanted experiments forced upon Lincoln and a majority of the North by the war. The wisdom of the move, the president asserted, was nevertheless manifest in the results: success on the battlefield and the enemy's loss of the labor of a hundred thousand slaves. But Lincoln, despite ample proof of black heroism in battles at Port Hudson and Milliken's Bend, Louisiana, at Fort Wagner, and along the South Carolina coast, chose only to say, "So far as tested, it is difficult to say they are not as good soldiers as any." Revealing his expectations, Lincoln expressed relief that "No servile insurrection, or tendency to violence or cruelty, has marked the measures of emancipation and arming the blacks." For those black soldiers who gave their lives for the Union and for an end to slavery—and at half the pay of the lowest-ranking white private—such praise was even more insulting than was Lincoln's continued support for colonization.

December 8, 1863

. . . The preliminary emancipation proclamation, issued in September, was running its assigned period to the beginning of the new year. A month later the final proclamation came, including the announcement that colored men of suitable condition would be received into the war service. The policy of emancipation, and of employing black soldiers, gave to the future a new aspect, about which hope, and fear, and doubt contended in uncertain conflict. According to our political system, as a matter of civil administration, the general government had no lawful power to effect emancipation in any State, and for a long time it had been hoped that the rebellion could be suppressed without resorting to it as a military measure. It was all the while deemed possible that the necessity for it might come, and that if it should, the crisis of the contest would then be presented. It came, and as was anticipated, it was followed by dark and doubtful days. Eleven months having now passed, we are permitted to take another review. The rebel borders are pressed still further back, and by the complete opening of the Mississippi the country dominated by the rebellion is divided into distinct parts, with no practical communication between them. Tennessee and Arkansas have been substantially cleared of insurgent control, and influential citizens in each, owners of slaves and advocates of slavery at the beginning of the rebellion, now declare openly for emancipation in their respective States. Of those States not included in the emancipation proclamation, Maryland, and Missouri, neither of which three years ago would tolerate any restraint upon the extension of slavery into new territories, only dispute now as to the best mode of removing it within their own limits.

Of those who were slaves at the beginning of the rebellion, full one hundred thousand are now in the United States military service, about one-half of which number actually bear arms in the ranks; thus giving the double advantage of taking so much labor from the insurgent cause, and supplying the places which otherwise must be filled with so many white men. So far as tested, it is difficult to say they are not as good soldiers as any. No servile insurrection, or tendency to violence or cruelty, has marked the measures of emancipation and arming the blacks. These measures have been much discussed in foreign countries, and contemporary with such discussion the tone of public sentiment there is much improved. . . .

But if it be proper to require, as a test of admission to the political body, an oath of allegiance to the Constitution of the United States, and to the Union under it, why also to the laws and proclamations in regard to slavery? Those laws and proclamations were enacted and put forth for the purpose of aiding in the suppression of the rebellion. To give them their fullest effect, there had to be a pledge for their maintenance. In my judgment they have aided, and will further aid, the cause for which they were intended. To now abandon them would be not only to relinquish a lever of power, but would also be a cruel and an astounding breach of faith. I may add at this point, that while I remain in my present position I shall not attempt to retract or modify the emancipation proclamation; nor shall I return to slavery any person who is free by the terms of that proclamation, or by any of the acts of Congress. For these and other reasons it is thought best that support of these measures shall be included in the oath; and it is believed the Executive may lawfully claim it in return for pardon and restoration of forfeited rights, which he has clear constitutional power to withhold altogether, or grant upon the terms which he shall deem wisest for the public interest. It should be observed, also, that this part of the oath is subject to the modifying and abrogating power of legislation and supreme judicial decision. . . .

63

Reply to New York Workingmen's Democratic Republican Association

CW, 7:259–260

In early 1864, trade unionists joined together to organize the Workingmen's Democratic-Republican Association of New York. Similar associations were later organized in Boston, Chicago, and Philadelphia. The association united Republicans and Democrats in support of Union candidates and educated workers on the issues surrounding the war. The organization's leadership sympathized with the abolitionist cause—believing that the institution of slavery threatened the rights of all workers. In March, the officers of the association visited President Lincoln, professed their support for his reelection, and bestowed upon him an honorary membership. The president happily accepted the membership and in response drew a connection between "African Slavery" and "the rights of all working people." Lincoln also alluded to the infamous New York City Draft Riots ("a disturbance in your city last summer") and the lynching of free blacks by the largely Irish rioters ("the hanging of some working people by other working people"). With careful political calculation, he elided expressing any direct sympathy for the city's black victims, since the Irish dominated the Workingmen's Democratic-Republican Association of New York, and their countrymen largely favored General George B. McClellan, the Democratic presidential challenger. Lincoln simply stated that such a condition "should never be so. The strongest bond of human sympathy, outside of the family relation, should be one uniting all working people, of all nations, and tongues, and kindreds." Democratic newspapers in New York, the *Jeffersonian* and the *Freeman's Journal and Catholic Register,* leapt to the attack, claiming that the president considered Irish citizens to be inferior to blacks and that he endorsed miscegenation. In November, the overwhelming majority of Irish Americans in New York voted for McClellan. However, thanks in part to the efforts of the Workingmen's Democratic-Republican Association of New York—and the timely capture of Atlanta, Georgia—Lincoln secured another term in the White House. For a discussion of the Workingmen's Association, see: Philip S. Foner, *History of the Labor Movement in the United States*, vol. 1, *From Colonial Times to the Founding of the American Federation of Labor* (New York: International Publishers, 1947).

March 21, 1864

Gentlemen of the Committee.

The honorary membership in your Association, as generously tendered, is gratefully accepted.

You comprehend, as your address shows, that the existing rebellion, means more, and tends to more, than the perpetuation of African Slavery—that it is, in fact, a war upon the rights of all working people. Partly to show that this view has not escaped my attention, and partly that I cannot better express myself, I read a passage from the Message to Congress in December 1861:

"It continues to develop that the insurrection * * * * * * * * * * till all of liberty shall be lost."

The views then expressed remain unchanged, nor have I much to add. None are so deeply interested to resist the present rebellion as the working people. Let them beware of prejudice, working division and hostility among themselves. The most notable feature of a disturbance in your city last summer, was the hanging of some working people by other working people. It should never be so. The strongest bond of human sympathy, outside of the family relation, should be one uniting all working people, of all nations, and tongues, and kindreds. Nor should this lead to a war upon property, or the owners of property. Property is the fruit of labor—property is desirable—is a positive good in the world. That some should be rich, shows that others may become rich, and hence is just encouragement to industry and enterprize. Let not him who is houseless pull down the house of another; but let him labor diligently and build one for himself, thus by example assuring that his own shall be safe from violence when built.

64

AL to Albert G. Hodges
CW, 7:281–282

Albert G. Hodges, editor of the Frankfort, Kentucky, *Commonwealth*, asked Lincoln to write out the substance of his remarks at an earlier meeting with Hodges, Kentucky governor Thomas E. Bramlette, a War Democrat, and Archibald Dixon, a former Whig Kentucky U.S. senator. The three men had visited the president because of intense opposition in their state over the recruitment of slaves into the Union army. As a border state, Kentucky retained its more than 225,000 slaves, and whites used every means possible, including murder, to halt the recruitment of their "property." When he first learned that the army intended to recruit Kentucky slaves, the governor predicted that the state would never see another day of peace. Despite intense white opposition, astonishingly, about 60 percent of the state's black men of military age served in the Union army. In words that countless biographers have cited, Lincoln had proclaimed his abhorrence of slavery: "I am naturally anti-slavery. If slavery is not wrong, nothing is wrong." The president, however, assured the Kentuckians that his personal feelings about the immorality of slavery had nothing to do with his oath as president to "preserve, protect, and defend the Constitution of the United States." No other issue, not even that of emancipation, would jeopardize his absolute commitment to the integrity of the nation. For Lincoln, as he had stated openly in his letter to Horace Greeley, the preservation of the Union and its principles remained the paramount duty of his presidency. To ease the Kentuckians' concerns, Lincoln reminded them that he had rejected emancipation by military force under General John C. Frémont early in the war in Missouri. He even opposed secretary of war Simon Cameron's desire to recruit black troops: "I objected, because I did not yet think it an indispensable necessity." Instead, he preferred to request that border state governments voluntarily liberate their slaves through a system of gradual, compensated emancipation, which Kentucky soundly rejected. Only then did Lincoln move toward the Emancipation Proclamation and the arming of black soldiers, "driven to the alternative of either surrendering the Union, and with it the Constitution, or of laying strong hand upon the colored element." Neither emancipation nor black recruitment was the president's goal, only preservation of the Constitution. As he famously wrote in this letter, "I claim not to have controlled events, but confess plainly that events have controlled me." For black recruitment in Kentucky, see: Richard D. Sears, *Camp Nelson, Kentucky: A Civil War History* (Lexington: University Press of Kentucky, 2002).

A. G. Hodges, Esq.   Executive Mansion,
Frankfort, Ky.   Washington, *April 4, 1864.*

. . . "I am naturally anti-slavery. If slavery is not wrong, nothing is wrong. I can not remember when I did not so think, and feel. And yet I have never understood that the Presidency conferred upon me an unrestricted right to act officially upon this judgment and feeling. It was in the oath I took that I would, to the best of my ability, preserve, protect, and defend the Constitution of the United States. I could not take the office without taking the oath. Nor was it my view that I might take an oath to get power, and break the oath in using the power. I understood, too, that in ordinary civil administration this oath even forbade me to practically indulge my primary abstract judgment on the moral question of slavery. I had publicly declared this many times, and in many ways. And I aver that, to this day, I have done no official act in mere deference to my abstract judgment and feeling on slavery. I did understand however, that my oath to preserve the constitution to the best of my ability, imposed upon me the duty of preserving, by every indispensable means, that government—that nation—of which that constitution was the organic law. Was it possible to lose the nation, and yet preserve the

constitution? By general law life *and* limb must be protected; yet often a limb must be amputated to save a life;
but a life is never wisely given to save a limb. I felt that
measures, otherwise unconstitutional, might become
lawful, by becoming indispensable to the preservation of
the constitution, through the preservation of the nation.
Right or wrong, I assumed this ground, and now avow it.
I could not feel that, to the best of my ability, I had even
tried to preserve the constitution, if, to save slavery, or any
minor matter, I should permit the wreck of government,
country, and Constitution all together. When, early in the
war, Gen. Fremont attempted military emancipation, I
forbade it, because I did not then think it an indispensable
necessity. When a little later, Gen. Cameron, then Secretary
of War, suggested the arming of the blacks, I objected,
because I did not yet think it an indispensable necessity.
When, still later, Gen. Hunter attempted military emancipation, I again forbade it, because I did not yet think
the indispensable necessity had come. When, in March,
and May, and July 1862 I made earnest, and successive
appeals to the border states to favor compensated emancipation, I believed the indispensable necessity for military
emancipation, and arming the blacks would come, unless
averted by that measure. They declined the proposition;
and I was, in my best judgment, driven to the alternative
of either surrendering the Union, and with it, the Constitution, or of laying strong hand upon the colored element.
I chose the latter. In choosing it, I hoped for greater gain
than loss; but of this, I was not entirely confident. More
than a year of trial now shows no loss by it in our foreign
relations, none in our home popular sentiment, none in
our white military force,—no loss by it any how or any
where. On the contrary, it shows a gain of quite a hundred
and thirty thousand soldiers, seamen, and laborers. These
are palpable facts, about which, as facts, there can be no
cavilling. We have the men; and we could not have had
them without the measure.

["]And now let any Union man who complains of the measure, test himself by writing down in one line that he is for subduing the rebellion by force of arms; and in the next, that he is for taking these hundred and thirty thousand men from the Union side, and placing them where they would be but for the measure he condemns. If he can not face his case so stated, it is only because he can not face the truth.["]

I add a word which was not in the verbal conversation. In telling this tale I attempt no compliment to my own sagacity. I claim not to have controlled events, but confess plainly that events have controlled me. Now, at the end of three years struggle the nation's condition is not what either party, or any man devised, or expected. God alone can claim it. Whither it is tending seems plain. If God now wills the removal of a great wrong, and wills also that we of the North as well as you of the South, shall pay fairly for our complicity in that wrong, impartial history will find therein new cause to attest and revere the justice and goodness of God.

Yours truly
A. Lincoln

65

AL to Edwin M. Stanton
CW, 7:345–346

On April 12, 1864, the Mississippi River ran red with the "blood of the slaughtered for 200 yards." Confederate general Nathan Bedford Forrest exulted over the black and white Union troops his men slaughtered after they surrendered their isolated Tennessee fort. For the remainder of the war, "Remember Fort Pillow!" tumbled from the lips of black Union soldiers, while others stitched those words onto their uniforms in defiance of the enemy they faced. All understood that if captured, they more likely would be shot than ever see the inside of a rebel prison camp. But by flying the "black flag," Confederates only increased the ferocity of the battlefield and the black soldiers' drive to win freedom for themselves and their brethren. Lincoln soon learned the details of the terrible slaughter and on April 18 in Baltimore publicly acknowledged what Forrest's men had done. He explained that because he had recruited black men into the army, it was his responsibility "to give him all the protection given to any other soldier." He did not question the government's obligation to protect its black troops but puzzled over how to do it: "The difficulty is not in stating the principle, but in practically applying it" (*CW*, 7:302). After an army inquiry—later followed by a congressional one—confirmed the horrifying details, Lincoln discussed a response with his cabinet in early May and then crafted but *never sent* the following letter to his secretary of war. Several members of the administration, William Henry Seward, Salmon P. Chase, Gideon Welles, and even Edwin M. Stanton, were willing to execute an equal number of rebel prisoners in the unlikely event that the Confederate government would take responsibility for Forrest's actions. Other members opposed killing innocent captives, but agreed to execute Forrest and officers in his command if they happen to fall into Union hands. Lincoln resisted his cabinet's suggestions, crafted these ambiguous and halting instructions for the War Department, and then decided against taking any action to protect the lives of his black Union soldiers. Forrest's quote is in Dudley T. Cornish, *The Sable Arm: Negro Union Troops in the Union Army, 1861–1865* (New York: W. W. Norton, 1966), 173; for the best book on Fort Pillow, see: John Cimprich, *Fort Pillow, a Civil War Massacre, and Public Memory* (Baton Rouge: Louisiana State University Press, 2005).

Hon. Secretary of War: Executive Mansion
Sir.   Washington, D. C. *May 17. 1864*

Please notify the insurgents, through the proper military channels and forms, that the government of the United States has satisfactory proof of the massacre, by insurgent forces, at Fort-Pillow, on the 12th. and 13th. days of April last, of fully white and colored officers and soldiers of the United States, after the latter had ceased resistance, and asked quarter of the former.

That with reference to said massacre. the government of the United States has assigned and set apart by name insurgent officers, theretofore, and up to that time, held by said government as prisoners of war.

That, as blood can not restore blood, and government should not act for revenge, any assurance, as nearly perfect as the case admits, given on or before the first day of July next, that there shall be no similar massacre, nor any officer or soldier of the United States, whether white or colored, now held, or hereafter captured by the insurgents, shall be treated other than according to the laws of war, will insure the replacing of said insurgent officers in the simple condition of prisoners of war.

That the insurgents having refused to exchange, or to give any account or explanation in regard to colored soldiers of the United States captured by them, a number of insurgent prisoners equal to the number of such colored soldiers supposed to have been captured by said insurgents will, from time to time, be assigned and set aside, with reference to such captured colored soldiers, and will, if the insurgents assent, be exchanged for such colored soldiers; but that if no satisfactory attention shall be given to this notice, by said insurgents, on or before the first day of July next, it will be assumed by the government of the United States, that said captured colored troops shall have been murdered, or subjected to Slavery, and that said government will, upon said assumption, take such action as may then appear expedient and just.

66

Interview with Alexander W. Randall and Joseph T. Mills
CW, 7:506–507

In discussions with Joseph T. Mills, a Wisconsin judge, and the former Wisconsin governor Alexander W. Randall, Lincoln recorded his impatience with the views of the Green Bay, Wisconsin, editor Charles D. Robinson. As a War Democrat, Robinson had supported the national administration, even after it issued the Emancipation Proclamation. War Democrats like Robinson understood Lincoln's approach to the war as outlined in the president's famous open letter to Horace Greeley: all actions aimed at restoration of the Union and only at restoration of the Union. As the Lincoln administration now insisted on the abolition of slavery as a prerequisite for reunion, Randall believed that War Democrats had to support General George B. McClellan in the fall elections. "This puts the question on a new basis, and takes us War Democrats clear off our feet, leaving us no ground to stand upon." Lincoln, with his reelection hopes fading, feared the response of men like Randall to the course of the war. His draft response and the comments Judge Mills recorded, however, clearly show that African Americans had pushed their way into the center of the president's policies, where they would remain. McClellan and the Democrats claimed to want to restore the Union "as it was," on the one hand, and, on the other, to conduct the war without black soldiers. But the North could not fight without its black troops—"we would be compelled to abandon the war in 3 weeks"—and the South would not return to the Union if it could retain the institution of slavery. "You cannot concilliate the South," he maintained, "when the mastery & control of millions of blacks makes them sure of ultimate success." Lincoln would not even consider a peace proposal if it meant reenslaving those black men who had fought bravely in the Union army. "I should

Columbia Demands her Children! *lithograph by Joseph E Baker, Boston, 1864. This antiwar print condemns a distracted and foolish Abraham Lincoln for the mounting cost of the Civil War. Columbia, the symbol of the nation, insists that Lincoln halt the endless demand for more soldiers. It is one of many Democratic efforts to whip up opposition to Lincoln and bring an end to the war. Library of Congress, Prints and Photographs Division, LC-USZ62-89748.*

be damned in time & in eternity for so doing." For information on the meeting with Mills and Randall and Robinson's views, see: *CW,* 7:501–502.

August 19, 1864

. . . My own experience has proven to me, that there is no program intended by the democratic party but that will result in the dismemberment of the Union. But Genl McClellan is in favor of crushing out the rebellion, & he will probably be the Chicago candidate. The slightest acquaintance with arithmetic will prove to any man that the rebel armies cannot be destroyed with democratic strategy. It would sacrifice all the white men of the north to do it. There are now between 1 & 200 thousand black men now in the service of the Union. These men will be disbanded, returned to slavery & we will have to fight two nations instead of one. I have tried it. You cannot concilliate the South, when the mastery & control of millions of blacks makes them sure of ultimate success. You cannot conciliate the South, when you place yourself in such a position, that they see they can achieve their independence. The war democrat depends upon conciliation. He must confine himself to that policy entirely. If he fights at all in such a war as this he must economise life & use all the means which God & nature puts in his power. Abandon all the posts now possessed by black men[,] surrender all these advantages to the enemy, & we would be compelled to abandon the war in 3 weeks. We have to hold territory. Where are the war democrats to do it. The field was open to them to have enlisted & put down this rebellion by force of arms, by concilliation, long before the present policy was inaugurated. There have been men who have proposed to me to return to slavery the black warriors of Port Hudson & Olustee to their masters to conciliate the South. I should be damned in time & in eternity for so doing. The world shall know that I will keep my faith to friends & enemies, come what will. My enemies say I am now carrying on this war for the sole purpose of abolition. It is & will be carried on so long as I am President for the sole purpose of restoring the Union. But no human power can subdue this rebellion without using the Emancipation lever as I have done. Freedom has given us the control of 200 000 able bodied men, born & raised on southern soil. It will give us more yet. Just so much it has sub[t]racted from the strength of our enemies, & instead of alienating the south from us, there are evidences of a fraternal feeling growing up between our own & rebel soldiers. My enemies condemn my emancipation policy. Let them prove by the history of this war, that we can restore the Union without it. . . .

67

Resolution Submitting the Thirteenth Amendment to the States
CW, 8:253

Although Lincoln believed in the necessity of a constitutional amendment to end slavery, he treated it largely as he handled all things that did not come under the authority of his office. As in the case of equal pay for black troops, the president refused to intervene in the matter—notwithstanding the crisis in the field and the pleas of many Union commanders and soldiers. Congress, he held, had sole authority in the matter. Similarly, Lincoln said nothing publicly about the Thirteenth Amendment throughout most of 1864 since the Constitution gave the presidency no role in the process. He may also have been worried about the upcoming election, one that seemed increasingly hopeless as the summer progressed. The president remained "indifferent" to the effort until December, although the Senate held a final vote approving the legislation on April 8, 1864. He then began lobbying for it in the House of Representatives, expressing his wish that Congress approve a resolution for a Thirteenth Amendment before he delivered his second inaugural address in March. Democrats tried to bargain with Lincoln, offering their support for the legislation in exchange for the administration's extending more serious peace feelers to the Confederate government. Senator Sumner pressured Lincoln, and mammoth petitions poured into the Congress demanding an amendment to end slavery once and for all time, an amendment that the House of Representatives finally approved on January 31, 1865. Although his signature was unnecessary, Lincoln signed the resolution, undoubtedly wanting his name on such a historic document. For Lincoln's role in adoption of the Thirteenth Amendment, see: Michael Vorenberg, *Final Freedom: The Civil War, the Abolition of Slavery, and the Thirteenth Amendment* (Cambridge: Cambridge University Press, 2001), 113–117, 125–127, 174–178, 206–210, 223–224.

February 1, 1865

Thirty-Eighth *Congress of the United States of America;*
At the second *Session,*
Begun and held at the City of Washington, on Monday,
the fifth *day of December, one thousand eight hundred*
and sixty-four.

A RESOLUTION

Submitting to the legislatures of the several States a proposition to amend the Constitution of the United States.

Resolved by the Senate and House of Representatives of the United States of America in Congress assembled, (two-thirds of both houses concurring), That the following article be proposed to the legislatures of the several States as an amendment to the constitution of the United States, which, when ratified by three-fourths of said Legislatures, shall be valid, to all intents and purposes, as a part of the said Constitution, namely: Article XIII. Section 1. Neither slavery nor involuntary servitude, except as a punishment for crime whereof the party shall have been duly convicted, shall exist within the United States, or any place subject to their jurisdiction. Section 2. Congress shall have power to enforce this article by appropriate legislation.

SCHUYLER COLFAX
Speaker of the House of Representatives.

H. HAMLIN
Vice President of the United States,
and President of the Senate.

Approved, *February 1. 1865.*
Abraham Lincoln

68

Second Inaugural Address
CW, 8:332–333

More than 618,000 Union and Confederate soldiers died during the Civil War; more than 470,000 were wounded. No accurate accounting of civilian losses is possible, but certainly thousands upon thousands suffered proportionately. The number of Americans who died in the Civil War exceeded the total number of combat deaths in all American wars combined. No family, North or South, escaped the consequences of the nation's most costly conflict. The overwhelming sacrifice burdened Lincoln's mind as he wrote the nation's most memorable presidential address. Wind and rain greeted inauguration day on March 4, 1865, transforming Washington, D.C.'s streets into rivers of mud. The new vice president, Andrew Johnson of Tennessee, gave a rambling and embarrassing speech in the Senate chambers after his swearing in. The president made sure that his running mate would not speak to the assembled throng outside. Later, as Lincoln readied himself on the platform at the front of the Capitol, the sun broke through the overcast sky. Many in the audience believed the change in weather foretold the future. "Fellow Countrymen," Lincoln then declared. He went on to trace the national descent into conflict. "All knew," he explained, that slavery "was, somehow, the cause of the war." He blamed the South for destroying the Union and so many lives, but with Calvinist resignation also explained that the whole nation should bear responsibility for the war's singular cause. If God willed it, he explained, the killing would continue "until all the wealth piled by the bond-man's two hundred and fifty years of unrequited toil shall be sunk, and until every drop of blood drawn with the lash, shall be paid by another drawn with the sword."

March 4, 1865

. . . On the occasion corresponding to this four years ago, all thoughts were anxiously directed to an impending civil-war. All dreaded it—all sought to avert it. While the inaugural address was being delivered from this place, devoted altogether to *saving* the Union without war, insurgent agents were in the city seeking to *destroy* it without war—seeking to dissol[v]e the Union, and divide effects, by negotiation. Both parties deprecated war; but one of them would *make* war rather than let the nation survive; and the other would *accept* war rather than let it perish. And the war came.

One eighth of the whole population were colored slaves, not distributed generally over the Union, but localized in the Southern part of it. These slaves constituted a peculiar and powerful interest. All knew that this interest was, somehow, the cause of the war. To strengthen, perpetuate, and extend this interest was the object for which the insurgents would rend the Union, even by war; while the government claimed no right to do more than to restrict the territorial enlargement of it. Neither party expected for the war, the magnitude, or the duration, which it has already attained. Neither anticipated that the *cause* of the conflict might cease with, or even before, the conflict itself should cease. Each looked for an easier triumph, and a result less fundamental and astounding. Both read the same Bible, and pray to the same God; and each invokes His aid against the other. It may seem strange that any men should dare to ask a just God's assistance in wringing their bread from the sweat of other men's faces; but let us judge not that we be not judged. The prayers of both could not be answered; that of neither has been answered fully. The Almighty has His own purposes. "Woe unto the world because of offences! for it must needs be that offences come; but woe to that man by whom the offence cometh!" If we shall suppose that American Slavery is one of those offences which, in the providence of God, must needs come, but which, having continued through His appointed time, He now wills to remove, and that He gives to both North and South, this terrible war, as the woe due to those by whom the offence came, shall we discern therein any departure from those divine attributes which the believers in a Living God always ascribe to Him? Fondly do we hope—fervently do we pray—that this mighty scourge of war may speedily pass away. Yet, if God wills that it continue, until all the wealth piled by the bond-man's two hundred and fifty years of unrequited toil shall be sunk, and until every drop of blood drawn with the lash, shall be paid by another drawn with the sword, as was said three thousand years ago, so still it must be said "the judgments of the Lord, are true and righteous altogether."

With malice toward none; with charity for all; with firmness in the right, as God gives us to see the right, let us strive on to finish the work we are in; to bind up the nation's wounds; to care for him who shall have borne the battle, and for his widow, and his orphan—to do all which may achieve and cherish a just, and a lasting peace, among ourselves, and with all nations. . . .

69

Speech to One Hundred Fortieth Indiana Regiment
CW, 8:360–361

At about four o'clock in the afternoon on March 17, 1865, Lincoln spoke from the balcony of National Hotel, at the corner of Pennsylvania Avenue and Sixth Street, in Washington, D.C. During the ceremony Lincoln presented to the governor of Indiana a rebel flag captured at Fort Anderson, North Carolina, by the 140th Indiana Regiment. He took the opportunity to reassert his opposition to slavery: "I have always thought that all men should be free." Primarily, he addressed rumors that slaves might be enlisted into the Confederate army, and what that move would mean. Throughout the Civil War rumors circulated concerning the arming of slaves to fight *against* the North. No rebel black units ever fought Union forces, although many slaves fought alongside their owners, and thousands more were compelled to labor for the Confederacy, rebuilding rail lines or constructing fortifications. As the Confederacy faced defeat in the closing months of the war, cries for the arming of slaves increased. Most Southerners rejected the call. Howell Cobb, who had been secretary of the treasury under President Buchanan and became a general commanding Georgia Confederate troops, exclaimed that "If slaves will make good soldiers our whole theory of slavery is wrong." Nevertheless, late in the war many state governors and commanders in the field cried out for more men—and the four millions of slaves represented the only fresh group available. Desperate to avoid defeat, President Jefferson Davis and his cabinet, in February 1865, approved the measure. When it obtained the blessing of General Robert E. Lee, Virginia organized a small contingent of poorly equipped and untrained slaves. Lincoln dismissed those blacks who joined such a unit as deserving the slavery they defended, not considering the possibility that such men faced little choice. More important to the president, the move proved that the Confederacy had reached "the bottom of the insurgent resources." On the issue of black troops fighting for the rebellion, see: James M. McPherson, *Battle Cry of Freedom: The Civil War Era* (New York: Oxford, 1988), 832–835.

March 17, 1865

... There are but few aspects of this great war on which I have not already expressed my views by speaking or writing. There is one—the recent effort of our erring bretheren, [*sic*] sometimes so-called, to employ the slaves in their armies. The great question with them has been; "will the negro fight for them?" They ought to know better than we; and, doubtless, do know better than we. I may incidentally remark, however, that having, in my life, heard many arguments,—or strings of words meant to pass for arguments,—intended to show that the negro ought to be a slave, that if he shall now really fight to keep himself a slave, it will be a far better argument why [he] should remain a slave than I have ever before heard. He, perhaps, ought to be a slave, if he desires it ardently enough to fight for it. Or, if one out of four will, for his own freedom, fight to keep the other three in slavery, he ought to be a slave for his selfish meanness. I have always thought that all men should be free; but if any should be slaves it should be first those who desire it for *themselves*, and secondly those who *desire* it for *others*. Whenever [I] hear any one, arguing for slavery I feel a strong impulse to see it tried on him personally.

There is one thing about the negroes fighting for the rebels which we can know as well [as] they can; and that is that they can not, at [the] same time fight in their armies, and stay at home and make bread for them. And this being known and remembered we can have but little concern whether they become soldiers or not. I am rather in favor of the measure; and would at any time if I could, have loaned them a vote to carry it. We have to reach the bottom of the insurgent resources; and that they employ, or seriously think of employing, the slaves as soldiers, gives us glimpses of the bottom. Therefore I am glad of what we learn on this subject. . . .

70

Last Public Address
CW, 8:401–404

On Palm Sunday, April 9, 1865, General Robert E. Lee surrendered his Army of Northern Virginia to General U. S. Grant. Five days earlier, Lincoln himself sailed up the James River to Richmond, the Confederate capital, and landed not far from the infamous Libby Prison. The president, Admiral David Dixon Porter, three other officers, and ten carbine-armed sailors then walked to the Confederate White House. It was a time for national thanksgiving, Lincoln remarked in his last public address. The Reconstruction experience in Louisiana, however, was foremost on his mind, and he defended his minimal requirements for states to return to the Union. He sought reconciliation and reunion, not radical reform and retribution. He refused to take the ground of a growing number of Republicans who contended that having seceded from the Union, the Southern states were now akin to territories and entirely subject to the authority of Congress. By labeling such a view "good for nothing" and a "pernicious abstraction," Lincoln moved away from, not toward, those who sought a more thorough Reconstruction of the South and greater rights for the former slaves. The president acknowledged that Louisiana blacks insisted on the right to vote. Yet he maintained that those who sought this end would bring it about sooner by supporting the current state government—based on 10 percent of the prewar voting population's taking an oath of allegiance to the Union—than by rejecting such governments in hopes of getting reformed ones more agreeable to radicals in Congress. Moreover, Lincoln asserted, by keeping Louisiana out of the Union, the Congress would be losing one more vote in favor of the Thirteenth Amendment to the Constitution ending slavery. Given Lincoln's record and limited goals for restoration of the Union, his Reconstruction policy meant that African Americans would never gain full equal rights.

April 11, 1865

. . . As a general rule, I abstain from reading the reports of attacks upon myself, wishing not to be provoked by that to which I can not properly offer an answer. In spite of this precaution, however, it comes to my knowledge that I am much censured for some supposed agency in setting up, and seeking to sustain, the new State Government of Louisiana. In this I have done just so much as, and no more than, the public knows. In the Annual Message of Dec. 1863 and accompanying Proclamation, I presented *a* plan of re-construction (as the phrase goes) which, I promised, if adopted by any State, should be acceptable to, and sustained by, the Executive government of the nation. I distinctly stated that this was not the only plan which might possibly be acceptable; and I also distinctly protested that the Executive claimed no right to say when, or whether members should be admitted to seats in Congress from such States. This plan was, in advance, submitted to the then Cabinet, and distinctly approved by every member of it. One of them suggested that I should then, and in that connection, apply the Emancipation Proclamation to the theretofore excepted parts of Virginia and Louisiana; that I should drop the suggestion about apprenticeship for freed-people, and that I should omit the protest against my own power, in regard to the admission of members to Congress; but even he approved every part and parcel of the plan which has since been employed or touched by the action of Louisiana. The new constitution of Louisiana, declaring emancipation for the whole State, practically applies the Proclamation to the part previously excepted. It does not adopt apprenticeship for freed-people. . . .

. . . I have been shown a letter on this subject, supposed to be an able one, in which the writer expresses regret that my mind has not seemed to be definitely fixed on the question whether the seceded States, so called, are in the Union or out of it. It would perhaps, add astonishment to his regret, were he to learn that since I have found professed Union men endeavoring to make that question, I have *purposely* forborne any public expression upon it. As appears to me that question has not been, nor yet is, a practically material one, and that any discussion of it, while it thus remains practically immaterial, could have no effect other than the mischievous one of dividing our friends. As yet, whatever it may hereafter become, that question is bad, as the basis of a controversy, and good for nothing at all—a merely pernicious abstraction.

We all agree that the seceded States, so called, are out of their proper practical relation with the Union; and that the sole object of the government, civil and military, in regard to those States is to again get them into that proper practical relation. I believe it is not only possible, but in fact, easier, to do this, without deciding, or even considering, whether these states have even been out of the Union, than with it. Finding themselves safely at home, it would be utterly immaterial whether they had ever been abroad. Let us all join in doing the acts necessary to restoring the proper practical relations between these states and the Union; and each forever after, innocently indulge his own opinion whether, in doing the acts, he brought the States from without, into the Union, or only gave them proper assistance, they never having been out of it.

The amount of constituency, so to to [*sic*] speak, on which the new Louisiana government rests, would be more satisfactory to all, if it contained fifty, thirty, or even twenty thousand, instead of only about twelve thousand, as it does. It is also unsatisfactory to some that the elective franchise is not given to the colored man. I would myself prefer that it were now conferred on the very intelligent, and on those who serve our cause as soldiers. Still the question is not whether the Louisiana government, as it stands, is quite all that is desirable. The question is "Will it be wiser to take it as it is, and help to improve it; or to reject, and disperse it?" "Can Louisiana be brought into proper practical relation with the Union *sooner* by *sustaining*, or by *discarding* her new State Government?"

Some twelve thousand voters in the heretofore slave-state of Louisiana have sworn allegiance to the Union, assumed to be the rightful political power of the State, held elections, organized a State government, adopted a free-state constitution, giving the benefit of public schools equally to black and white, and empowering the Legislature to confer the elective franchise upon the colored man. Their Legislature has already voted to ratify the constitutional amendment recently passed by Congress, abolishing slavery throughout the nation. These twelve thousand persons are thus fully committed to the Union, and to perpetual freedom in the state—committed to the very things, and nearly all the things the nation wants—and they ask the nations recognition, and it's assistance to make good their committal. Now, if we reject, and spurn them, we do our utmost to disorganize and disperse them. We in effect say to the white men "You are worthless, or worse—we will neither help you, nor be helped by you." To the blacks we say "This cup of liberty which these, your old masters, hold to your lips, we will dash from you, and leave you to the chances of gathering the spilled and scattered contents in some vague and undefined when, where, and how." If this course, discouraging and paralyzing both white and black, has any tendency to bring Louisiana into proper practical relations with the Union, I have, so far, been unable to perceive it. If, on the contrary, we recognize, and sustain the new government of Louisiana the converse of all this is made true. We encourage the hearts, and nerve the arms of the twelve thousand to adhere to their work, and argue for it, and proselyte for it, and fight for it, and feed it, and grow it, and ripen it to a complete success. The colored man too, in seeing all united for him, is inspired with vigilance, and energy, and daring, to the same end. Grant that he desires the elective franchise, will he not attain it sooner by saving the already advanced steps toward it, than by running backward over them? Concede that the new government of Louisiana is only to what it should be as the egg is to the fowl, we shall sooner have the fowl by hatching the egg than by smashing it? Again, if we reject Louisiana, we also reject one vote in favor of the proposed amendment to the national constitution. To meet this proposition, it has been argued that no more than three fourths of those States which have not attempted secession are necessary to validly ratify the amendment. I do not commit myself against this, further than to say that such a ratification would be questionable, and sure to be persistently questioned; while a ratification by three fourths of all the States would be unquestioned and unquestionable.

I repeat the question. "Can Louisiana be brought into proper practical relation with the Union *sooner* by *sustaining* or by *discarding* her new State Government? . . ."

Appendix

Lincoln, Race, and Humor

No nineteenth-century politician more adeptly employed humor for political effect than did Abraham Lincoln. During his rise as a successful lawyer and Whig political organizer, Lincoln used self-deprecating humor to diminish the elitism associated with both his profession and his party. Through humor he could display his knowledge and wisdom without appearing threatening, and could exercise leadership without distancing himself from those whose votes he required. During the famed debates with Stephen A. Douglas, Lincoln's clever folksiness rallied audiences to his side and heaped ridicule upon his opponent's assertions, making them appear unworthy of the voters' credence. But what proved eminently respectable to both candidates was contempt for African Americans. It should come as no surprise that racism tinged Lincoln's public and private humor. Even when his jokes served to buttress his opposition to the expansion of slavery, they relied on racist cultural assumptions. Indeed for such humor to work, it must affirm stereotypes. Like minstrelsy, racial humor created bonds and established cultural boundaries for whites, serving as an effective instrument of repression and dehumanization. Sexual themes appeared most commonly in the race jokes of the nineteenth century. As in Lincoln's story of the razor stropping, they expressed fantasies of black male sexuality and white sexual inferiority. Such jokes affirmed white fear of unrestrained black sexuality—and what it implied for white womanhood—and simultaneously assuaged that fear by reducing blacks to helplessness and leaving ultimate power (the razor) in white hands. Lincoln jokes abound, but relatively few can be authenticated by exacting modern standards. The ones reproduced below are from Lincoln's writings, from those of his contemporaries, or from reliable recollections of contemporaries. Many not included are from nineteenth-century sources with questionable political motives. For the full range of Lincoln humor, see: Paul M. Zall, ed., *Abe*

Lincoln's Legacy of Laughter: Humorous Stories by and about Abraham Lincoln (Knoxville: University of Tennessee Press, 2007). For a discussion of the problem of using reminiscence material, see Rodney O. Davis, "William Herndon, Memory and Lincoln Biography," *Journal of Illinois History* 1 (Winter 1998): 99–112.

> But his [Lincoln's] easy good-nature was sometimes imposed upon by inconsiderate acquaintances; and Mr. [Samuel] Hill relates one of the devices by which he sought to stop the abuse. "One Elmore Johnson, an ignorant but ostentatious, proud man, used to go to Lincoln's post-office [in New Salem] every day,—sometimes three or four times a day, if in town,—and inquire, 'Anything for me?' This bored Lincoln, yet it amused him. Lincoln fixed a plan,—wrote a letter to Johnson as coming from a negress in Kentucky, saying many good things about opossum, dances, corn-shuckings, &c.; 'John's! come and see me; and old master won't kick you out of the kitchen any more!' Elmore took it out; opened it; couldn't read a word; pretended to read it; went away; got some friends to read it; they read it correctly; he thought the reader was fooling him, and went to others with the same result. At last he said he would get *Lincoln* to read it, and presented it to Lincoln. It was almost too much for Lincoln, but he read it. The man never asked afterwards, 'Anything here for me?'"

Ward H. Lamon, *The Life of Abraham Lincoln; from his Birth to his Inauguration as President* (Boston: J. R. Osgood, 1872), 148–149.

[In a 30 March 1849 letter, Congressman Moses Hampton of Pittsburgh, Pennsylvania, reminded Lincoln of a story he had once told him.] "Do you remember the story of the old Virginian stropping his razor on a certain *member* of

a young negro's body which you told and connected with
my mission to Brazil—"

*Lincoln Papers; the Story of the Collection, with Selections to July 4,
1861,* ed. David Chambers Mearns, intro. Carl Sandburg, 2 vols.
(Garden City, N.Y.: Doubleday, 1948), 1:169.

The speaker said we had selected and elected a Republican
State ticket. We have done what we supposed to be our
duty. It is now the duty of those elected to give us a good
Republican Administration. In regard to the Governor-
elect, Col. [William Henry] Bissell, —[Loud and long-
continued cheers and waving of handkerchiefs]—he referred to the opposite party saying that "he couldn't take
the oath." Well, they said "he couldn't be elected," and
as they were mistaken once, he thought they were not
unlikely to be mistaken again. "They wouldn't take such
an oath!" Oh, no! [Laughter.] "They would cut off their
right arm first." He would like to know one of them who
would not part with his right arm to have the privilege
of taking the oath. Their conduct reminded him of the
darky who, when a bear had put its head into the hole and
shut out the daylight, cried out, "What was darkening de
hole?" "Ah," cried the other darky, who was on to the tail
of the animal, "if de tail breaks you'll find out." [Laughter
and cheers.] Those darkies at Springfield see something
darkening the hole, but wait till the tail breaks on the 1st
of January, and they will see. [Cheers.]

Abraham Lincoln, "Speech at a Republican Banquet, Chicago, Illinois, December 10, 1856," *Collected Works of Abraham Lincoln* (New
Brunswick, N.J.: Rutgers University Press, 1953), 2:383–384.

Now gentlemen, I don't want to read at any greater
length, but this is the true complexion of all I have ever
said in regard to the institution of slavery and the black

race. This is the whole of it, and anything that argues me into his idea of perfect social and political equality with the negro, is but a specious and fantastic arrangement of words, by which a man can prove a horse chestnut to be a chestnut horse. [Laughter.] I will say here, while upon this subject, that I have no purpose directly or indirectly to interfere with the institution of slavery in the States where it exists.

Abraham Lincoln, "First Debate with Stephen A. Douglas at Ottawa, Illinois, August 21, 1858," *Collected Works of Abraham Lincoln* (New Brunswick, N.J.: Rutgers University Press, 1953), 3:16.

At Memphis Douglas told his audience that he was for the negro against the crocodile, but for the white man against the negro. This was not a sudden thought spontaneously thrown off at Memphis. He said the same thing many times in Illinois last summer and autumn, though I am not sure it was reported then. It is a carefully framed illustration of the estimate he places upon the negro and the manner he would have him dealt with. It is a sort of proposition in proportion. "As the negro is to the crocodile, so the white man is to the negro." As the negro ought to treat the crocodile as a beast, so the white man ought to treat the negro as a beast. Gentlemen of the South, is not that satisfactory? Will you give Douglas no credit for impressing that sentiment on the Northern mind for your benefit? Why, you should magnify him to the utmost, in order that he may impress it the more deeply, broadly, and surely.

Abraham Lincoln, "Notes for Speeches at Columbus and Cincinnati, Ohio [September 16, 17, 1859]," *Collected Works of Abraham Lincoln* (New Brunswick, N.J.: Rutgers University Press, 1953), 3:431–432.

It has ever since been a source of regret that I omitted at the time to jot down some of the delightful sayings and amusing anecdotes related by Lincoln in Leonard Volk's studio in Chicago in mid-April in 1860. A single Southern story is, after almost half a century, the only one I can recall, and I cannot remember what led Mr. Lincoln to relate the incident, for he rarely told a story without a purpose. A balloon ascension occurred in New Orleans "befo' de wa'," and after sailing in the air several hours, the aeronaut, who was arrayed in silks and spangles like a circus performer, descended in a cotton field, where a gang of slaves were at work. The frightened negroes took to the woods—all but one venerable darkey, who was rheumatic and could not run, and who, as the resplendent aeronaut approached, having apparently just dropped from heaven, said: "Good mawning, Massa Jesus; how's your Pa?"

James Grant Wilson, "Recollections of Lincoln," in *Putnam's Monthly and the Reader: A Magazine of Literature, Art and Life* (New Rochelle, N.Y.: G. P. Putnam's Sons, Knickerbocker Press, 1909), 5:671–672.

Walking over with him [Lincoln] at his request, —to divert his mind, I repeated a story told me the night previous concerning a 'contraband' who had fallen into the hands of some good pious people, and was being taught by them to read and pray. Going off by himself one day, he was overheard to commence a prayer by the introduction of himself as "Jim Williams—a berry good nigga' to wash windows; 'spec's you know me now?"

An amusing illustration of the fact that whatever the nature of an incident related to the President, it never failed to remind him of something silimar, [*sic*] followed. After a hearty laugh at what he called this "direct way of putting the case," he said: "The story that suggests to me, has resemblance to it save in the 'washing windows' part. A lady in Philadelphia had a pet poodle dog, which mysteriously disappeared. Rewards were offered for him, and a great ado made without effect. Some weeks passed, and all hope of the favorite's return had been given up, when a servant brought him in one day, in the filthiest condition imaginable. The lady was overjoyed to see her pet again, but horrified at his appearance. 'Where *did* you find him?' she exclaimed. 'Oh,' replied the man, very unconcernedly, 'a negro down the street had him tied to the end of a pole, *swabbing* windows.'"

F. B. Carpenter, *Six Months at the White House with Abraham Lincoln: The Story of a Picture* (New York: Hurd and Houghton, 1867), 158–159.

But little of importance was done at the Cabinet-meeting. Several subjects discussed. Seward was embarrassed about the Dominican question. To move either way threatened difficulty. On one side Spain, on the other side the negro. The President remarked that the dilemma reminded him of the interview between two negroes, one of whom was a preacher endeavoring to admonish and enlighten the other. "There are," said Josh, the preacher, "two roads for you, Joe. Be careful which you take. One ob dem leads straight to hell, de odder go right to damnation." Joe opened his eyes under the impressive eloquence and awful future and exclaimed, "Josh, take which road you please; I go troo de wood." "I am not disposed to take any new trouble," said the President, "just at this time, and shall neither go for Spain nor the negro in this matter, but shall take to the woods."

Gideon Welles, "February 2, 1864," *Diary of Gideon Welles, Secretary of the Navy under Lincoln and Johnson,* vol. 1, ed. Edgar Thaddeus (Boston: Houghton, Mifflin & Co., 1911), 519–520.

We were about to retire, but he [Lincoln] insisted on our remaining longer. Dismissing the present state of the country, he entertained us with reminiscences of the past—of the discussions between himself & Douglass.

[*sic*] He said he was accused of of [*sic*] joking. In his later speeches, the seriousness of the theme prevented him from using anecdotes. Mr. Harris a democratic orator of Ill, once appealed to his audience in this way. If these republicans get into power, the darkies will be allowed to come to the polls & vote. Here comes forward a white man, & you ask him who will you vote for. I will vote for S A Douglass. Next comes up a sleek pampered negro. Well Sambo, who do you vote for. I vote for Massa Lincoln. Now asked the orator, what do you think of that. Some old farmer cried out, I think the darkey showd a damd sight of more sense than the white man. It is such social tete a tetes among his friends that enables Mr Lincoln to endure mental toils & application that would crush any other man.

"Interview with Alexander W. Randall and Joseph T. Mills, August 19, 1864," *Collected Works of Abraham Lincoln* (New Brunswick, N.J.: Rutgers University Press, 1953), 7:507–508.

He [Lincoln] remarked that, in reckoning the number of those who had perished in the war, a fair per-centage must be deducted for ordinary mortality, which would have carried off under any circumstances a certain proportion of the men, all of whom were generally set down as victims of the sword. He also remarked that very exaggerated accounts of the carnage had been produced by including among the killed large numbers of men whose term of enlistment had expired, and who had been on that account replaced by others, or had reenlisted themselves; and he told in illustration of this remark one of his characteristic stories:—"A negro had been learning arithmetic. Another negro asked him, if he shot at three pigeons sitting on a fence and killed one, how many would remain. 'One,' replied the arithmetician. 'No,' said the other negro, 'the other two would fly away.'" In the course of the conversation he told two or three more of these stories—if stories they could be called,—always by way of illustrating some remark he had made, rather than for the sake of the anecdote itself.

Goldwin Smith, "President Lincoln," *MacMillan's Magazine* 11 (February 1865): 301.

[Charles Almerin] Tinker records that one day Secretary Seward, who was not renowned as a joker, said he had been told that a short time before, on a street crossing, Lincoln had been seen to turn out in the mud to give a colored woman a chance to pass. "Yes," said Lincoln, "it has been a rule of my life that if people would not turn out for me, I would turn out for them. Then you avoid collisions."

David Homer Bates, *Lincoln in the Telegraph Office: Recollections of the United States Military Telegraph Corps During the Civil War* (New York: The Century Co., 1907), 204.

"They tell me that if the Republicans prevail, slavery will be abolished, and whites will marry and form a mongrel race. Now, I have a sister-in-law down in Kentucky, and if any one can show me that if Fremont is elected she will have to marry a negro, I will vote against Fremont, and if that isn't an argumentum ad hominem it is an argument ad womanum." The joke never failed to bring down the house.

George W. Shaw, *Personal Reminiscences of Abraham Lincoln* (Moline, Ill.: Carlson, 1924), 18.

Index

Gates argues that Lincoln's views on race and equality evolved throughout his career while Wilentz argued that Lincolns views altered with the views of his constituents. Both G + W ~~agree~~ recognize that L's views and opinions changed on these subjects, but they disagree on the reason. G fails to recognize the impact that being a politician had on Lincoln.